WEREWOLF!

Novels By Bill Pronzini

NIGHT SCREAMS (with Barry N. Malzberg)
TWOSPOT (with Collin Wilcox)
ACTS OF MERCY (with Barry N. Malzberg)
BLOWBACK
GAMES
THE RUNNING OF BEASTS (with Barry N. Malzberg)
SNOWBOUND
UNDERCURRENT
THE VANISHED
PANIC!
THE SNATCH
THE STALKER

Anthologies Edited By Bill Pronzini

WEREWOLF!
DARK SINS, DARK DREAMS (with Barry N. Malzberg)
THE END OF SUMMER: SCIENCE FICTION OF THE
FIFTIES (with Barry N. Malzberg)
MIDNIGHT SPECIALS
TRICKS AND TREATS (with Joe Gores)

WERE

WOLF!

Edited by Bill Pronzini

ARBOR HOUSE
NEW YORK

ACKNOWLEDGMENTS

"Loups-Garous," by Avram Davidson. Copyright © 1971 by Mercury Press, Inc. First published in *The Magazine of Fantasy and Science Fiction.* Reprinted by permission of the author and his agent, Kirby McCauley, Ltd.

"Gabriel-Ernest," by Saki (H.H. Munro). From *The Complete Short Stories of Saki (H.H. Munro).* Copyright © 1930, 1958 by The Viking Press, Inc. Reprinted by permission of The Viking Press.

"There Shall Be No Darkness," by James Blish. Copyright © 1950 by Standard Magazines, Inc. First published in *Thrilling Wonder Stories.* Reprinted by permission of Robert P. Mills, Ltd., agent for the estate of James Blish.

"Nightshapes," by Barry N. Malzberg. Copyright © 1979 by Barry N. Malzberg. An original story published by permission of the author.

"The Hound," by Fritz Leiber. Copyright © 1942 by Weird Tales, Inc. First published in *Weird Tales.* Reprinted by permission of the author.

"Wolves Don't Cry," by Bruce Elliott. Copyright © 1954 by Fantasy House, Inc. First published in *The Magazine of Fantasy and Science Fiction.* Reprinted by permission of Scott Meredith Literary Agency, Inc., 845 Third Avenue, New York, N.Y. 10022, agents for the estate of Bruce Elliott.

"Lila the Werewolf," by Peter S. Beagle. Copyright © 1974 by Capra Press. Reprinted by permission of Capra Press, 631 State Street, Santa Barbara, CA 93101.

"A Prophecy of Monsters," by Clark Ashton Smith. Copyright © 1954 by Fantasy House, Inc. First published in *The Magazine of Fantasy and Science Fiction.* Reprinted by permission of Arkham

The editor would like to thank those individuals who assisted in various ways with this anthology: Clyde Taylor, Bill Blackbeard of the San Francisco Academy of Art, Barry N. Malzberg, and Charles Cockey. Their help was invaluable and is much appreciated.

CONTENTS

Introduction
Loups-Garous, by Avram Davidson   1

PART ONE: **CLASSIC STORIES**   3

The Were-Wolf, by Clemence Housman   5
The Wolf, by Guy de Maupassant   42
The Mark Of The Beast, by Rudyard Kipling   49
Dracula's Guest, by Bram Stoker   63
Gabriel-Ernest, by Saki (H.H. Munro)   77

PART TWO: **CONTEMPORARY TALES AND VARIATIONS**

There Shall Be No Darkness, by James Blish   87
Nightshapes, by Barry N. Malzberg   145
The Hound, by Fritz Leiber   153
Wolves Don't Cry, by Bruce Elliott   168
Lila The Werewolf, by Peter S. Beagle   181

PART THREE: **TWO VIEWS OF TOMORROW**

A Prophecy Of Monsters, by Clark Ashton Smith   207
Full Sun, by Brian W. Aldiss   211

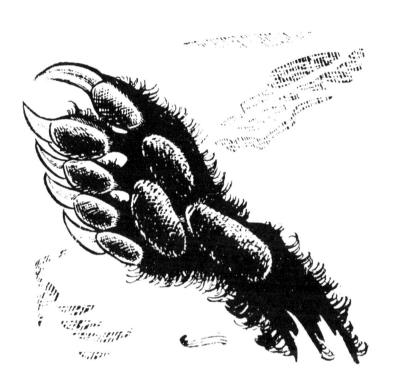

INTRODUCTION

Even a man who is pure in heart
And says his prayers by night
May become a wolf when the wolfsbane blooms
And the autumn moon is bright.
                    —ANCIENT GYPSY RHYME

Consider the werewolf.

He is quite different from any other supernatural or preternatural being of legend and myth, any monster born in the imaginations of writers and filmmakers. He is not a creature fashioned of human parts and brought to life in a madman's laboratory. He is not a member of the undead—a zombie resurrected by the magic of a voodoo priest; nor the mummy of an Egyptian king kept alive for centuries by sorcery and tana leaves; nor a vampire who must drink blood in order to maintain his unnatural life, who can change himself at will into a bat, who must sleep during the day because exposure to sunlight will cause him to shrivel and perish. He does not have the evil powers of a witch, a warlock, or one of Satan's demons. He is not a thing that flies, or crawls, or scuttles; not a rodent or an insect mutated into monstrous and deadly size.

He is just a man, a woman, a mortal human being.

Who is cursed.

By day he walks among other humans, lives among them, and few if any suspect his terrible secret. It is only by night, those autumn nights when the moon is full and the wolfsbane blooms, that the change overtakes him. That the fur begins to grow on his body and his teeth become long and sharp; that his hands and feet alter shape, the fingers and toes turn into pads and gleaming claws, and he drops down onto all fours; that the mind and soul of a man are transmogrified into those of a ravening wolf. Only then that he leaves the world of *Homo sapiens* to run free in the moonlight and the shadows, to hunt the unsuspecting and the unwary who will become his prey.

Hunger is what possesses him on those nights—the overpowering, all-consuming lust for human flesh, human blood. The soft throat, the living organs are his goal and his fare; he knows nothing else, desires nothing else.

And when the night is done, when he has killed and ravaged and fed, he returns, sated, to his human lair to await the change that will again make him a man. It comes at the first light of dawn, that second change, and after it is complete and his intellect is restored, he remembers. The hunt, the kill, the blood—he remembers all of this, and perhaps the memory fills him with pain and torment. Perhaps, because he is not a vampire, not a zombie or a mummy or a monster created in a laboratory—because he is a man—perhaps he is repulsed and sickened by the savage acts he was compelled to perform and he wishes with all that is left of his soul for the release of death.

But death will not come easy for him. He is doomed, he is cursed; the forces of evil control him, and the evil that he does, even his suffering, pleases them. Someday he will die, yes, from natural causes or perhaps when a bullet or other weapon made of silver pierces his flesh; he is not immortal. Until that day, he can only wait with a sense of dread—and a sense of lupine anticipation, too—for another full moon, another change, another night of hunting. And another feast of blood.

Consider the werewolf.

For he is the most terrifying—and the most tragic—of them all.

The origin of the werewolf superstition is lost in antiquity. It may have begun, as scholars of the supernatural Sabine Baring-Gould and Montague Summers believe, with those primitive tribes of man who practiced the rites of cannibalism. Evolution brought about a gradual civilizing of these tribes, or of splinter groups among them, and led to both the abolition of cannibalistic practices and a fear and loathing of their brothers who continued to consume human flesh. The man-eaters were then considered to have the souls of animals, predators. And the predator most universally reviled—"the eternal symbol of ferocity and inordinate evil appetite, hard by which rides cruel devouring lust," as Summers writes in his classic study, *The Werewolf*—has always been the wolf.

With the passage of centuries, this fear and hatred developed into superstition: the cannibals not only had the souls of wolves, they were actually able, through magic or witchcraft, to turn themselves into beasts in order to satisfy their bloodlust. The ancient Greeks were the first to give the superstition a name, one of the two by which we know it today. Lycanthropy, from the Greek words *lukos* (wolf) and *anthropos* (man); the physical transformation—or, in modern medical parlance, the psychotic delusion that one is able to effect such a transformation—of man into animal. (The second term by which we know this phenomenon, of course, is "were-ism," which derives from "wer," the Old English word for man.)

The legend exists in every country and every culture; in those places where there are no wolves, such as Africa, the belief is in weretigers, wereleopards, werebears—whatever are the most savage and most feared predators. The myth of the werewolf is particularly strong in Scandinavia and in southern and eastern Europe. Most of our modern lore comes from Germany, Hungary, Czechoslovakia; stories of the *vlkolak,* the werewolf, have been told and retold for centuries by the wandering gypsy tribes of these regions, most notably those from the Carpathian Mountains.

Both Sabine Baring-Gould and Montague Summers offer numerous accounts of lycanthropy throughout history. Perhaps the most famous—and most obscene—of these cases, recounted by Baring-Gould in his *The Book of Werewolves,* is that of Gilles de Laval, the Maréchal de Retz.

Laval, one of the most powerful noblemen in France, was brought to trial in 1440 to answer charges that he was responsible for the disappearance and death of scores of beggar and peasant children. Terrible atrocities involving these children were said to have been performed in the Castle of Machecoul, a gloomy fortress comprised of massive towers and surrounded by deep moats; peasants spoke of nights when "a fierce red glare" irradiated a casement high up in an isolated tower, and of "sharp cries ringing out of it, through the hushed woods, to be answered only by the howl of the wolf as it rose from its lair."

During the trial, the testimony of two of Laval's servants revealed that the charges were true: he had murdered not scores but hundreds upon hundreds of children in an eight-year period, by beheading, strangulation, mutilation, and other hideous means. He experienced intense pleasure in their agonies, Laval stated in his confession, and often bathed in their blood. He was convicted and sent to the gallows—a rather pallid end for one of the most depraved of all human monsters.

Baring-Gould's description of Laval at the trial is significant: "His hair and moustache were light brown, and his beard was clipped to a point. This beard, which resembled no other beard, was black, but under certain lights it assumed a blue hue, and it was this peculiarity which obtained for the Sire de Retz the surname of Bluebeard, a name which has attached to him in popular romance . . .

"But on closer examination of the countenance of Gilles de Retz, contraction of the muscles of the face, nervous quivering of the mouth, spasmodic twitchings of the brows, and above all, the sinister expression of the eyes, showed that there was something strange and frightful in the man. At intervals he ground his teeth like a wild beast preparing to dash upon his prey . . ."

Other such cases abound in history—including recent history; several accounts of the modern, twentieth-century lycanthrope are related in Robert Eisler's fact-crime book, *Man Into Wolf.* These cases, of course, like that of Gilles de Laval, may all be explained as lycanthropic madness: the disease, the delusion, rather than actual transmogrification.

But there are others, from centuries past, which may not be so easily accounted for by natural laws. No doubt the facts in such instances were distorted or exaggerated, as the result of superstitious ignorance; no doubt they are either apocryphal or explainable as all the rest. The literal werewolf does not exist and never has. He is only a myth, only a creature of the mind.

Of course he is.

We all know that, don't we?

Fiction writers have spun tales of the werewolf for close to three centuries. One of the earliest works, listed by Summers, is Laurent

Bordelon's *L'Histoire des Imaginations Extravagantes de Monsieur Oufle,* published in France in 1710. But although there have been many novels and stories since then, in English, French, German, and other languages, none may be considered as *the* definitive work on the subject of lycanthropy.

Perhaps the best of all the werewolf novels, that which comes closest to being its *Dracula* or its *Frankenstein,* is Guy Endore's *The Werewolf of Paris.* First published in the U.S. in 1933, Endore's powerful and savage tale of Bertrand Caillet and the Paris of 1870 has achieved a certain amount of fame among aficionados of supernatural horror. Yet despite the fact that it is still in print today, and despite such accolades as *The Saturday Review*'s "an unsurpassed calendar of horrors," it remains little known among general readers.

Other novels worthy of note, but which are also even more obscure, include Alexandre Dumas's *The Wolf-Leader* (1857), Samuel Rutherford Crockett's *The Black Douglas* (1899), *House of Fear* (1927) by Robert W. Service (the poet of "The Shooting of Dan McGrew" fame), Jack Mann's *Grey Shapes* (1938), and Jack Williamson's *Darker Than You Think* (1948). The Williamson is an especially fine and gripping tale. A new werewolf novel, Whitley Strieber's *The Wolfen,* published last year, has a fascinating premise—that werewolves are not men who turn into beasts but a mutated canine race that has survived in packs for thousands of years and which today infests large cities, masquerading as dogs when glimpsed by humans, preying on the weak and the derelict. But it is a flawed work and leaves too many questions unanswered.

Films have done much to popularize the werewolf superstition in the past four decades. The first werewolf film was a silent, *The Werewolf,* made in 1913 and seldom seen today. If there is one screen classic, it is *The Wolf Man* (1941), which had good production values and an excellent cast—Lon Chaney, Jr., Claude Rains, Bela Lugosi, Maria Ouspenskaya—and which made accurate use of werewolf lore.

There are a handful of other interesting and well-made films, such as the richly atmospheric 1963 Hammer production, *Curse of the Werewolf,* based on the Guy Endore novel, but unfortunately, most of the screen attempts dealing with the subject have unintentionally satirized and cheapened it. These include such forgettable titles as *Cry of the Werewolf, She-Wolf of London, The Werewolf* (a 1956 film, not the silent previously mentioned), *Werewolf in a Girl's Dormitory,* and *The Boy Who Cried Werewolf.* One made-for-TV movie, *Death Moon,* has to be seen to be disbelieved.

Which brings us to the short story and the contents of this anthology. There have been hundreds of shorter works on the lycanthropy theme, a good percentage of them (as is the case in fiction of all types) of mediocre or poor quality. But some of those that are good are very good indeed and rank with the finest of supernatural horror tales. Clemence Housman's "The Were-Wolf" is one; Saki's "Gabriel-Ernest," Rudyard Kipling's "The Mark of the Beast," James Blish's "There Shall Be No Darkness," and Fritz Leiber's "The Hound" are a few of the others. All are included here.

None of these stories, as you'll see, is of the stereotypical "B horror-movie" type. Each is different from the other in style, approach, thematic variation, and setting (locales and time periods include ancient Scandinavia, eighteenth-century France, nineteenth-century Germany and India, twentieth-century England, Scotland, and the United States—and places here and abroad in the far future). Horror is the dominant motif in each tale, of course, but there is also a good deal of irony, high tragedy, leavening humor, and social and historical commentary and satire.

A little something for every taste, in short.

Not to mention plenty of bite.

And now—

The autumn moon is full, the wolfsbane is in bloom. In the shadows, where a human form stood moments ago, there is a soft howling cry—and a fearful gray shape glides away into the night. A ravenous hunger gnaws in the beast's belly; the smell of blood is in his nostrils.

The feast is about to begin.

—Bill Pronzini
San Francisco, California
October 1978

WEREWOLF!

LOUPS-GAROUS
by AVRAM DAVIDSON

Avram Davidson is a man of many literary faces—all of them bright and inimitable. He has written novels and stories of fantasy, mystery, history, and science fiction; poems and light verse; and essays, book reviews, and magazine articles on a wide range of topics. He is also an editor emeritus of the much-lauded Magazine of Fantasy and Science Fiction.

"Loups-Garous" is a fine example of his short verse and makes a most fitting epigram to this anthology.

 It was late when I arrived at Dr. Glosspan's office.
Overhead, the replenished moon
Rode high, spending itself
Upon the aquiescent earth.
He was none too pleased to see me. Indeed,

As he explained, under the glare of the framed vellum and the
  framed sheepskin,
He had agreed to do so only to explain again
How impossible it was
For him to take me as a patient—
His work-load was already so heavy,
Dr. Glosspan said. I seized his cold, reluctant hands
And poured out my plaints and pleas.
I told him how I was tortured by dreadful dreams
Of running, naked, on all fours
Swiftly, fleetly, through the endless woods and fields—
And all the rest of it—the chase, the quarry, the hazard, and the
  blood.
Oh, the blood! Oh, the blood!
Scarcely had I begun to realize
That the hand I held had a hairy palm, when
Dr. Glosspan groaned.
We watched each other's faces push out to muzzles
And our teeth grow long and white and sharp
And hair grow thick and grey on all our changing limbs.
Together we slipped from alien clothes and,
Laughing, laughing, howling, growling, we leaped
Through the open window
To run forever through the endless woods and fields
Beneath the festering fullness of the moon:
The chase, the hazard, the quarry, and the blood.
Oh, the blood! Oh, the blood!

Part One:
CLASSIC STORIES

THE WERE-WOLF
by CLEMENCE HOUSMAN

Considered by many horror-fantasy enthusiasts to be among the two or three finest werewolf stories ever written, "The Were-Wolf" was first published in the British magazine Atalanta *in 1896. Later that year it simultaneously appeared in book form in England and in this country (Way and Williams, Chicago). Montague Summers calls it an "exquisite prose-poem"; its eloquent and lyrical style, poignant evocation of life in ancient Scandinavia, and quiet account of lycanthropic horror affirm those words of high praise.*

Whether by accident or design, Clemence Housman appears to have neither sought nor received notoriety as an author; little is known about him or his work (or if, indeed, he wrote any other supernatural tales during his lifetime). It is probable that he was related to A.E. Housman, the respected British poet and classical scholar: Laurence Housman, A.E.'s brother, contributed several illustrations to the first book editions of "The Were-Wolf."

If this is, in fact, Clemence Housman's only work of fantasy, its quality is all the more remarkable for its "one-shot" status. The reader may wonder why he chose not to continue writing, and what other tales he might have told had he kept on setting pen to paper.

The great farm hall was ablaze with the fire-light, and noisy with laughter and talk and many-sounding work. None could be idle but the very young and the very old—little Rol, who was hugging a puppy, and old Trella, whose palsied hand fumbled over her knitting. The early evening had closed in, and the farm servants had come in from the outdoor work and assembled in the ample hall, which had space for scores of workers. Several of the men were engaged in carving, and to these were yielded the best place and light; others made or re-paired fishing tackle and harness, and a great seine net occupied three pairs of hands. Of the women, most were sorting and mix-ing eider feather and chopping straw of the same. Looms were there, though not in present use, but three wheels whirred emu-lously, and the finest and swiftest thread of the three ran be-tween the fingers of the house mistress. Near her were some children, busy, too, plaiting wicks for candles and lamps. Each group of workers had a lamp in its center, and those farthest from the fire had extra warmth from two braziers filled with glowing wood embers, replenished now and again from the gen-erous hearth. But the flicker of the great fire was manifest to re-motest corners, and prevailed beyond the limits of the lesser lights.

Little Rol grew tired of his puppy, dropped it incontinently, and made an onslaught on Tyr, the old wolfhound, who basked, dozing, whimpering and twitching in his hunting dreams. Prone went Rol beside Tyr, his young arms round the shaggy neck, his curls against the black jowl. Tyr gave a perfunctory lick, and stretched with a sleepy sigh. Rol growled and rolled and shoved invitingly, but could gain nothing from the old dog but placid toleration and a half-

observant blink. "Take that, then!" said Rol, indignant at this ignoring of his advances, and sent the puppy sprawling against the dignity
that disdained him as playmate. The dog took no notice, and the
child wandered off to find amusement elsewhere.

The baskets of white eider feathers caught his eye far off in a
distant corner. He slipped under the table and crept along on all-
fours, the ordinary commonplace custom of walking down a room
upright not being to his fancy. When close to the women he lay still
for a moment watching, with his elbows on the floor and his chin
in his palms. One of the women seeing him nodded and smiled, and
presently he crept out behind her skirts and passed, hardly noticed,
from one to another, till he found opportunity to possess himself
of a large handful of feathers. With these he traversed the length of
the room, under the table again, and emerged near the spinners. At
the feet of the youngest he curled himself round, sheltered by her
knees from the observation of the others, and disarmed her of
interference by secretly displaying his handful with a confiding
smile. A dubious nod satisfied him, and presently he proceeded with
the play he had planned. He took a tuft of the white down, and
gently shook it free of his fingers close to the whirl of the wheel. The
wind of the swift motion took it, spun it round and round in widen-
ing circles, till it floated above like a slow white moth. Little Rol's
eyes danced, and the row of his small teeth shone in a silent laugh
of delight. Another and another of the white tufts was sent whirling
round like a winged thing in a spider's web, and floating clear at last.
Presently the handful failed.

Rol sprawled forward to survey the room and contemplate another journey under the table. His shoulder thrusting forward
checked the wheel for an instant; he shifted hastily. The wheel flew
on with a jerk and the thread snapped. "Naughty Rol!" said the girl.
The swiftest wheel stopped also, and the house mistress, Rol's aunt,
leaned forward and sighting the low curly head, gave a warning
against mischief, and sent him off to old Trella's corner.

Rol obeyed, and, after a discreet period of obedience, sidled out
again down the length of the room farthest from his aunt's eye. As
he slipped in among the men, they looked up to see that their tools
might be, as far as possible, out of reach of Rol's hands, and close
to their own. Nevertheless, before long he managed to secure a fine

chisel and take off its point on the leg of the table. The carver's strong objections to this disconcerted Rol, who for five minutes thereafter effaced himself under the table.

During this seclusion he contemplated the many pairs of legs that surrounded him and almost shut out the light of the fire. How very odd some of the legs were; some were curved where they should be straight; some were straight where they should be curved; and as Rol said to himself, "They all seemed screwed on differently." Some were tucked away modestly, under the benches, others were thrust far out under the table, encroaching on Rol's own particular domain. He stretched out his own short legs and regarded them critically, and, after comparison, favorably. Why were not all legs made like this, or like his?

These legs approved by Rol were a little apart from the rest. He crawled opposite and again made comparison. His face grew quite solemn as he thought of the innumerable days to come before his legs could be as long and strong. He hoped they would be just like those, his models, as straight as to bone, as curved as to muscle.

A few moments later Sweyn of the long legs felt a small hand caressing his foot, and looking down met the upturned eyes of his little cousin Rol. Lying on his back, still softly patting and stroking the young man's foot, the child was quiet and happy for a good while. He watched the movements of the strong, deft hands and the shifting of the bright tools. Now and then minute chips of wood puffed off by Sweyn fell down upon his face. At last he raised himself very gently, lest a jog should wake impatience in the carver, and crossing his own legs round Sweyn's ankle, clasping with his arms too, laid his head against the knee. Such an act is evidence of a child's most wonderful hero worship. Quite content was Rol, and more than content when Sweyn paused a minute to joke, and pat his head and pull his curls. Quiet he remained, as long as quiescence is possible to limbs young as his. Sweyn forgot he was near, hardly noticed when his leg was gently released, and never saw the stealthy abstraction of one of his tools.

Ten minutes thereafter was a lamentable wail from low on the floor, rising to the full pitch of Rol's healthy lungs, for his hand was gashed across and the copious bleeding terrified him. Then there was soothing and comforting, washing and binding, and a modicum of scolding, till the loud outcry sank into occasional sobs, and the child, tear-stained and subdued, was returned to the chimney-corner, where Trella nodded.

In the reaction after pain and fright, Rol found that the quiet of that firelit corner was to his mind. Tyr, too, disdained him no longer, but, roused by his sobs, showed all the concern and sympathy that a dog can by licking and wistful watching. A little shame weighed also upon his spirits. He wished he had not cried quite so much. He remembered how once Sweyn had come home with his arm torn down from the shoulder, and a dead bear; and how he had never winced nor said a word, though his lips turned white with pain. Poor little Rol gave an extra sighing sob over his own faint-hearted shortcomings.

The light and motion of the great fire began to tell strange stories to the child, and the wind in the chimney roared a corroborative note now and then. The great black mouth of the chimney, impending high over the hearth, received the murky coils of smoke and brightness of aspiring sparks as into a mysterious gulf, and beyond, in the high darkness, were muttering and wailing and strange doings, so that sometimes the smoke rushed back in panic, and curled out and up to the roof, and condensed itself to invisibility among the rafters. And then the wind would rage after its lost prey, rattling and shrieking at window and door.

In a lull, after one such loud gust, Rol lifted his head in surprise and listened. A lull had also come on the babble of talk, and thus could be heard with strange distinctness a sound without the door —the sound of a child's voice, a child's hands. "Open, open; let me in!" piped the little voice from low down, lower than the handle, and the latch rattled as though a tiptoe child reached up to it, and soft small knocks were struck. One near the door sprang up and opened it. "No one is here," he said. Tyr lifted his head and gave utterance to a howl, loud, prolonged, most dismal.

Sweyn, not able to believe that his ears had deceived him, got up and went to the door. It was a dark night; the clouds were heavy with snow, that had fallen fitfully when the wind lulled. Untrodden snow lay up to the porch; there was no sight nor sound of any human being. Sweyn strained his eyes far and near, only to see dark sky, pure snow, and a line of black fir trees on a hill brow, bowing down before the wind. "It must have been the wind," he said, and closed the door.

Many faces looked scared. The sound of a child's voice had been so distinct—and the words, "Open, open; let me in!" The wind might creak the wood or rattle the latch, but could not speak with a child's voice; nor knock with the soft plain blows that a plump fist gives. And the strange unusual howl of the wolfhound was an omen to be feared, be the rest what it might. Strange things were said by one and other, till the rebuke of the house mistress quelled them into far-off whispers. For a time after there was uneasiness, constraint, and silence; then the chill fear thawed by degrees, and the babble of talk flowed on again.

Yet half an hour later a very slight noise outside the door sufficed to arrest every hand, every tongue. Every head was raised, every eye fixed in one direction. "It is Christian; he is late," said Sweyn.

No, no; this is a feeble shuffle, not a young man's tread. With the sound of uncertain feet came the hard tap-tap of a stick against the door, and the high-pitched voice of eld, "Open, open; let me in!" Again Tyr flung up his head in a long doleful howl.

Before the echo of the tapping stick and the high voice had fairly died away, Sweyn had sprung across to the door and flung it wide. "No one again," he said in a steady voice, though his eyes looked startled as he stared out. He saw the lonely expanse of snow, the clouds swagging low, and between the two the line of dark fir trees bowing in the wind. He closed the door without word of comment, and recrossed the room.

A score of blanched faces were turned to him as though he were the solver of the enigma. He could not be unconscious of this mute eye-questioning, and it disturbed his resolute air of composure. He hesitated, glanced toward his mother, the house mistress, then back at the frightened folk, and gravely, before them all, made the sign of the cross. There was a flutter of hands as the sign was repeated by all, and the dead silence was stirred as by a huge sigh, for the held breath of many was freed as if the sign gave magic relief.

Even the house mistress was perturbed. She left her wheel and crossed the room to her son, and spoke with him for a moment in a low tone that none could overhear. But a moment later her voice was high-pitched and loud, so that all might benefit by her rebuke of the "heathen chatter" of one of the girls. Perhaps she essayed to silence thus her own misgivings and forebodings.

No other voice dared speak now with its natural fulness. Low tones made intermittent murmurs, and now and then silence drifted over the whole room. The handling of tools was as noiseless as might be, and suspended on the instant if the door rattled in a gust of wind. After a time Sweyn left his work, joined the group nearest the door, and loitered there on the pretense of giving advice and help to the unskillful.

A man's tread was heard outside in the porch. "Christian!" said Sweyn and his mother simultaneously, he confidently, she authoritatively, to set the checked wheels going again. But Tyr flung up his head with an appalling howl.

"Open, open; let me in!"

It was a man's voice, and the door shook and rattled as a man's strength beat against it. Sweyn could feel the planks quivering, as on the instant his hand was upon the door, flinging it open, to face the blank porch, and beyond only snow and sky, and firs aslant in the wind.

He stood for a long minute with the open door in his hand. The bitter wind swept in with its icy chill, but a deadlier chill of fear came swifter, and seemed to freeze the beating of hearts. Sweyn snatched up a great bearskin cloak.

"Sweyn, where are you going?"

"No farther than the porch, mother," and he stepped out and closed the door.

He wrapped himself in the heavy fur, and leaning against the most sheltered wall of the porch, steeled his nerves to face the devil and all his works. No sound of voices came from within; but he could hear the crackle and roar of the fire.

It was bitterly cold. His feet grew numb, but he forebore stamping them into warmth lest the sound should strike panic within; nor would he leave the porch, nor print a footmark on the untrodden snow that testified conclusively to no human voices and hands having approached the door since snow fell two hours or more ago. "When the wind drops there will be more snow," thought Sweyn.

For the best part of an hour he kept his watch, and saw no living thing—heard no unwonted sound. "I will freeze here no longer," he muttered, and re-entered.

One woman gave a half-suppressed scream as his hand was laid on the latch, and then a gasp of relief as he came in. No one questioned him, only his mother said, in a tone of forced unconcern, "Could you not see Christian coming?" as though she were made anxious only by the absence of her younger son. Hardly had Sweyn stamped near to the fire than clear knocking was heard at the door. Tyr leaped from the hearth—his eyes red as the fire—his fangs showing white in the black jowl—his neck ridged and bristling; and overleaping Rol, ramped at the door, barking furiously.

Outside the door a clear, mellow voice was calling. Tyr's bark made the words undistinguishable.

No one offered to stir toward the door before Sweyn.

He stalked down the room resolutely, lifted the latch, and swung back the door.

A white-robed woman glided in.

No wraith! Living—beautiful—young.

Tyr leapt upon her.

Lithely she balked the sharp fangs with folds of her long fur robe, and snatching from her girdle a small two-edged axe, whirled it up for a blow of defense.

Sweyn caught the dog by the collar and dragged him off, yelling and struggling. The stranger stood in the doorway motionless, one foot set forward, one arm flung up, till the house mistress hurried down the room, and Sweyn, relinquishing to others the furious Tyr, turned again to close the door and offer excuses for so fierce a greeting. Then she lowered her arm, slung the axe in its place at her waist, loosened the furs about her face, and shook over her shoulder the long white robe—all, as it were, with the sway of one movement.

She was a maiden, tall and very fair. The fashion of her dress was strange—half masculine, yet not unwomanly. A fine fur tunic, reaching but little below the knee, was all the skirt she wore; below were the cross-bound shoes and leggings that a hunter wears. A white fur cap was set low upon the brows, and from its edge strips of fur fell lappet-wise about her shoulders, two of which at her entrance had been drawn forward and crossed about her throat, but now, loosened and thrust back, left unhidden long plaits of fair hair that lay forward on shoulder and breast, down to the ivory-studded girdle where the axe gleamed.

Sweyn and his mother led the stranger to the hearth without question or sign of curiosity, till she voluntarily told her tale of a long journey to distant kindred, a promised guide unmet, and signals and landmarks mistaken.

"Alone!" exclaimed Sweyn, in astonishment. "Have you journeyed thus far—a hundred leagues—alone?"

She answered "Yes," with a little smile.

"Over the hills and the wastes! Why, the folk there are savage and wild as beasts."

She dropped her hand upon her axe with a laugh of scorn.

"I fear neither man nor beast; some few fear me," and then she told strange tales of fierce attack and defense, and of the bold, free huntress life she had led.

Her words came a little slowly and deliberately, as though she spoke in a scarce familiar tongue; now and then she hesitated, and stopped in a phrase, as if for lack of some word.

She became the center of a group of listeners. The interest she excited dissipated, in some degree, the dread inspired by the mysterious voices. There was nothing ominous about this bright, fair reality, though her aspect was strange.

Little Rol crept near, staring at the stranger with all his might. Unnoticed, he softly stroked and patted a corner of her soft white robe that reached to the floor in ample folds. He laid his cheek against it caressingly, and then edged close up to her knees.

"What is your name?" he asked.

The stranger's smile and ready answer, as she looked down, saved Rol from the rebuke merited by his question.

"My real name," she said, "would be uncouth to your ears and tongue. The folk of this country have given me another name, and from this"—she laid her hand on the fur robe—"they call me 'White Fell.'"

Little Rol repeated it to himself, stroking and patting as before. "White Fell, White Fell."

The fair face, and soft, beautiful dress pleased Rol. He knelt up, with his eyes on her face and an air of uncertain determination, like a robin's on a doorstep, and plumped his elbows into her lap with a little gasp at his own audacity.

"Rol!" exclaimed his aunt; but, "Oh, let him!" said White Fell, smiling and stroking his head; and Rol stayed.

He advanced farther, and, panting at his own adventurousness, in the face of his aunt's authority, climbed up on to her knees. Her welcoming arms hindered any protest. He nestled happily, fingering the axe head, the ivory studs in her girdle, the ivory clasp at her throat, the plaits of fair hair; rubbing his head against the softness of her fur-clad shoulder, with a child's confidence in the kindness of beauty.

White Fell had not uncovered her head, only knotted the pendant fur loosely behind her neck. Rol reached up his hand toward it, whispering her name to himself, "White Fell, White Fell," then slid his arms round her neck, and kissed her—once—twice. She laughed delightedly and kissed him again.

"The child plagues you?" said Sweyn.

"No, indeed," she answered, with an earnestness so intense as to seem disproportionate to the occasion.

Rol settled himself again on her lap and began to unwind the bandage bound round his hand. He paused a little when he saw where the blood had soaked through, then went on till his hand was bare and the cut displayed, gaping and long, though only skin-deep. He held it up toward White Fell, desirous of her pity and sympathy.

At sight of it and the blood-stained linen she drew in her breath suddenly, clasped Rol to her—hard, hard—till he began to struggle. Her face was hidden behind the boy, so that none could see its expression. It had lighted up with a most awful glee.

Afar, beyond the fir grove, beyond the low hill behind, the absent Christian was hastening his return. From daybreak he had been afoot, carrying summons to a bear hunt to all the best hunters of the farms and hamlets that lay within a radius of twelve miles. Nevertheless, having been detained till a late hour, he now broke into a run, going with a long smooth stride that fast made the miles diminish.

He entered the midnight blackness of the fir grove with scarcely slackened pace, though the path was invisible, and, passing through into the open again, sighted the farm lying a furlong off down the slope. Then he sprang out freely, and almost on the instant gave one great sideways leap and stood still. There in the snow was the track of a great wolf.

His hand went to his knife, his only weapon. He stooped, knelt down, to bring his eyes to the level of a beast, and peered about, his teeth set, his heart beating—a little harder than the pace of his running had set it. A solitary wolf, nearly always savage and of large size, is a formidable beast that will not hesitate to attack a single man. This wolf track was the largest Christian had ever seen, and, as far as he could judge, recently made. It led from under the fir trees down the slope. Well for him, he thought, was the delay that had so vexed him before; well for him that he had not passed through the dark fir grove when that danger of jaws lurked there. Going warily, he followed the track.

It led down the slope, across a broad ice-bound stream, along the level beyond, leading toward the farm. A less sure knowledge than Christian's might have doubted of it being a wolf track, and guessed it to be made by Tyr or some large dog; but he was sure, and knew better than to mistake between a wolf's and a dog's footmark.

Straight on—straight on toward the farm.

Christian grew surprised and anxious at a prowling wolf daring so near. He drew his knife and pressed on, more hastily, more keenly eyed. Oh, that Tyr were with him!

Straight on, straight on, even to the very door, where the snow failed. His heart seemed to give a great leap and then stop. There the track ended.

Nothing lurked in the porch, and there was no sign of return. The firs stood straight against the sky, the clouds lay low; for the wind had fallen and a few snowflakes came drifting down. In a horror of surprise, Christian stood dazed a moment; then he lifted the latch and went in. His glance took in all the old familiar forms and faces, and with them that of the stranger, fur-clad and beautiful. The awful truth flashed upon him. He knew what she was.

Only a few were startled by the rattle of the latch as he entered. The room was filled with bustle and movement, for it was the supper hour, and all tools were being put aside and trestles and tables shifted. Christian had no knowledge of what he said and did; he moved and spoke mechanically, half thinking that soon he must wake from this horrible dream. Sweyn and his mother supposed him to be cold and dead-tired, and spared all unnecessary questions. And he found himself seated beside the hearth, opposite that dreadful Thing that looked like a beautiful girl, watching her every movement, curdling with horror to see her fondle Rol.

Sweyn stood near them both, intent upon White Fell also, but how differently! She seemed unconscious of the gaze of both—neither aware of the chill dread in the eyes of Christian, nor of Sweyn's warm admiration.

These two brothers, who were twins, contrasted greatly, despite their striking likeness. They were alike in regular profile, fair brown hair, and deep blue eyes; but Sweyn's features were perfect as a young god's, while Christian's showed faulty details. Thus, the line of his mouth was set too straight, the eyes shelved too deeply back, and the contour of the face flowed in less generous curves than Sweyn's. Their height was the same, but Christian was too slender for perfect proportion, while Sweyn's well-knit frame, broad shoulders and muscular arms made him pre-eminent for manly beauty as well as for strength. As a hunter Sweyn was without rival; as a fisher without rival. All the countryside acknowledged him to be the best wrestler, rider, dancer, singer. Only in speed could he be surpassed, and in that only by his younger brother. All others Sweyn could distance fairly; but Christian could outrun him easily. Aye, he could keep pace with Sweyn's most breathless burst, and laugh and talk the while. Christian took little pride in his fleetness of foot, counting a man's legs to be the least worthy of his limbs. He had no envy of his brother's athletic superiority, though to several feats he had made a moderate second. He loved as only a twin can love—proud of all that Sweyn did, content with all that Sweyn was, humbly content also that his own great love should not be so exceedingly returned, since he knew himself to be so far less loveworthy.

Christian dared not, in the midst of women and children, launch the horror that he knew into words. He waited to consult his brother; but Sweyn did not, or would not, notice the signal he made, and kept his face always turned toward White Fell. Christian drew away from the hearth, unable to remain passive with that dread upon him.

"Where is Tyr?" he said, suddenly. Then catching sight of the dog in a distant corner, "Why is he chained there?"

"He flew at the stranger," one answered.

Christian's eyes glowed. "Yes?" he said interrogatively, and, rising, went without a word to the corner where Tyr was chained. The dog rose up to meet him, as piteous and indignant as a dumb beast can be. He stroked the black head. "Good Tyr! Brave dog!"

They knew—they only—and the man and the dumb dog had comfort of each other.

Christian's eyes turned again toward White Fell. Tyr's also, and he strained against the length of the chain. Christian's hand lay on the dog's neck, and he felt it ridge and bristle with the quivering of impotent fury. Then he began to quiver in like manner, with a fury born of reason, not instinct; as impotent morally as was Tyr physically. Oh, the woman's form that he dare not touch! Anything but that, and he with Tyr, would be free to kill or be killed.

Then he returned to ask fresh questions.

"How long has the stranger been here?"

"She came about half an hour before you."

"Who opened the door to her?"

"Sweyn. No one else dared."

The tone of the answer was mysterious.

"Why?" queried Christian. "Has anything strange happened? Tell me?"

For answer he was told in a low undertone of the summons at the door, thrice repeated, without human agency; and of Tyr's ominous howls, and of Sweyn's fruitless watch outside.

Christian turned toward his brother in a torment of impatience for a word apart. The board was spread and Sweyn was leading White Fell to the guest's place. This was more awful! She would break bread with them under the roof tree.

He started forward and, touching Sweyn's arm, whispered an urgent entreaty. Sweyn stared, and shook his head in angry impatience.

Thereupon Christian would take no morsel of food.

His opportunity came at last. White Fell questioned of the landmarks of the country, and of one Cairn Hill, which was an appointed meeting place at which she was due that night. The house mistress and Sweyn both exclaimed:

"It is three long miles away," said Sweyn, "with no place for shelter but a wretched hut. Stay with us this night and I will show you the way tomorrow."

White Fell seemed to hesitate. "Three miles," she said, "then I should be able to see or hear a signal."

"I will look out," said Sweyn; "then, if there be no signal, you must not leave us."

He went to the door. Christian silently followed him out.

"Sweyn, do you know what she is?"

Sweyn, surprised at the vehement grasp and low hoarse voice, made answer:

"She? Who? White Fell?"

"Yes."

"She is the most beautiful girl I have ever seen."

"She is a were-wolf."

Sweyn burst out laughing. "Are you mad?" he asked.

"No; here, see for yourself."

Christian drew him out of the porch, pointing to the snow where the footmarks had been—had been, for now they were not. Snow was falling, and every dint was blotted out.

"Well?" asked Sweyn.

"Had you come when I signed to you, you would have seen for yourself."

"Seen what?"

"The footprints of a wolf leading up to the door; none leading away."

It was impossible not to be startled by the tone alone, though it was hardly above a whisper. Sweyn eyed his brother anxiously, but in the darkness could make nothing of his face. Then he laid his hands kindly and reassuringly on Christian's shoulders and felt how he was quivering with excitement and horror.

"One sees strange things," he said, "when the cold has got into the brain behind the eyes; you came in cold and worn out."

"No," interrupted Christian. "I saw the track first on the brow of the slope, and followed it down right here to the door. This is no delusion."

Sweyn in his heart felt positive that it was. Christian was given to daydreams and strange fancies, though never had he been possessed with so mad a notion before.

"Don't you believe me?" said Christian desperately. "You must. I swear it is sane truth. Are you blind? Why, even Tyr knows."

"You will be clearer-headed tomorrow, after a night's rest. Then come, too, if you will, with White Fell, to the Hill Cairn, and, if you have doubts still, watch and follow, and see what footprints she leaves."

Galled by Sweyn's evident contempt, Christian turned abruptly to the door. Sweyn caught him back.

"What now, Christian? What are you going to do?"

"You do not believe me; my mother shall."

Sweyn's grasp tightened. "You shall not tell her," he said, authoritatively.

Customarily Christian was so docile to his brother's mastery that it was now a surprising thing when he wrenched himself free vigorously and said as determinedly as Sweyn: "She shall know." But Sweyn was nearer the door, and would not let him pass.

"There has been scare enough for one night already. If this notion of yours will keep, broach it tomorrow." Christian would not yield.

"Women are so easily scared," pursued Sweyn, "and are ready to believe any folly without proof. Be a man, Christian, and fight this notion of a were-wolf by yourself."

"If you would believe me," began Christian.

"I believe you to be a fool," said Sweyn, losing patience. "Another, who was not your brother, might think you a knave, and guess that you had transformed White Fell into a were-wolf because she smiled more readily on me than on you."

The jest was not without foundation, for the grace of White Fell's bright looks had been bestowed on him—on Christian never a whit. Sweyn's coxcombry was always frank and most forgivable, and not without justifiableness.

"If you want an ally," continued Sweyn, "confide in old Trella. Out of her stores of wisdom—if her memory holds good—she can instruct you in the orthodox manner of tackling a were-wolf. If I remember aright, you should watch the suspected person till midnight, when the beast's form must be resumed, and retained ever after if a human eye sees the change; or, better still, sprinkle hands and feet with holy water, which is certain death! Oh, never fear, but old Trella will be equal to the occasion."

Sweyn's contempt was no longer good-humored, for he began to feel excessively annoyed at this monstrous doubt of White Fell. But Christian was too deeply distressed to take offense.

"You speak of them as old wives' tales, but if you had seen the proof I have seen, you would be ready at least to wish them true, if not also to put them to the test."

"Well," said Sweyn, with a laugh that had a little sneer in it, "put them to the test—I will not mind that, if you will only keep your notions to yourself. Now, Christian, give me your word for silence, and we will freeze here no longer."

Christian remained silent.

Sweyn put his hands on his shoulders again and vainly tried to see his face in the darkness.

"We have never quarreled yet, Christian?"

"I have never quarreled," returned the other, aware for the first time that his dictatorial brother had sometimes offered occasion for quarrel, had he been ready to take it.

"Well," said Sweyn, emphatically, "if you speak against White Fell to any other, as tonight you have spoken to me—we shall."

He delivered the words like an ultimatum, turned sharp round and re-entered the house. Christian, more fearful and wretched than before, followed.

"Snow is falling fast—not a single light is to be seen."

White Fell's eyes passed over Christian without apparent notice, and turned bright and shining upon Sweyn.

"Nor any signal to be heard?" she queried. "Did you not hear the sound of a sea-horn?"

"I saw nothing and heard nothing; and signal or no signal, the heavy snow would keep you here perforce."

She smiled her thanks beautifully. And Christian's heart sank like lead with a deadly foreboding, as he noted what a light was kindled in Sweyn's eyes by her smile.

That night, when all others slept, Christian, the weariest of all, watched outside the guest chamber till midnight was past. No sound, not the faintest, could be heard. Could the old tale be true of the midnight change? What was on the other side of the door— a woman or a beast—he would have given his right hand to know. Instinctively he laid his hand on the latch, and drew it softly, though believing that bolts fastened the inner side. The door yielded to his hand; he stood on the threshold; a keen gust of air cut at him. The window stood open; the room was empty.

So Christian could sleep with a somewhat lightened heart.

In the morning there was surprise and conjecture when White Fell's absence was discovered. Christian held his peace; not even to his brother did he say how he knew that she had fled before midnight; and Sweyn, though evidently greatly chagrined, seemed to disdain reference to the subject of Christian's fears.

The elder brother alone joined the bear hunt; Christian found pretext to stay behind. Sweyn, being out of humor, manifested his contempt by uttering not one expostulation.

All that day, and for many a day after, Christian would never go out of sight of his home. Sweyn alone noticed how he maneuvered for this, and was clearly annoyed by it. White Fell's name was never mentioned between them, though not seldom was it heard in general talk. Hardly a day passed without little Rol asking when White Fell would come again; pretty White Fell, who kissed like a snowflake. And if Sweyn answered, Christian would be quite sure that the light in his eyes, kindled by White Fell's smile, had not yet died out.

Little Rol! Naughty, merry, fair-haired little Rol! A day came when his feet raced over the threshold never to return; when his chatter and laugh were heard no more; when tears of anguish were wept by eyes that never would see his bright head again—never again—living or dead.

He was seen at dusk for the last time, escaping from the house with his puppy, in freakish rebellion against old Trella. Later, when his absence had begun to cause anxiety, his puppy crept back to the farm, cowed, whimpering, and yelping—a pitiful, dumb lump of terror—without intelligence or courage to guide the frightened search.

Rol was never found, nor any trace of him. How he had perished was known only by an awful guess—a wild beast had devoured him.

Christian heard the conjecture, "a wolf," and a horrible certainty flashed upon him that he knew what wolf it was. He tried to declare what he knew, but Sweyn saw him start at the words with white face and struggling lips, and, guessing his purpose, pulled him back and kept him silent, hardly, by his imperious grip and wrathful eyes, and one low whisper. Again Christian yielded to his brother's stronger words and will, and against his own judgment consented to silence.

Repentance came before the new moon—the first of the year—was old. White Fell came again, smiling as she entered as though assured of a glad and kindly welcome; and, in truth, there was only one who saw again her fair face and strange white garb without pleasure. Sweyn's face glowed with delight, while Christian's grew pale and rigid as death. He had given his word to keep silence, but he had not thought that she would dare to come again. Silence was impossible—face to face with that Thing—impossible. Irrepressibly he cried out:

"Where is Rol?"

Not a quiver disturbed White Fell's face; she heard, yet remained bright and tranquil—Sweyn's eyes flashed round at his brother dangerously. Among the women some tears fell at the poor child's name, but none caught alarm from its sudden utterance, for the thought of Rol rose naturally. Where was Rol, who had nestled in the stranger's arms, kissing her, and watched for her since, and prattled of her daily?

Christian went out silently. Only one thing there was that he could do, and he must not delay. His horror overmastered any curiosity to hear White Fell's glib excuses and smiling apologies for her strange and uncourteous departure; or her easy tale of the circumstances of her return; or to watch her bearing as she heard the sad tale of little Rol.

The swiftest runner of the countryside had started on his hardest race—little less than three leagues and back, which he reckoned to accomplish in two hours, though the night was moonless and the way rugged. He rushed against the still cold air till it felt like a wind upon his face. The dim homestead sank below the ridges at his back, and fresh ridges of snowlands rose out of the obscure horizon level to drive past him as the stirless air drove, and sink away behind into obscure level again. He took no conscious heed of landmarks, not even when all sign of a path was gone under depths of snow. His will was set to reach his goal with unexampled speed, and thither by instinct his physical forces bore him, without one definite thought to guide.

And the idle brain lay passive, inert, receiving into its vacancy, restless siftings of past sights and sounds; Rol weeping, laughing, playing, coiled in the arms of that dreadful Thing; Tyr—O Tyr!— white fangs in the black jowl; the women who wept on the foolish puppy, precious for the child's last touch; footprints from pinewood to door; the smiling face among furs, of such womanly beauty— smiling—smiling; and Sweyn's face.

"Sweyn, Sweyn, O Sweyn, my brother!"

Sweyn's angry laugh possessed his ear within the sound of the wind of his speed; Sweyn's scorn assailed more quick and keen than the biting cold at his throat. And yet he was unimpressed by any thought of how Sweyn's scorn and anger would rise if this errand were known.

To the younger brother all life was a spiritual mystery, veiled from his clear knowledge by the density of flesh. Since he knew his own body to be linked to the complex and antagonistic forces that constitute one soul, it seemed to him not impossibly strange that one spiritual force should possess divers forms for widely various manifestation. Nor, to him, was it great effort to believe that as pure water washes away all natural foulness, so water holy by consecration must needs cleanse God's world from that supernatural evil Thing. Therefore, faster than ever man's foot had covered those leagues, he sped under the dark, still night, over the waste trackless snow ridges to the faraway church where salvation lay in the holy-water stoop at the door. His faith was as firm as any that wrought miracles in days past, simple as a child's wish, strong as a man's will.

He was hardly missed during these hours, every second of which was by him fulfilled to its utmost extent by extremest effort that sinews and nerves could attain. Within the homestead the while the easy moments went bright with words and looks of unwonted animation, for the kindly hospitable instincts of the inmates were roused into cordial expression of welcome and interest by the grace and beauty of the returned stranger.

But Sweyn was eager and earnest, with more than a host's courteous warmth. The impression that at her first coming had charmed him, that had lived since through memory, deepened now in her actual presence. Sweyn, the matchless among men, acknowledged in this fair White Fell a spirit high and bold as his own, and a frame so firm and capable that only bulk was lacking for equal strength. Yet the white skin was moulded most smoothly, without such muscular swelling as made his might evident. Such love as his frank self-love could concede was called forth by an ardent admiration for this supreme stranger. More admiration than love was in his passion, and therefore he was free from a lover's hesitancy, and delicate reserve and doubts. Frankly and boldly he courted her favor by looks and tones, and an address that was his by natural ease.

Nor was she a woman to be wooed otherwise. Tender whispers and sighs would never gain her ear; but her eyes would brighten and shine if she heard of a brave feat, and her prompt hand in sympathy fall swiftly on the axe haft and clasp it hard. That movement ever fired Sweyn's admiration anew; he watched for it, strove to elicit it and glowed when it came. Wonderful and beautiful was that wrist, slender and steel-strong; the smooth shapely hand that curved so fast and firm, ready to deal instant death.

Desiring to feel the pressure of these hands, this bold lover schemed with palpable directness, proposing that she should hear how their hunting songs were sung, with a chorus that signaled hands to be clasped. So his splendid voice gave the verses, and, as the chorus was taken up, he claimed her hands, and, even through the easy grip, felt, as he desired, the strength that was latent, and the vigor that quickened the very fingertips, as the song fired her, and her voice was caught out of her by the rhythmic swell and rang clear on the top of the closing surge.

Afterward she sang alone. For contrast, or in the pride of swaying moods by her voice, she chose a mournful song that drifted along in a minor chant, sad as a wind that dirges:

> "Oh, let me go!
> Around spin wreaths of snow;
> The dark earth sleeps below.

"Far up the plain
Moans on a voice of pain:
"Where shall my babe be lain?

"In my white breast
Lay the sweet life to rest!
Lay, where it can be best!

" 'Hush! hush!' it cries;
'Tense night is on the skies;
'Two stars are in thine eyes.'

"Come, babe away!
But lie thou till dawn be gray,
Who must be dead by day.

"This cannot last;
But, o'er the sickening blast,
All sorrows shall be past;

"All kings shall be
Low bending at thy knee,
Worshiping life from thee.

"For men long sore
To hope of what's before—
To leave the things of yore.

"Mine, and not thine,
How deep their jewels shine!
Peace laps thy head, not mine!"

Old Trella came tottering from her corner, shaken to additional palsy by an aroused memory. She strained her dim eyes toward the singer, and then bent her head that the one ear yet sensible to sound might avail of every note. At the close, groping forward, she murmured with the high-pitched quaver of old age:

"So she sang, my Thora; my last and brightest. What is she like —she, whose voice is like my dead Thora's? Are her eyes blue?"

"Blue as the sky."

"So were my Thora's! Is her hair fair and in plaits to the waist?"

"Even so," answered White Fell herself, and met the advancing hands with her own, and guided them to corroborate her words by touch.

"Like my dead Thora's," repeated the old woman; and then her trembling hands rested on the fur-clad shoulders and she bent forward and kissed the smooth fair face that White Fell upturned, nothing loath to receive and return the caress.

So Christian saw them as he entered.

He stood a moment. After the starless darkness and the icy night air, and the fierce silent two hours' race, his senses reeled on sudden entrance into warmth and light and the cheery hum of voices. A sudden unforeseen anguish assailed him, as now first he entertained the possibility of being overmatched by her wiles and her daring, if at the approach of pure death she should start up at bay transformed to a terrible beast, and achieve a savage glut at the last. He looked with horror and pity on the harmless helpless folk, so unwitting of outrage to their comfort and security. The dreadful Thing in their midst, that was veiled from their knowledge by womanly beauty, was a center of pleasant interest. There, before him, signally impressive, was poor old Trella, weakest and feeblest of all, in fond nearness. And a moment might bring about the revelation of a monstrous horror—a ghastly, deadly danger, set loose and at bay, in a circle of girls and women, and careless, defenseless men.

And he alone of the throng prepared!

For one breathing space he faltered, no longer than that, while over him swept the agony of compunction that yet could not make him surrender his purpose.

He alone? Nay, but Tyr also, and he crossed to the dumb sole sharer of his knowledge.

So timeless is thought that a few seconds only lay between his lifting of the latch and his loosening of Tyr's collar; but in those few seconds succeeding his first glance, as lightning-swift had been the impulses of others, their motion as quick and sure. Sweyn's vigilant eye had darted upon him, and instantly his every fiber was alert with hostile instinct; and half divining, half incredulous, of Christian's object in stooping to Tyr, he came hastily, wary, wrathful, resolute to oppose the malice of his wild-eyed brother.

But beyond Sweyn rose White Fell, blanching white as her furs, and with eyes grown fierce and wild. She leapt down the room to the door, whirling her long robe closely to her. "Hark!" she panted. "The signal horn! Hark, I must go!" as she snatched at the latch to be out and away.

For one precious moment Christian had hesitated on the half-loosened collar; for, except the womanly form were exchanged for the bestial, Tyr's jaws would gnash to rags his honor of manhood. He heard her voice, and turned—too late.

As she tugged at the door, he sprang across grasping his flask, but Sweyn dashed between and caught him back irresistibly, so that a most frantic effort only availed to wrench one arm free. With that, on the impulse of sheer despair, he cast at her with all his force. The door swung behind her, and the flask flew into fragments against it. Then, as Sweyn's grasp slackened, and he met the questioning astonishment of surrounding faces, with a hoarse inarticulate cry: "God help us all!" he said; "she is a were-wolf!"

Sweyn turned upon him, "Liar, coward!" and his hands gripped his brother's throat with deadly force as though the spoken word could be killed so, and, as Christian struggled, lifted him clear off his feet and flung him crashing backward. So furious was he that, as his brother lay motionless, he stirred him roughly with his foot, till their mother came between, crying, "Shame!" and yet then he stood by, his teeth set, his brows knit, his hands clenched, ready to enforce silence again violently, as Christian rose, staggering and bewildered.

But utter silence and submission was more than he expected, and turned his anger into contempt for one so easily cowed and held in subjection by mere force. "He is mad!" he said, turning on his heel as he spoke, so that he lost his mother's look of pained reproach at this sudden free utterance of what was a lurking dread within her.

Christian was too spent for the effort of speech. His hard-drawn breath labored in great sobs; his limbs were powerless and unstrung in utter relax after hard service. His failure in this endeavor induced a stupor of misery and despair. In addition was the wretched humiliation of open violence and strife with his brother, and the distress of hearing misjudging contempt expressed without reserve, for he was aware that Sweyn had turned to allay the scared excitement half by imperious mastery, half by explanation and argument that showed painful disregard of brotherly consideration.

Sweyn the while was observant of his brother, despite the continual check of finding, turn and glance where he would, Christian's eyes always upon him, with a strange look of helpless distress, discomposing enough to the angry aggressor. "Like a beaten dog!" he said to himself, rallying contempt to withstand compunction. Observation set him wondering on Christian's exhausted condition. The heavy laboring breath and the slack, inert fall of the limbs told surely of unusual and prolonged exertion. And then why had close upon two hours' absence been followed by manifestly hostile behavior toward White Fell? Suddenly, the fragments of the flask giving a clue, he guessed all, and faced about to stare at his brother in amaze. He forgot that the motive scheme was against White Fell, demanding derision and resentment from him; that was swept out of remembrance by astonishment and admiration for the feat of speed and endurance.

That night Sweyn and his mother talked long and late together, shaping into certainty the suspicion that Christian's mind had lost its balance, and discussing the evident cause. For Sweyn, declaring his own love for White Fell, suggested that his unfortunate brother with a like passion—they being twins in love as in birth—had through jealousy and despair turned from love to hate, until reason failed at the strain, and a craze developed, which the malice and treachery of madness made a serious and dangerous force.

So Sweyn theorized; convincing himself as he spoke; convincing afterward others who advanced doubts against White Fell; fettering his judgment by his advocacy, and by his staunch defense of her hurried flight, silencing his own inner consciousness of the unaccountability of her action.

But a little time and Sweyn lost his vantage in the shock of a fresh horror at the homestead. Trella was no more, and her end a mystery. The poor old woman crawled out in a bright gleam to visit a bed-ridden gossip living beyond the fir grove. Under the trees she was last seen halting for her companion, sent back for a forgotten present. Quick alarm sprang, calling every man to the search. Her stick was found among the brushwood near the path, but no track or stain, for a gusty wind was sifting the snow from the branches and hid all sign of how she came by her death.

So panic-stricken were the farm folk that none dared go singly on the search. Known danger could be braced, but not this stealthy Death that walked by day invisible, that cut off alike the child in his play and the aged woman so near to her quiet grave.

"Rol she kissed; Trella she kissed!" So rang Christian's frantic cry again and again, till Sweyn dragged him away and strove to keep him apart from the rest of the household.

But thenceforward all Sweyn's reasoning and mastery could not uphold White Fell above suspicion. He was not called upon to defend her from accusation, when Christian had been brought to silence again; but he well knew the significance of this fact, that her name, formerly uttered freely and often, he never heard now—it was huddled away into whispers that he could not catch.

For a time the twins' variance was marked on Sweyn's part by an air of rigid indifference, on Christian's by heavy downcast silence, and a nervous, apprehensive observation of his brother. Superadded to his remorse and foreboding, Sweyn's displeasure weighed upon him intolerably, and the remembrance of their violent rupture was ceaseless misery. The elder brother, self-sufficient and insensitive, could little know how deeply his unkindness stabbed. A depth and force of affection such as Christian's was unknown to him, and his brother's ceaseless surveillance annoyed him greatly. Therefore, that suspicion might be lulled, he judged it wise to make overtures for peace. Most easily done. A little kindliness, a few evidences of consideration, a slight return of the old brotherly imperiousness, and Christian replied by a gratefulness and relief that might have touched him had he understood all, but instead increased his secret contempt.

So successful was his finesse that when, late on a day, a message summoning Christian to a distance was transmitted by Sweyn no doubt of its genuineness occurred. When, his errand proving useless, he set out to return, mistake or misapprehension was all that he surmised. Not till he sighted the homestead, lying low between the night-gray snow ridges, did vivid recollection of the time when he had tracked that horror to the door rouse an intense dread, and with it a hardly defined suspicion.

His grasp tightened on the bear-spear that he carried as a staff; every sense was alert, every muscle strung; excitement urged him on, caution checked him, and the two governed his long stride, swiftly, noiselessly to the climax he felt was at hand.

As he drew near to the outer gates, a light shadow stirred and went, as though the gray of the snow had taken detached motion. A darker shadow stayed and faced Christian.

Sweyn stood before him, and surely the shadow that went was White Fell.

They had been together—close. Had she not been in his arms, near enough for lips to meet?

There was no moon, but the stars gave light enough to show that Sweyn's face was flushed and elated. The flush remained, though the expression changed quickly at sight of his brother. How, if Christian had seen all, should one of his frenzied outbursts be met and managed—by resolution? By indifference? He halted between the two, and as a result, he swaggered.

"White Fell?" questioned Christian, breathlessly.

"Yes?" Sweyn's answer was a query, with an intonation that implied he was clearing the ground for action.

From Christian came, "Have you kissed her?" like a bolt direct, staggering Sweyn by its sheer, prompt temerity.

He flushed yet darker, and yet half smiled over this earnest of success he had won. Had there been really between himself and Christian the rivalry that he imagined, his face had enough of the insolence of triumph to exasperate jealous rage.

"You dare ask this!"

"Sweyn, O Sweyn, I must know! You have!"

The ring of despair and anguish in his tone angered Sweyn, misconstruing it. Jealousy so presumptuous was intolerable.

"Mad fool!" he said, constraining himself no longer. "Win for yourself a woman to kiss. Leave mine without question. Such a one as I should desire to kiss is such a one as shall never allow a kiss to you."

Then Christian fully understood his supposition.

"I—I—!" he cried. "White Fell—that deadly Thing! Sweyn, are you blind, mad? I would save you from her—a were-wolf!"

Sweyn maddened again at the accusation—a dastardly way of revenge, as he conceived; and instantly, for the second time, the brothers were at strife violently. But Christian was now too desperate to be scrupulous; for a dim glimpse had shot a possibility into his mind, and to be free to follow it the striking of his brother was a necessity. Thank God! he was armed, and so Sweyn's equal.

Facing his assailant with the bear-spear, he struck up his arms, and with the butt end hit so hard that he fell. Then the matchless runner leapt away, to follow a forlorn hope.

Sweyn, on regaining his feet, was as amazed as angry at this unaccountable flight. He knew in his heart that his brother was no coward, and that it was unlike him to shrink from an encounter because defeat was certain, and cruel humiliation from a vindictive victor probable. Of the uselessness of pursuit he was well aware; he must abide his chagrin until his time for advantage should come. Since White Fell had parted to the right, Christian to the left, the event of a sequent encounter did not occur to him.

And now Christian, acting on the dim glimpse he had had, just as Sweyn turned upon him, of something that moved against the sky along the ridge behind the homestead, was staking his only hope on a chance, and his own superlative speed. If what he saw was really White Fell, he guessed she was bending her steps toward the open wastes; and there was just a possibility that, by a straight dash, and a desperate, perilous leap over a sheer bluff, he might yet meet her or head her. And then—he had no further thought.

It was past, the quick, fierce race, and the chance of death at the leap, and he halted in a hollow to fetch his breath and to look—did she come? Had she gone?

She came.

She came with a smooth, gliding, noiseless speed, that was neither walking nor running; her arms were folded in her furs that were drawn tight about her body; the white lappets from her head were wrapped and knotted closely beneath her face; her eyes were set on a far distance. Then the even sway of her going was startled to a pause by Christian.

"Fell!"

She drew a quick, sharp breath at the sound of her name thus mutilated, and faced Sweyn's brother. Her eyes glittered; her upper lip was lifted and showed the teeth. The half of her name, impressed with an ominous sense as uttered by him, warned her of the aspect of a deadly foe. Yet she cast loose her robes till they trailed ample, and spoke as a mild woman.

"What would you?"

Christian answered with his solemn, dreadful accusation:

"You kissed Rol—and Rol is dead! You kissed Trella—she is dead! You have kissed Sweyn, my brother, but he shall not die!"

He added: "You may live till midnight."

The edge of the teeth and the glitter of the eyes stayed a moment, and her right hand also slid down to the axe haft. Then, without a word, she swerved from him, and sprang out and away swiftly over the snow.

And Christian sprang out and away, and followed her swiftly over the snow, keeping behind, but half a stride's length from her side.

So they went running together, silent, toward the vast wastes of snow where no living thing but they two moved under the stars of night.

Never before had Christian so rejoiced in his powers. The gift of speed and the training of use and endurance were priceless to him now. Though midnight was hours away he was confident that go where that Fell Thing would hasten as she would, she could not outstrip him, nor escape from him. Then, when came the time for transformation, when the woman's form made no longer a shield against a man's hand, he could slay or be slain to save Sweyn. He had struck his dear brother in dire extremity, but he could not, though reason urged, strike a woman.

For one mile, for two miles they ran; White Fell ever foremost, Christian ever at an equal distance from her side, so near that, now and again, her outflying furs touched him. She spoke no word; nor he. She never turned her head to look at him, nor swerved to evade him; but, with set face looking forward, sped straight on, over rough, over smooth, aware of his nearness by the regular beat of his feet, and the sound of his breath behind.

In a while she quickened her pace. From the first Christian had judged of her speed as admirable, yet with exulting security in his own excelling and enduring whatever her efforts. But, when the pace increased, he found himself put to the test as never had been done before in any race. Her feet indeed flew faster than his; it was only by his length of stride that he kept his place at her side. But his heart was high and resolute, and he did not fear failure yet.

So the desperate race flew on. Their feet struck up the powdery snow, their breath smoked into the sharp, clear air, and they were gone before the air was cleared of snow and vapor. Now and then Christian glanced up to judge, by the rising of the stars, of the coming of midnight. So long—so long!

White Fell held on without slack. She, it was evident, with confidence in her speed proving matchless, as resolute to outrun her pursuer, as he to endure till midnight and fulfill his purpose. And Christian held on, still self-assured. He could not fail; he would not fail. To avenge Rol and Trella was motive enough for him to do what man could do; but for Sweyn more. She had kissed Sweyn, but he should not die, too—with Sweyn to save he could not fail.

Never before was such a race as this; no, not when in old Greece man and maid raced together with two fates at stake; for the hard running was sustained unabated, while star after star rose and went wheeling up toward midnight—for one hour, for two hours.

Then Christian saw and heard what shot him through with fear. Where a fringe of trees hung round a slope he saw something dark moving, and heard a yelp, followed by a full, horrid cry, and the dark spread out upon the snow—a pack of wolves in pursuit.

Of the beasts alone he had little cause for fear; at the pace he held he could distance them, four-footed though they were. But of White Fell's wiles he had infinite apprehension, for how might she not avail herself of the savage jaws of these wolves, akin as they were to half her nature. She vouchsafed to them nor look nor sign; but Christian, on an impulse, to assure himself that she should not escape him, caught and held the back-flung edge of her furs, running still.

She turned like a flash with a beastly snarl, teeth and eyes gleaming again. Her axe shone on the upstroke, on the downstroke, as she hacked at his hand. She had lopped it off at the wrist, but that he parried with the bear-spear. Even then she shore through the shaft and shattered the bones of the hand, so that he loosed perforce.

Then again they raced on as before, Christian not losing a pace, though his left hand swung bleeding and broken.

The snarl, indubitably, though modified from a woman's organs; the vicious fury revealed in teeth and eyes; the sharp, arrogant pain of her maiming blow, caught away Christian's heed of the beasts behind, by striking into him close, vivid realization of the infinitely greater danger that ran before him in that deadly Thing.

When he bethought him to look behind, lo! the pack had but reached their tracks, and instantly slunk aside, cowed; the yell of pursuit changing to yelps and whines. So abhorrent was that Fell creature to beast as to man.

She had drawn her furs more closely to her, disposing them so that, instead of flying loose to her heels, no drapery hung lower than her knees, and this without a check to her wonderful speed, nor embarrassment by the cumbering of the folds. She held her head as before; her lips were firmly set, only the tense nostrils gave her breath; not a sign of distress witnessed to the long sustaining of that terrible speed.

But on Christian by now the strain was telling palpably. His head weighed heavy, and his breath came laboring in great sobs; the bear-spear would have been a burden now. His heart was beating like a hammer, but such a dullness oppressed his brain that it was only by degrees he could realize his helpless state; wounded and weaponless, chasing that Thing, that was a fierce, desperate, axe-armed woman, except she should assume the beast with fangs yet more deadly.

And still the far, slow stars went lingering nearly an hour from midnight.

So far was his brain astray that an impression took him that she was fleeing from the midnight stars, whose gain was by such slow degrees that a time equalling days and days had gone in the race round the northern circle of the world, and days and days as long might last before the end—except she slackened, or except he failed.

But he would not fail yet.

How long had he been praying so? He had started with a self-confidence and reliance that had felt no need for that aid; and now it seemed the only means by which to restrain his heart from swelling beyond the compass of his body; by which to cherish his brain from dwindling and shriveling quite away. Some sharp-toothed creature kept tearing and dragging on his maimed left hand; he never could see it, he could not shake it off, but he prayed it off at times.

The clear stars before him took to shuddering and he knew why; they shuddered at sight of what was behind him. He had never divined before that strange Things hid themselves from men, under pretense of being snow-clad mounds of swaying trees; but now they came slipping out from their harmless covers to follow him, and mock at his impotence to make a kindred Thing resolve to truer form. He knew the air behind him was thronged; he heard the hum of innumerable murmurings together; but his eyes could never catch them—they were too swift and nimble; but he knew they were there, because, on a backward glance, he saw the snow mounds surge as they groveled flatlings out of sight; he saw the trees reel as they screwed themselves rigid past recognition among the boughs.

And after such glance the stars for a while returned to steadfastness, and an infinite stretch of silence froze upon the chill, gray world, only deranged by the swift, even beat of the flying feet, and his own—slower from the longer stride, and the sound of his breath. And for some clear moments he knew that his only concern was to sustain his speed regardless of pain and distress, to deny with every nerve he had her power to outstrip him or to widen the space between them, till the stars crept up to midnight.

A hideous check came to the race. White Fell swirled about and leapt to the right, and Christian, unprepared for so prompt a lurch, found close at his feet a deep pit yawning, and his own impetus past control. But he snatched at her as he bore past, clasping her right arm with his one whole hand, and the two swung together upon the brink.

And her straining away in self-preservation was vigorous enough to counterbalance his headlong impulse, and brought them reeling together to safety.

Then, before he was verily sure that they were not to perish so, crashing down, he saw her gnashing in wild, pale fury, as she wrenched to be free; and since her right arm was in his grasp, used her axe left-handed, striking back at him.

The blow was effectual enough even so; his right arm dropped powerless, gashed and with the lesser bone broken that jarred with horrid pain when he let it swing, as he leaped out again, and ran to recover the few feet she had gained from his pause at the shock.

The near escape and this new, quick pain made again every faculty alive and intense. He knew that what he followed was most surely Death animate; wounded and helpless, he was utterly at her mercy if so she should realize and take action. Hopeless to avenge, hopeless to save, his very despair for Sweyn swept him on to follow and follow and precede the kiss-doomed to death. Could he yet fail to hunt that Thing past midnight, out of the womanly form, alluring and treacherous, into lasting restraint of the bestial, which was the last shred of hope left from the confident purpose of the outset.

The last hour from midnight had lost half its quarters, and the stars went lifting up the great minutes, and again his greatening heart and his shrinking brain and the sickening agony that swung at either side conspired to appall the will that had only seeming empire over his feet.

Now White Fell's body was so closely enveloped that not a lap nor an edge flew free. She stretched forward strangely aslant, leaning from the upright poise of a runner. She cleared the ground at times by long bounds, gaining an increase of speed that Christian agonized to equal.

He grew bewildered, uncertain of his own identity, doubting of his own true form. He could not be really a man, no more than that running Thing was really a woman; his real form was only hidden under embodiment of a man, but what it was he did not know. And Sweyn's real form he did not know. Sweyn lay fallen at his feet, where he had struck him down—his own brother—he; he stumbled over him and had to overleap him and race harder because she who had kissed Sweyn leapt so fast. "Sweyn—Sweyn—O Sweyn!"

Why did the stars stop to shudder? Midnight else had surely come!

The leaning, leaping Thing looked back at him a wild, fierce look, and laughed in savage scorn and triumph. He saw in a flash why, for within a time measurable by seconds she would have escaped him utterly. As the land lay a slope of ice sunk on the one hand; on the other hand a steep rose, shouldering forward; between the two was space for a foot to be planted, but none for a body to stand; yet a juniper bough, thrusting out, gave a handhold secure enough for one with a resolute grasp to swing past the perilous place, and pass on safe.

Though the first seconds of the last moment were going, she dared to flash back a wicked look, and laugh at the pursuer who was impotent to grasp.

The crisis struck convulsive life into his last supreme effort; his will surged up indomitable, his speed proved matchless yet. He leapt with a rush, passed her before her laugh had time to go out, and turned short, barring the way, and braced to withstand her.

She came hurling desperate, with a feint to the right hand, and then launched herself upon him with a spring like a wild beast when it leaps to kill. And he, with one strong arm and a hand that could not hold, with one strong hand and an arm that could not guide and sustain, he caught and held her even so. And they fell together. And because he felt his whole arm slipping and his whole hand loosing, to slack the dreadful agony of the wrenched bone above, he caught and held with his teeth the tunic at her knee, as she struggled up and wrung off his hands to overleap him victorious.

Like lightning she snatched her axe, and struck him on the neck —deep—once—twice—his life-blood gushed out, staining her feet.

The stars touched midnight.

The death scream he heard was not his, for his set teeth had hardly yet relaxed when it rang out. And the dreadful cry began with a woman's shriek, and changed and ended as the yell of a beast. And before the final blank overtook his dying eyes, he saw the She gave place to It; he saw more, that Life gave place to Death—incomprehensibly.

For he did not dream that no holy water could be more holy, more potent to destroy an evil thing than the life-blood of a pure heart poured out for another in willing devotion.

His own true hidden reality that he had desired to know grew palpable, recognizable. It seemed to him just this: a great, glad, abounding hope that he had saved his brother; too expansive to be contained by the limited form of a sole man, it yearned for a new embodiment infinite as the stars.

What did it matter to that true reality that the man's brain shrank, shrank, till it was nothing; that the man's body could not retain the huge pain of his heart, and heaved it out through the red exit riven at the neck: that hurtling blackness blotted out forever the man's sight, hearing, sense?

In the early gray of day Sweyn chanced upon the footprints of a man—of a runner, as he saw by the shifted snow; and the direction they had taken aroused curiosity, since a little farther their line must be crossed by the edge of a sheer height. He turned to trace them. And so doing, the length of the stride struck his attention—a stride long as his own if he ran. He knew he was following Christian.

In his anger he had hardened himself to be indifferent to the night-long absence of his brother; but now, seeing where the footsteps went, he was seṭed with compunction and dread. He had failed to give thought and care to his poor, frantic twin, who might —was it possible?—have rushed to a frantic death.

His heart stood still when he came to the place where the leap had been taken. A piled edge of snow had fallen, too, and nothing lay below when he peered. Along the upper edge he ran for a furlong, till he came to a dip where he could slip and climb down, and then back again on the lower level to the pile of fallen snow. There he saw that the vigorous running had started afresh.

He stood pondering; vexed that any man should have taken that leap where he had not ventured to follow; vexed that he had been beguiled to such painful emotions; guessing vainly at Christian's object in this mad freak. He began sauntering along half-unconsciously following his brother's track, and so in a while he came to the place where the footprints were doubled.

Small prints were these others, small as a woman's, though the pace from one to another was longer than that which the skirts of women allow.

Did not White Fell tread so?

A dreadful guess appalled him—so dreadful that he recoiled from belief. Yet his face grew ashy white, and he gasped to fetch back motion to his checkered heart. Unbelievable? Closer attention showed how the smaller footfall had altered for greater speed, striking into the snow with a deeper onset and a lighter pressure on the heels. Unbelievable? Could any woman but White Fell run so? Could any man but Christian run so? The guess becamɔ a certainty.

He was following where alone in the dark night White Fell had fled from Christian pursuing.

Such villainy set heart and brain on fire with rage and indignation —such villainy in his own brother, till lately loveworthy, praise-worthy, though a fool for meekness. He would kill Christian; had he lives as many as the footprints he had trodden, vengeance should demand them all. In a tempest of murderous hate he followed on in haste, for the track was plain enough; starting with such a burst of speed as could not be maintained, but brought him back soon to a plod for the spent, sobbing breath to be regulated.

Mile after mile he traveled with a bursting heart; more piteous, more tragic, seemed the case at this evidence of White Fell's splen-did supremacy, holding her own so long against Christian's famous speed. So long, so long, that his love and admiration grew more and more boundless, and his grief and indignation therewith also. Whenever the track lay clear he ran, with such reckless prodigality of strength that it was soon spent, and he dragged on heavily, till, sometimes on the ice of a mere, sometimes on a wind-swept place, all signs were lost; but, so undeviating had been their line, that a course straight on, and then short questing to either hand recovered them again.

Hour after hour had gone by through more than half that winter day, before ever he came to the place where the trampled snow showed that a scurry of feet had come and gone! Wolves' feet—and gone most amazingly! Only a little beyond he came to the lopped point of Christian's bear-spear—farther on he would see where the remnant of the useless shaft had been dropped. The snow here was dashed with blood, and the footsteps of the two had fallen closer together. Some hoarse sound of exultation came from him that might have been a laugh had breath sufficed. "O White Fell, my poor brave love! Well struck!" he groaned, torn by his pity and great admiration, as he guessed surely how she had turned and dealt a blow.

The sight of the blood inflamed him as it might a beast that ravens. He grew mad with a desire to once again have Christian by the throat, not to loose this time till he had crushed out his life— or beat out his life—or stabbed out his life—or all of these, and torn him piecemeal likewise—and ah! then, not till then, bleed his heart with weeping, like a child, like a girl, over the piteous fate of his poor lost love.

On—on—on—through the aching time, toiling and straining in the track of those two superb runners, aware of the marvel of their endurance, but unaware of the marvel of their speed that in the three hours before midnight had overpassed all that vast distance that he could only traverse from twilight to twilight. For clear daylight was passing when he came to the edge of an old marlpit, and saw how the two who had gone before had stamped and trampled together in desperate peril on the verge. And here fresh blood stains spoke to him of a valiant defense against his infamous brother; and he followed where the blood had dripped till the cold had staunched its flow, taking a savage gratification from the evidence that Christian had been gashed deeply, maddening afresh with desire to do likewise more excellently and so slake his murderous hate. And he began to know that through all his despair he had entertained a germ of hope, that grew apace, rained upon by his brother's blood.

He strove on as best he might, wrung now by an access of hope —now of despair, in agony to reach the end, however terrible, sick with the aching of the toiled miles that deferred it.

And the light went lingering out of the sky, giving place to uncertain stars.

He came to the finish.

Two bodies lay in a narrow place. Christian's was one, but the other beyond not White Fell's. There where the footsteps ended lay a great white wolf. At the sight Sweyn's strength was blasted; body and soul he was struck down groveling.

The stars had grown sure and intense before he stirred from where he had dropped prone. Very feebly he crawled to his dead brother, and laid his hands upon him, and crouched so, afraid to look or stir further.

Cold—stiff—hours dead. Yet the dead body was his only shelter and stay in that most dreadful hour. His soul, stripped bare of all comfort, cowered, shivering, naked, abject, and the living clung to the dead out of piteous need for grace from the soul that had passed away.

He rose to his knees, lifting the body. Christian had fallen face forward in the snow, with his arms flung up and wide, and so had the frost made him rigid; strange, ghastly, unyielding to Sweyn lifting, so that he laid him down again and crouched above, with his arms fast round him and a low, heart-wrung groan.

When at last he found force to raise his brother's body and gather it in his arms, tight clasped to his breast, he tried to face the Thing that lay beyond. The sight set his limbs in a palsy with horror and dread. His senses had failed and fainted in utter cowardice, but for the strength that came from holding dead Christian in his arms, enabling him to compel his eyes to endure the sight, and take into the brain the complete aspect of the Thing. No wound—only blood stains on the feet. The great, grim jaws had a savage grin, though dead-stiff. And his kiss—he could bear it no longer, and turned away, nor ever looked again.

And the dead man in his arms, knowing the full horror, had followed and faced it for his sake; had suffered agony and death for his sake; in the neck was the deep death-gash, one arm and both hands were dark with frozen blood, for his sake! Dead he knew him —as in life he had not known him—to give the right meed of love and worship. He longed for annihilation, that so he might lose the agony of knowing himself so unworthy of such perfect love. The frozen calm of death on the face appalled him. He dared not touch it with lips that had cursed so lately, with lips fouled by a kiss of the Horror that had been Death.

He struggled to his feet, still clasping Christian. The dead man stood upright within his arms, frozen rigid. The eyes were not quite closed; the head had stiffened, bowed slightly to one side; the arms stayed straight and wide. It was the figure of one crucified, the blood-stained hands also conforming.

So living and dead went back along the track, that one had passed in the deepest passion of love, and one in the deepest passion of hate. All that night Sweyn toiled through the snow, bearing the weight of dead Christian, treading back along the steps he before had trodden when he was wronging with vilest thoughts and cursing with murderous hate the brother who all the while lay dead for his sake.

THE WOLF
by GUY DE MAUPASSANT

In "The Wolf," Montague Summers writes in The Werewolf, *"we meet with savage beasts and men more savage yet than they." An apt description of this vivid tale of revenge, in which the Marquis d'Arville relates at a dinner party why none of his family has joined in a hunt since 1764—the year two of his forebears set out after a wolf who had been terrorizing the countryside. An extraordinary wolf, fierce and colossal, "who had eaten two children, gnawed off a woman's arm . . . and penetrated without fear into the farm-yards to come snuffling under the doors. The people in the houses affirmed that they had felt his breath, and that it made the flame of the lights flicker . . ."*

Guy de Maupassant (born in Normandy in 1850) was a disciple of French novelist Gustave Flaubert and learned from him the art of writing fiction. Maupassant published several novels and more than two hundred short stories between 1880 and his death in 1893; that he was one of the all-time masters of the short-story form is beyond question. The qualities for which his work is most noted—simplicity of style, realism, and the recurring theme of man's inherent cruelty—are clearly in evidence in "The Wolf."

Here is what the old Marquis d'Arville told us towards the end of St. Hubert's dinner at the house of the Baron des Ravels.

We had killed a stag that day. The marquis was the only one of the guests who had not taken any part in this chase, for he never hunted.

All through that long repast we had talked about hardly anything but the slaughter of animals. The ladies themselves were interested in tales sanguinary and often unlikely, and the orators imitated the attacks and the combats of men against beasts, raised their arms, romanced in a thundering voice.

M. d'Arville talked well, with a certain poetry of style somewhat high-sounding, but full of effect. He must have repeated this story often, for he told it fluently, not hesitating on words, choosing them with skill to produce a picture—

Gentlemen, I have never hunted; neither did my father, nor my grandfather, nor my great-grandfather. This last was the son of a man who hunted more than all of you put together. He died in 1764. I will tell you how.

His name was Jean. He was married, father of that child who became my ancestor, and he lived with his younger brother, François d'Arville, in our castle in Lorraine, in the middle of the forest.

François d'Arville had remained a bachelor for love of the chase.

They both hunted from one end of the year to the other, without repose, without stopping, without fatigue. They loved only that, understood nothing else, talked only of that, lived only for that.

They had at heart that one passion, which was terrible and inexorable. It consumed them, having entirely invaded them, leaving place for no other.

They had given orders that they should not be interrupted in the chase, for any reason whatever. My great-grandfather was born while his father was following a fox, and Jean d'Arville did not stop his pursuit, but he swore: "Name of a name, that rascal there might have waited till after the view-halloo!"

His brother François showed himself still more infatuated. On rising he went to see the dogs, then the horses; then he shot little birds about the castle until the moment for departing to hunt down some great beast.

In the countryside they were called M. le Marquis and M. le Cadet, the nobles then not doing at all like the chance nobility of our time, which wishes to establish an hereditary hierarchy in titles; for the son of a marquis is no more a count, nor the son of a viscount a baron, than the son of a general is a colonel by birth. But the mean vanity of today finds profit in that arrangement.

I return to my ancestors.

They were, it seems, immeasurably tall, bony, hairy, violent, and vigorous. The younger, still taller than the older, had a voice so strong that, according to a legend of which he was proud, all the leaves of the forests shook when he shouted.

And when they both mounted to go off to the hunt, that must have been a superb spectacle to see those two giants straddling their huge horses.

Now towards the midwinter of that year, 1764, the frosts were excessive, and the wolves became ferocious.

They even attacked belated peasants, roamed at night about the houses, howled from sunset to sunrise, and depopulated the stables.

And soon a rumor began to circulate. People talked of a colossal wolf, with gray fur, almost white, who had eaten two children, gnawed off a woman's arm, strangled all the dogs of the *garde du pays,* and penetrated without fear into the farm-yards to come snuffling under the doors. The people in the houses affirmed that they had felt his breath, and that it made the flame of the lights flicker. And soon a panic ran through all the province. No one dared go out any more after night-fall. The shades seemed haunted by the image of the beast.

The brothers d'Arville resolved to find and kill him, and several times they assembled all the gentlemen of the country to a great hunting.

In vain. They might beat the forest and search the coverts; they never met him. They killed wolves, but not that one. And every night after a *battue,* the beast, as if to avenge himself, attacked some traveller or devoured someone's cattle, always far from the place where they had looked for him.

Finally one night he penetrated into the pig-pen of the Château d'Arville and ate the two finest pigs.

The brothers were inflamed with anger, considering this attack as a bravado of the monster, an insult direct, a defiance. They took their strong blood-hounds used to pursue formidable beasts, and they set off to hunt, their hearts swollen with fury.

From dawn until the hour when the empurpled sun descended behind the great naked trees, they beat the thickets without finding anything.

At last, furious and disconsolate, both were returning, walking their horses along an *allée* bordered with brambles, and they marvelled that their woodcraft should be crossed so by this wolf, and they were seized suddenly with a sort of mysterious fear.

The elder said:

"That beast there is not an ordinary one. You would say it thought like a man."

The younger answered:

"Perhaps we should have a bullet blessed by our cousin, the bishop, or pray some priest to pronounce the words which are needed."

Then they were silent.

Jean continued:

"Look how red the sun is. The great wolf will do some harm tonight."

He had hardly finished speaking when his horse reared; that of François began to kick. A large thicket covered with dead leaves opened before them, and a colossal beast, quite gray, sprang up and ran off across the wood.

Both uttered a kind of groan of joy, and, bending over the necks of their heavy horses, they threw them forward with an impulse from their whole bodies, hurling them on at such a pace, exciting them, hurrying them away, maddening them so with the voice, with gesture, and with spur that the strong riders seemed rather to be carrying the heavy beasts between their thighs and to bear them off as if they were flying.

Thus they went, *ventre à terre,* bursting the thickets, cleaving the beds of streams, climbing the hillsides, descending the gorges, and blowing on the horn with full lungs to attract their people and their dogs.

And now, suddenly, in that mad race, my ancestor struck his forehead against an enormous branch which split his skull; and he fell stark dead on the ground, while his frightened horse took himself off, disappearing in the shade which enveloped the woods.

The cadet of Arville stopped short, leaped to the earth, and seized his brother in his arms. He saw that the brains ran from the wound with the blood.

Then he sat down beside the body, rested the head, disfigured and red, on his knees, and waited, contemplating that immobile face of the elder brother. Little by little a fear invaded him, a strange fear which he had never felt before, the fear of the dark, the fear of solitude, the fear of the deserted wood, and the fear also of the fantastic wolf who had just killed his brother to avenge himself upon them both.

The shadows thickened; the acute cold made the trees crack. François got up, shivering, unable to remain there longer, feeling himself almost growing faint. Nothing was to be heard, neither the voice of the dogs nor the sound of the horns—all was silent along the invisible horizon; and this mournful silence of the frozen night had something about it frightening and strange.

He seized in his colossal hands the great body of Jean, straightened it and laid it across the saddle to carry it back to the château; then he went on his way softly, his mind troubled as if he were drunken, pursued by horrible and surprising images.

And abruptly, in the path which the night was invading, a great shape passed. It was the beast. A shock of terror shook the hunter; something cold, like a drop of water, glided along his veins, and, like a monk haunted of the devil, he made a great sign of the cross, dismayed at this abrupt return of the frightful prowler. But his eyes fell back upon the inert body laid before him, and suddenly, passing abruptly from fear to anger, he shook with an inordinate rage.

Then he spurred his horse and rushed after the wolf.

He followed it by the copses, the ravines, and the tall trees, traversing woods which he no longer knew, his eyes fixed on the white speck which fled before him through the night now fallen upon the earth.

His horse also seemed animated by a force and an ardor hitherto unknown. It galloped, with outstretched neck, straight on, hurling against the trees, against the rocks, the head and the feet of the dead man thrown across the saddle. The briers tore out the hair; the brow, beating the huge trunks, spattered them with blood; the spurs tore their ragged coats of bark. And suddenly the beast and the horseman issued from the forest and rushed into a valley, just as the moon appeared above the mountains. This valley was stony, closed by enormous rocks, without possible issue; and the wolf was cornered and turned round.

François then uttered a yell of joy which the echoes repeated like a rolling of thunder, and he leaped from his horse, his cutlass in his hand.

The beast, with bristling hair, the back arched, awaited him; its eyes glistened like two stars. But, before offering battle, the strong hunter, seizing his brother, seated him on a rock, and, supporting with stones his head, which was no more than a blot of blood, he shouted in the ears as if he was talking to a deaf man, "Look, Jean; look at this!"

Then he threw himself upon the monster. He felt himself strong enough to overturn a mountain, to bruise stones in his hands. The beast tried to bite him, seeking to strike in at his stomach; but he had seized it by the neck, without even using his weapon, and he strangled it gently, listening to the stoppage of the breathings in its throat and the beatings of its heart. And he laughed, rejoicing madly, pressing closer and closer his formidable embrace, crying in a delirium of joy, "Look, Jean, look!" All resistance ceased; the body of the wolf became lax. He was dead.

Then François, taking him up in his arms, carried him off and went and threw him at the feet of the elder brother, repeating, in a tender voice, "There, there, there, my little Jean, see him!"

Then he replaced on the saddle the two bodies one upon the other; and he went his way.

He returned to the château, laughing and crying, like Gargantua at the birth of Pantagruel, uttering shouts of triumph and stamping with joy in relating the death of the beast, and moaning and tearing his beard in telling that of his brother.

And often, later, when he talked again of that day, he said, with tears in his eyes, "If only that poor Jean could have seen me strangle the other, he would have died content. I am sure of it!"

The widow of my ancestor inspired her orphan son with that horror of the chase which has transmitted itself from father to son as far down as myself.

The Marquis d'Arville was silent. Someone asked:

"That story is a legend, isn't it?"

And the storyteller answered:

"I swear to you that it is true from one end to the other."

Then a lady declared, in a little, soft voice:

"All the same, it is fine to have passions like that."

THE MARK OF THE BEAST
RUDYARD KIPLING

No other author wrote so prolifically or so well of life in India under British colonial rule than Rudyard Kipling. Born in Bombay in 1865, educated in England, Kipling published his first volume of satirical verse, Departmental Ditties, *at the age of twenty-one and continued to produce quality stories, novels, poems, and nonfiction until his death in 1936. Among his finest works are the collected animal stories in* The Jungle Book *(1894), the novel* Kim *(1901), and the verse collection* Barrack-Room Ballads *(1892), which contains his famous popular poems "Gunga Din," "Mandalay," and "Danny Deever."*

"The Mark of the Beast" is vintage Kipling in its evocative portrait of India at the turn of the century and in its strong and probing examination of the darker side of the human condition. It is also a memorable tale of lycanthropy, of course, particularly for its unique variation on the theme—the soul of a wolf implanted in a man as the result of a leper's curse—and for such chilling passages as:

"I understood then how men and women and little children can endure to see a witch burnt alive; for the beast was moaning on the floor, and though the Silver Man had no face, you could see horrible feelings passing through the slab that took its place, exactly as waves of heat play across red-hot iron . . ."

East of Suez, some hold, the direct control of Providence ceases; Man being there handed over to the power of the Gods and Devil of Asia, and the Church of England Providence only exercising an occasional and modified supervision in the case of Englishmen.

This theory accounts for some of the more unnecessary horrors of life in India: it may be stretched to explain my story.

My friend Strickland of the Police, who knows as much of natives of India as is good for any man, can bear witness to the facts of the case. Dumoise, our doctor, also saw what Strickland and I saw. The inference which he drew from the evidence was entirely incorrect. He is dead now; he died, in a rather curious manner, which has been elsewhere described.

When Fleete came to India, he owned a little money and some land in the Himalayas, near a place called Dharmsala. Both properties had been left him by an uncle, and he came out to finance them. He was a big, heavy, genial, and inoffensive man. His knowledge of natives was, of course, limited, and he complained of the difficulties of the language.

He rode in from his place in the hills to spend New Year in the station, and he stayed with Strickland. On New Year's Eve there was a big dinner at the club, and the night was excusably wet. When men foregather from the uttermost ends of the Empire, they have a right to be riotous. The Frontier had sent down a contingent o' Catch-'em-Alive-O's who had not seen twenty white faces for a year, and were used to ride fifteen miles to dinner at the next Fort at the risk of a Khyberee bullet where their drinks should lie. They profited by their new security, for they tried to play pool with a curled-up hedgehog found in the garden, and one of them carried the marker round the room in his teeth. Half a dozen planters had come in from the south and were talking "horse" to the Biggest Liar in Asia, who was trying to cap all their stories at once. Everybody was there, and there was a general closing up of ranks and taking stock of our losses in dead or disabled that had fallen during the past year.

It was a very wet night, and I remember that we sang "Auld Lang Syne" with our feet in the Polo Championship Cup, and our heads among the stars, and swore that we were all dear friends. Then some of us went away and annexed Burma, and some tried to open up the Soudan and were opened up by Fuzzies in that cruel scrub outside Suakim, and some found stars and medals, and some were married, which was bad, and some did other things which were worse, and the others of us stayed in our chains and strove to make money on insufficient experiences.

Fleete began the night with sherry and bitters, drank champagne steadily up to dessert, then raw, rasping Capri with all the strength of whisky, took Benedictine with his coffee, four or five whiskies and sodas to improve his pool strokes, beer and bones at half-past two, winding up with old brandy. Consequently, when he came out, at half-past three in the morning, into fourteen degrees of frost, he was very angry with his horse for coughing, and tried to leapfrog into the saddle. The horse broke away and went to his stables; so Strickland and I formed a Guard of Dishonor to take Fleete home.

Our road lay through the bazaar, close to a little temple of Hanuman, the Monkey-god, who is a leading divinity worthy of respect. All gods have good points, just as have all priests. Personally, I attach much importance to Hanuman, and am kind to his people—the great gray apes of the hills. One never knows when one may want a friend.

There was a light in the temple, and as we passed, we could hear voices of men chanting hymns. In a native temple, the priests rise at all hours of the night to do honor to their god. Before we could stop him, Fleete dashed up the steps, patted two priests on the back, and was gravely grinding the ashes of his cigar butt into the forehead of the red stone image of Hanuman. Strickland tried to drag him out, but he sat down and said solemnly:

"Shee that? 'Mark of the B—beasht! *I* made it. Ishn't it fine?"

In half a minute the temple was alive and noisy, and Strickland, who knew what came of polluting gods, said that things might occur. He, by virtue of his official position, long residence in the country, and weakness for going among the natives, was known to the priests and he felt unhappy. Fleete sat on the ground and refused to move. He said that "good old Hanuman" made a very soft pillow.

Then, without any warning, a Silver Man came out of a recess behind the image of the god. He was perfectly naked in that bitter, bitter cold, and his body shone like frosted silver, for he was what the Bible calls "a leper as white as snow." Also he had no face, because he was a leper of some years' standing and his disease was heavy upon him. We two stooped to haul Fleete up, and the temple was filling and filling with folk who seemed to spring from the earth, when the Silver Man ran in under our arms, making a noise exactly like the mewing of an otter, caught Fleete round the body and dropped his head on Fleete's breast before we could wrench him away. Then he retired to a corner and sat mewing while the crowd blocked all the doors.

The priests were very angry until the Silver Man touched Fleete. That nuzzling seemed to sober them.

At the end of a few minutes' silence one of the priests came to Strickland and said, in perfect English, "Take your friend away. He was done with Hanuman, but Hanuman has not done with him." The crowd gave room and we carried Fleete into the road.

Strickland was very angry. He said that we might all three have been knifed, and that Fleete should thank his stars that he had escaped without injury.

Fleete thanked no one. He said that he wanted to go to bed. He was gorgeously drunk.

We moved on, Strickland silent and wrathful, until Fleete was taken with violent shivering fits and sweating. He said that the smells of the bazaar were overpowering, and he wondered why slaughter-houses were permitted so near English residences. "Can't you smell the blood?" said Fleete.

We put him to bed at last, just as the dawn was breaking, and Strickland invited me to have another whisky and soda. While we were drinking he talked of the trouble in the temple, and admitted that it baffled him completely. Strickland hates being mystified by natives, because his business in life is to overmatch them with their own weapons. He has not yet succeeded in doing this, but in fifteen or twenty years he will have made some small progress.

"They should have mauled us," he said, "instead of mewing at us. I wonder what they meant. I don't like it one little bit."

I said that the Managing Committee of the temple would in all probability bring a criminal action against us for insulting their religion. There was a section of the Indian Penal Code which exactly met Fleete's offense. Strickland said he only hoped and prayed that they would do this. Before I left I looked into Fleete's room and saw him lying on his right side, scratching his left breast. Then I went to bed cold, depressed, and unhappy, at seven o'clock in the morning.

At one o'clock I rode over to Strickland's house to inquire after Fleete's head. I imagined that it would be a sore one. Fleete was breakfasting and seemed unwell. His temper was gone, for he was abusing the cook for not supplying him with an underdone chop. A man who can eat raw meat after a wet night is a curiosity. I told Fleete this and he laughed.

"You breed queer mosquitoes in these parts," he said. "I've been bitten to pieces, but only in one place."

"Let's have a look at the bite," said Strickland. "It may have gone down since this morning."

While the chops were being cooked, Fleete opened his shirt and showed us, just over his left breast, a mark, the perfect double of the black rosettes—the five or six irregular blotches arranged in a circle—on a leopard's hide. Strickland looked and said, "It was only pink this morning. It's grown black now."

Fleete ran to a glass.

"By Jove!" he said, "this is nasty. What is it?"

We could not answer. Here the chops came in, all red and juicy, and Fleete bolted three in a most offensive manner. He ate on his right grinders only, and threw his head over his right shoulder as he snapped the meat. When he had finished, it struck him that he had been behaving strangely, for he said apologetically, "I don't think I ever felt so hungry in my life. I've bolted like an ostrich."

After breakfast Strickland said to me, "Don't go. Stay here, and stay for the night."

Seeing that my house was not three miles from Strickland's, this request was absurd. But Strickland insisted, and was going to say something when Fleete interrupted by declaring in a shamefaced way that he felt hungry again. Strickland sent a man to my house to fetch over my bedding and a horse, and we three went down to Strickland's stables to pass the hours until it was time to go out for a ride. The man who has a weakness for horses never wearies of inspecting them; and when two men are killing time in this way they gather knowledge and lies the one from the other.

There were five horses in the stables, and I shall never forget the scene as we tried to look them over. They seemed to have gone mad. They reared and screamed and nearly tore up their pickets; they sweated and shivered and lathered and were distraught with fear. Strickland's horses used to know him as well as his dogs; which made the matter more curious. We left the stable for fear of the brutes throwing themselves in their panic. Then Strickland turned back and called me. The horses were still frightened, but they let us "gentle" and make much of them, and put their heads in our bosoms.

"They aren't afraid of *us*," said Strickland. "D'you know, I'd give three months' pay if *Outrage* here could talk."

But *Outrage* was dumb, and could only cuddle up to his master and blow out his nostrils, as is the custom of horses when they wish to explain things but can't. Fleete came up when we were in the stalls, and as soon as the horses saw him, their fright broke out afresh. It was all that we could do to escape from the place unkicked. Strickland said, "They don't seem to love you, Fleete."

"Nonsense," said Fleete; "my mare will follow me like a dog." He went to her; she was in a loose-box; but as he slipped the bars she plunged, knocked him down, and broke away into the garden. I laughed, but Strickland was not amused. He took his moustache in both fists and pulled at it till it nearly came out. Fleete, instead of going off to chase his property, yawned, saying that he felt sleepy. He went to the house to lie down, which was a foolish way of spending New Year's Day.

Strickland sat with me in the stables and asked if I had noticed anything peculiar in Fleete's manner. I said that he ate his food like a beast; but that this might have been the result of living alone in the hills out of the reach of society as refined and elevating as ours for instance. Strickland was not amused. I do not think that he listened to me, for his next sentence referred to the mark on Fleete's breast, and I said that it might have been caused by blister-flies, or that it was possibly a birthmark newly born and now visible for the first time. We both agreed that it was unpleasant to look at, and Strickland found occasion to say that I was a fool.

"I can't tell you what I think now," said he, "because you would call me a madman; but you must stay with me for the next few days, if you can. I want you to watch Fleete, but don't tell me what you think till I have made up my mind."

"But I am dining out tonight," I said.

"So am I," said Strickland, "and so is Fleete. At least if he doesn't change his mind."

We walked about the garden smoking, but saying nothing—because we were friends, and talking spoils good tobacco—till our pipes were out. Then we went to wake up Fleete. He was wide awake and fidgeting about his room.

"I say, I want some more chops," he said. "Can I get them?"

We laughed and said, "Go and change. The ponies will be round in a minute."

"All right," said Fleete. "I'll go when I get the chops—underdone ones, mind."

He seemed to be quite in earnest. It was four o'clock, and we had had breakfast at one; still, for a long time, he demanded those underdone chops. Then he changed into riding clothes and went out into the verandah. His pony—the mare had not been caught—would not let him come near. All three horses were unmanageable —mad with fear—and finally Fleete said that he would stay at home and get something to eat. Strickland and I rode out wondering. As we passed the temple of Hanuman, the Silver Man came out and mewed at us.

"He is not one of the regular priests of the temple," said Strickland. "I think I should peculiarly like to lay my hands on him."

There was no spring in our gallop on the racecourse that evening. The horses were stale, and moved as though they had been ridden out.

"The fright after breakfast has been too much for them," said Strickland.

That was the only remark he made through the remainder of the ride. Once or twice I think he swore to himself; but that did not count.

We came back in the dark at seven o'clock, and saw that there were no lights in the bungalow. "Careless ruffians my servants are!" said Strickland.

My horse reared at something on the carriage drive, and Fleete stood up under its nose.

"What are you doing, grovelling about the garden?" said Strickland.

But both horses bolted and nearly threw us. We dismounted by the stables and returned to Fleete, who was on his hands and knees under the orange bushes.

"What the devil's wrong with you?" said Strickland.

"Nothing, nothing in the world," said Fleete, speaking very quickly and thickly. "I've been gardening—botanizing you know. The smell of the earth is delightful. I think I'm going for a walk—a long walk—all night."

Then I saw that there was something excessively out of order somewhere, and I said to Strickland, "I am not dining out."

"Bless you!" said Strickland. "Here, Fleete, get up. You'll catch fever there. Come in to dinner and let's have the lamps lit. We'll all dine at home."

Fleete stood up unwillingly, and said, "No lamps—no lamps. It's much nicer here. Let's dine outside and have some more chops—lots of 'em and underdone—bloody ones with gristle."

Now a December evening in Northern India is bitterly cold, and Fleete's suggestion was that of a maniac.

"Come in," said Strickland sternly. "Come in at once."

Fleete came, and when the lamps were brought, we saw that he was literally plastered with dirt from head to foot. He must have been rolling in the garden. He shrank from the light and went to his room. His eyes were horrible to look at. There was a green light behind them, not in them, if you understand, and the man's lower lip hung down.

Strickland said, "There is going to be trouble—big trouble—tonight. Don't change your riding things."

We waited and waited for Fleete's reappearance, and ordered dinner in the meantime. We could hear him moving about his own room, but there was no light there. Presently from the room came the long-drawn howl of a wolf.

People write and talk lightly of blood running cold and hair standing up and things of that kind. Both sensations are too horrible to be trifled with. My heart stopped as though a knife had been driven through it, and Strickland turned white as the tablecloth.

The howl was repeated, and was answered by another howl far across the fields.

That set the gilded roof on the horror. Strickland dashed into Fleete's room. I followed, and we saw Fleete getting out of the window. He made beast-noises in the back of his throat. He could not answer us when we shouted at him. He spat.

I don't quite remember what followed, but I think that Strickland must have stunned him with the long boot-jack or else I should never have been able to sit on his chest. Fleete could not speak, he could only snarl, and his snarls were those of a wolf, not of a man. The human spirit must have been giving way all day and have died out with the twilight. We were dealing with a beast that had once been Fleete.

The affair was beyond any human and rational experience. I tried to say "hydrophobia," but the word wouldn't come, because I knew that I was lying.

We bound this beast with leather thongs of the punkah-rope, and tied its thumbs and big toes together, and gagged it with a shoe-horn, which makes a very efficient gag if you know how to arrange it. Then we carried it into the dining room, and sent a man to Dumoise, the doctor, telling him to come over at once. After we had despatched the messenger and were drawing breath, Strickland said, "It's no good. This isn't any doctor's work." I, also, knew that he spoke the truth.

The beast's head was free, and it threw it about from side to side.

Any one entering the room would have believed that we were curing a wolf's pelt. That was the most loathsome accessory of all.

Strickland sat with his chin in the heel of his fist, watching the beast as it wriggled on the ground, but saying nothing. The shirt had been torn open in the scuffle and showed the black rosette mark on the left breast. It stood out like a blister.

In the silence of the watching we heard something without mewing like a she-otter. We both rose to our feet, and, I answer for myself, not Strickland, felt sick—actually and physically sick. We told each other, as did the men in *Pinafore,* that it was the cat.

Dumoise arrived, and I never saw a little man so unprofessionally shocked. He said that it was a heartrending case of hydrophobia, and that nothing could be done. At least any palliative measures would only prolong the agony. The beast was foaming at the mouth. Fleete, as we told Dumoise, had been bitten by dogs once or twice. Any man who keeps half a dozen terriers must expect a nip now and again. Dumoise could offer no help. He could only certify that Fleete was dying of hydrophobia. The beast was then howling, for it had managed to spit out the shoe-horn. Dumoise said that he would be ready to certify to the cause of death, and that the end was certain. He was a good little man, and he offered to remain with us; but Strickland refused the kindness. He did not wish to poison Dumoise's New Year. He would only ask him not to give the real cause of Fleete's death to the public.

So Dumoise left, deeply agitated; and as soon as the noise of the cartwheels had died away, Strickland told me, in a whisper, his suspicions. They were so wildly improbable that he dared not say them out aloud; and I, who entertained all Strickland's beliefs, was so ashamed of owning to them that I pretended to disbelieve.

"Even if the Silver Man had bewitched Fleete for polluting the image of Hanuman, the punishment could not have fallen so quickly."

As I was whispering this the cry outside the house rose again, and the beast fell into a fresh paroxysm of struggling till we were afraid that the thongs that held it would give way.

"Watch!" said Strickland. "If this happens six times I shall take the law into my own hands. I order you to help me."

He went into his room and came out in a few minutes with the barrels of an old shotgun, a piece of fishing-line, some thick cord, and his heavy wooden bedstead. I reported that the convulsions had followed the cry by two seconds in each case, and the beast seemed perceptibly weaker.

Strickland muttered, "But he can't take away the life! He can't take away the life!"

I said, though I knew that I was arguing against myself, "It may be a cat. It must be a cat. If the Silver Man is responsible, why does he dare to come here?"

Strickland arranged the wood on the hearth, put the gun barrels into the glow of the fire, spread the twine on the table and broke a walking stick in two. There was one yard of fishing-line, gut, lapped with wire, such as is used for *mahseer*-fishing, and he tied the two ends together in a loop.

Then he said, "How can we catch him? He must be taken alive and unhurt."

I said that we must trust in Providence, and go out softly with polo sticks into the shrubbery at the front of the house. The man or animal that made the cry was evidently moving round the house as regularly as a night watchman. We could wait in the bushes till he came by and knock him over.

Strickland accepted this suggestion, and we slipped out from a bathroom window into the front verandah and then across the carriage drive into the bushes.

In the moonlight we could see the leper coming round the corner of the house. He was perfectly naked, and from time to time he mewed and stopped to dance with his shadow. It was an unattractive sight, and thinking of poor Fleete, brought to such degradation by so foul a creature, I put away all my doubts and resolved to help Strickland from the heated gun barrels to the loop of twine—from the loins to the head and back again—with all tortures that might be needful.

The leper halted in the front porch for a moment and we jumped out on him with the sticks. He was wonderfully strong, and we were afraid that he might escape or be fatally injured before we caught him. We had an idea that lepers were frail creatures, but this proved to be incorrect. Strickland knocked his legs from under him and I put my foot on his neck. He mewed hideously, and even through my riding boots I could feel that his flesh was not the flesh of a clean man.

He struck at us with his hand and feet-stumps. We looped the lash of a dog whip round him, under the armpits and dragged him backwards into the hall and so into the dining room where the beast lay. There we tied him with trunk straps. He made no attempt to escape, but mewed.

When we confronted him with the beast the scene was beyond description. The beast doubled backwards into a bow as though he had been poisoned with strychnine, and moaned in the most pitiable fashion. Several other things happened also, but they cannot be put down here.

"I think I was right," said Strickland. "Now we will ask him to cure this case."

But the leper only mewed. Strickland wrapped a towel round his hand and took the gun barrels out of the fire. I put the half of the broken walking stick through the loop of fishing-line and buckled the leper comfortably to Strickland's bedstead. I understood then how men and women and little children can endure to see a witch burnt alive; for the beast was moaning on the floor, and though the Silver Man had no face, you could see horrible feelings passing through the slab that took its place, exactly as waves of heat play across red-hot iron—gun barrels for instance.

Strickland shaded his eyes with his hands for a moment and we got to work. This part is not to be printed.

The dawn was beginning to break when the leper spoke. His mewings had not been satisfactory up to that point. The beast had fainted from exhaustion and the house was very still. We unstrapped the leper and told him to take away the evil spirit. He crawled to the beast and laid his hand upon the left breast. That was all. Then he fell face down and whined, drawing in his breath as he did so.

We watched the face of the beast, and saw the soul of Fleete coming back into the eyes. Then a sweat broke out on the forehead and the eyes—they were human eyes—closed. We waited for an hour but Fleete still slept. We carried him to his room and bade the leper go, giving him the bedstead, and the sheet on the bedstead to cover his nakedness, the gloves and the towels with which we had touched him, and the whip that had been hooked round his body. He put the sheet about him and went out into the early morning without speaking or mewing.

Strickland wiped his face and sat down. A night-gong, far away in the city, made seven o'clock.

"Exactly four-and-twenty hours!" said Strickland. "And I've done enough to ensure my dismissal from the service, besides permanent quarters in a lunatic asylum. Do you believe that we are awake?"

The red-hot gun barrel had fallen on the floor and was singeing the carpet. The smell was entirely real.

That morning at eleven we two together went to wake up Fleete. We looked and saw that the black leopard-rosette on his chest had disappeared. He was very drowsy and tired, but as soon as he saw us, he said, "Oh! Confound you fellows. Happy New Year to you. Never mix your liquors. I'm nearly dead."

"Thanks for your kindness, but you're over time," said Strickland. "Today is the morning of the second. You've slept the clock round with a vengeance."

The door opened, and little Dumoise put his head in. He had come on foot, and fancied that we were laying out Fleete.

"I've brought a nurse," said Dumoise. "I suppose that she can come in for . . . what is necessary."

"By all means," said Fleete cheerily, sitting up in bed. "Bring on your nurses."

Dumoise was dumb. Strickland led him out and explained that there must have been a mistake in the diagnosis. Dumoise remained dumb and left the house hastily. He considered that his professional reputation had been injured, and was inclined to make a personal matter of the recovery. Strickland went out too. When he came back, he said that he had been to call on the Temple of Hanuman to offer redress for the pollution of the god, and had been solemnly assured that no white man had ever touched the idol and that he was an incarnation of all the virtues laboring under a delusion. "What do you think?" said Strickland.

I said, " 'There are more things . . .' "

But Strickland hates that quotation. He says that I have worn it threadbare.

One other curious thing happened which frightened me as much as anything in all the night's work. When Fleete was dressed he came into the dining room and sniffed. He had a quaint trick of moving his nose when he sniffed. "Horrid doggy smell, here," said he. "You should really keep those terriers of yours in better order. Try sulphur, Strick."

But Strickland did not answer. He caught hold of the back of a chair, and, without warning, went into an amazing fit of hysterics. It is terrible to see a strong man overtaken with hysteria. Then it struck me that we had fought for Fleete's soul with the Silver Man in that room, and had disgraced ourselves as Englishmen forever, and I laughed and gasped and gurgled just as shamefully as Strickland, while Fleete thought that we had both gone mad. We never told him what we had done.

Some years later, when Strickland had married and was a churchgoing member of society for his wife's sake, we reviewed the incident dispassionately, and Strickland suggested that I should put it before the public.

I cannot myself see that this step is likely to clear up the mystery; because, in the first place, no one will believe a rather unpleasant story, and, in the second, it is well known to every rightminded man that the gods of the heathen are stone and brass, and any attempt to deal with them otherwise is justly condemned.

DRACULA'S GUEST
by BRAM STOKER

The name Dracula has become synonymous with vampirism—and conjures up immediate images of a foreboding Eastern European castle, bats flying in the night, a sinister Count who looks strangely like Bela Lugosi (or perhaps Christopher Lee), and coffins occupied by pale young women with long, sharp incisors. Bram Stoker wrote the novel which began it all, of course; first published in England in 1897, Dracula *ranks with Mary Shelley's* Frankenstein *as the greatest and most popular of all supernatural horror stories.*

Not many people know, however, that prior to its publication Stoker excised the novel's first chapter at the behest of his publishers, who felt the book was too long and needed trimming. That first chapter, which is a complete enough entity to be read as a short story, subsequently became the title piece in an 1899 collection of Stoker's macabre tales. It is, as you'll have surmised, "Dracula's Guest."

But the obvious question is: What is the excised first chapter of Dracula *doing in an anthology of werewolf stories? Answer: "Dracula's Guest" is not about vampires, but about certain strange and fearful happenings on Walpurgis Night in the German countryside—and about a gigantic wolf with "two great flaming eyes." Not precisely a werewolf, perhaps—or is it? You may draw your own conclusions after you've finished reading this chilling and atmospheric piece; I've already drawn mine.*

Bram Stoker was born in Dublin, served as literary and dramatic critic on various publications in the Irish capital, and left Ireland in 1876 to join British actor Sir Henry Irving in the management of London's Lyceum

Theatre; he remained associated with Irving for the next thirty years. In addition to his supernatural fiction, Stoker also wrote such nonfiction books as Personal Reminiscences of Henry Irving *(1906). He died in 1912 at the age of sixty-seven.*

When we started for our drive the sun was shining brightly on Munich, and the air was full of the joyousness of early summer. Just as we were about to depart, Herr Delbrück (the maître d'hôtel of the Quatre Saisons, where I was staying) came down, bareheaded, to the carriage and, after wishing me a pleasant drive, said to the coachman, still holding his hand on the handle of the carriage door:

"Remember you are back by nightfall. The sky looks bright but there is a shiver in the north wind that says there may be a sudden storm. But I am sure you will not be late." Here he smiled, and added, "for you know what night it is."

Johann answered with an emphatic, "Ja, mein Herr," and, touching his hat, drove off quickly. When we had cleared the town, I said, after signalling to him to stop:

"Tell me, Johann, what is tonight?"

He crossed himself, as he answered laconically: "Walpurgis Nacht." Then he took out his watch, a great, old-fashioned German silver thing as big as a turnip, and looked at it, with his eyebrows gathered together and a little impatient shrug of his shoulders. I realized that this was his way of respectfully protesting against the unnecessary delay, and sank back in the carriage, merely motioning him to proceed. He started off rapidly, as if to make up for lost time. Every now and then the horses seemed to throw up their heads and sniffed the air suspiciously. On such occasions I often looked round in alarm. The road was pretty bleak, for we were traversing a sort of high, wind-swept plateau. As we drove, I saw a road that looked but little used, and which seemed to dip through a little, winding valley. It looked so inviting that, even at the risk of offending him, I called Johann to stop—and when he had pulled up, I told him I would like to drive down that road. He made all sorts of excuses, and frequently crossed himself as he spoke. This somewhat piqued my curiosity, so I asked him various questions. He answered fencingly, and repeatedly looked at his watch in protest. Finally I said:

"Well, Johann, I want to go down this road. I shall not ask you to come unless you like; but tell me why you do not like to go, that is all I ask." For answer he seemed to throw himself off the box, so quickly did he reach the ground. Then he stretched out his hands appealingly to me, and implored me not to go. There was just enough of English mixed with the German for me to understand the drift of his talk. He seemed always just about to tell me something —the very idea of which evidently frightened him; but each time he pulled himself up, saying, as he crossed himself: "Walpurgis Nacht!"

I tried to argue with him, but it was difficult to argue with a man when I did not know his language. The advantage certainly rested with him, for although he began to speak in English, of a very crude and broken kind, he always got excited and broke into his native tongue—and every time he did so, he looked at his watch. Then the horses became restless and sniffed the air. At this he grew very pale, and, looking around in a frightened way, he suddenly jumped forward, took them by the bridles and led them on some twenty feet. I followed, and asked why he had done this. For answer he crossed himself, pointed to the spot we had left and drew his carriage in the direction of the other road, indicating a cross, and said, first in German, then in English: "Buried him—him what killed themselves."

I remembered the old custom of burying suicides at cross-roads: "Ah! I see, a suicide. How interesting!" But for the life of me I could not make out why the horses were frightened.

Whilst we were talking, we heard a sort of sound between a yelp and a bark. It was far away; but the horses got very restless, and it took Johann all his time to quiet them. He was pale, and said, "It sounds like a wolf—but yet there are no wolves here now."

"No?" I said, questioning him; "isn't it long since the wolves were so near the city?"

"Long, long," he answered, "in the spring and summer; but with the snow the wolves have been here not so long."

Whilst he was petting the horses and trying to quiet them, dark clouds drifted rapidly across the sky. The sunshine passed away, and a breath of cold wind seemed to drift past us. It was only a breath, however, and more in the nature of a warning than a fact, for the sun came out brightly again. Johann looked under his lifted hand at the horizon and said:

"The storm of snow, he comes before long time." Then he looked at his watch again, and, straightaway holding his reins firmly—for the horses were still pawing the ground restlessly and shaking their heads—he climbed to his box as though the time had come for proceeding on our journey.

I felt a little obstinate and did not at once get into the carriage.

"Tell me," I said, "about this place where the road leads," and I pointed down.

Again he crossed himself and mumbled a prayer, before he answered, "It is unholy."

"What is unholy?" I enquired.

"The village."

"Then there is a village?"

"No, no. No one lives there hundreds of years." My curiosity was piqued. "But you said there was a village."

"There was."

"Where is it now?"

Whereupon he burst out into a long story in German and English, so mixed up that I could not quite understand exactly what he said, but roughly I gathered that long ago, hundreds of years, men had died there and been buried in their graves; and sounds were heard under the clay, and when the graves were opened, men and women were found rosy with life, and their mouths red with blood. And so, in haste to save their lives (aye, and their souls!—and here he crossed himself) those who were left fled away to other places, where the living lived, and the dead were dead and not—not something. He was evidently afraid to speak the last words. As he proceeded with his narration, he grew more and more excited. It seemed as if his imagination had got hold of him, and he ended in a perfect paroxysm of fear—white-faced, perspiring, trembling and looking round him, as if expecting that some dreadful presence would manifest itself there in the bright sunshine on the open plain. Finally, in an agony of desperation, he cried:

"Walpurgis Nacht!" and pointed to the carriage for me to get in. All my English blood rose at this, and, standing back, I said:

"You are afraid, Johann—you are afraid. Go home; I shall return alone; the walk will do me good." The carriage door was open. I took from the seat my oak walking stick—which I always carry on my holiday excursions—and closed the door, pointing back to Munich, and said, "Go home, Johann—Walpurgis Nacht doesn't concern Englishmen."

The horses were now more restive than ever, and Johann was trying to hold them in, while excitedly imploring me not to do anything so foolish. I pitied the poor fellow, he was deeply in earnest; but all the same I could not help laughing. His English was quite gone now. In his anxiety he had forgotten that his only means of making me understand was to talk my language, so he jabbered away in his native German. It began to be a little tedious. After giving the direction, "Home!" I turned to go down the cross-road into the valley.

With a despairing gesture, Johann turned his horses towards Munich. I leaned on my stick and looked after him. He went slowly along the road for a while: then there came over the crest of the hill a man tall and thin. I could see so much in the distance. When he drew near the horses, they began to jump and kick about, then to scream with terror. Johann could not hold them in; they bolted down the road, running away madly. I watched them out of sight, then looked for the stranger, but I found that he, too, was gone.

With a light heart I turned down the side road through the deepening valley to which Johann had objected. There was not the slightest reason, that I could see, for his objection; and I daresay I tramped for a couple of hours without thinking of time or distance, and certainly without seeing a person or a house. So far as the place was concerned, it was desolation itself. But I did not notice this particularly till, on turning a bend in the road, I came upon a scattered fringe of wood; then I recognized that I had been impressed unconsciously by the desolation of the region through which I had passed.

I sat down to rest myself, and began to look around. It struck me that it was considerably colder than it had been at the commencement of my walk—a sort of sighing sound seemed to be around me, with, now and then, high overhead, a sort of muffled roar. Looking upwards I noticed that great thick clouds were drifting rapidly across the sky from north to south at a great height. There were signs of coming storm in some lofty stratum of the air. I was a little chilly, and, thinking that it was the sitting still after the exercise of walking, I resumed my journey.

The ground I passed over was now much more picturesque. There were no striking objects that the eye might single out; but in all there was a charm of beauty. I took little heed of time and it was only when the deepening twilight forced itself upon me that I began to think of how I should find my way home. The brightness of the day had gone. The air was cold, and the drifting of clouds high overhead was more marked. They were accompanied by a sort of far-away rushing sound, through which seemed to come at intervals that mysterious cry which the driver had said came from a wolf. For a while I hesitated. I had said I would see the deserted village, so on I went, and presently came on a wide stretch of open country, shut in by hills all around. Their sides were covered with trees which spread down to the plain, dotting, in clumps, the gentler slopes and hollows which showed here and there. I followed with my eye the winding of the road, and saw that it curved close to one of the densest of these clumps and was lost behind it.

As I looked there came a cold shiver in the air, and the snow began to fall. I thought of the miles and miles of bleak country I had passed, and then hurried on to seek the shelter of the wood in front. Darker and darker grew the sky, and faster and heavier fell the snow, till the earth before and around me was a glistening white carpet the further edge of which was lost in misty vagueness. The road was here but crude, and when on the level its boundaries were not so marked, as when it passed through the cuttings; and in a little while I found that I must have strayed from it, for I missed underfoot the hard surface, and my feet sank deeper in the grass and moss. Then the wind grew stronger and blew with ever-increasing force, till I was fain to run before it. The air became icy-cold, and in spite of my exercise I began to suffer. The snow was now falling so thickly and whirling around me in such rapid eddies that I could hardly keep my eyes open. Every now and then the heavens were torn asunder by vivid lightning, and in the flashes I could see ahead of me a great mass of trees, chiefly yew and cypress all heavily coated with snow.

I was soon amongst the shelter of the trees, and there, in comparative silence, I could hear the rush of the wind high overhead. Presently the blackness of the storm had become merged in the darkness of the night. By-and-by the storm seemed to be passing away: it now only came in fierce puffs or blasts. At such moments the weird sound of the wolf appeared to be echoed by many similar sounds around me.

Now and again, through the black mass of drifting cloud, came a straggling ray of moonlight, which lit up the expanse, and showed me that I was at the edge of a dense mass of cypress and yew trees. As the snow had ceased to fall, I walked out from the shelter and began to investigate more closely. It appeared to me that, amongst so many old foundations as I had passed, there might be still standing a house in which, though in ruins, I could find some sort of shelter for a while. As I skirted the edge of the copse, I found that a low wall encircled it, and following this I presently found an opening. Here the cypresses formed an alley leading up to a square mass of some kind of building. Just as I caught sight of this, however, the drifting clouds obscured the moon, and I passed up the path in darkness. The wind must have grown colder, for I felt myself shiver as I walked; but there was hope of shelter, and I groped my way blindly on.

I stopped, for there was a sudden stillness. The storm had passed; and, perhaps in sympathy with nature's silence, my heart seemed to cease to beat. But this was only momentarily; for suddenly the moonlight broke through the clouds, showing me that I was in a graveyard, and that the square object before me was a great massive tomb of marble, as white as the snow that lay on and all around it. With the moonlight there came a fierce sigh of the storm, which appeared to resume its course with a long, low howl, as of many dogs or wolves. I was awed and shocked, and felt the cold perceptibly grow upon me till it seemed to grip me by the heart. Then while the flood of moonlight still fell on the marble tomb, the storm gave further evidence of renewing, as though it was returning on its track. Impelled by some sort of fascination, I approached the sepulchre to see what it was, and why such a thing stood alone in such a place. I walked around it, and read, over the Doric door, in German:

COUNTESS DOLINGEN OF GRATZ
IN STYRIA
SOUGHT AND FOUND DEATH
1801

On the top of the tomb, seemingly driven through the solid marble—for the structure was composed of a few vast blocks of stone —was a great iron spike or stake. On going to the back I saw, graven in great Russian letters:

The dead travel fast.

There was something so weird and uncanny about the whole thing that it gave me a turn and made me feel quite faint. I began to wish, for the first time, that I had taken Johann's advice. Here a thought struck me, which came under almost mysterious circumstances and with a terrible shock. This was Walpurgis Night!

Walpurgis Night, when, according to the belief of millions of people, the devil was abroad—when the graves were opened and the dead came forth and walked. When all evil things of earth and air and water held revel. This very place the driver had specially shunned. This was the depopulated village of centuries ago. This was where the suicide lay; and this was the place where I was alone —unmanned, shivering with cold in a shroud of snow with a wild storm gathering again upon me! It took all my philosophy, all the religion I had been taught, all my courage, not to collapse in a paroxysm of fright.

And now a perfect tornado burst upon me. The ground shook as though thousands of horses thundered across it; and this time the storm bore on its icy wings, not snow, but great hailstones which drove with such violence that they might have come from the thongs of Balearic slingers—hailstones that beat down leaf and branch and made the shelter of the cypresses of no more avail than though their stems were standing-corn. At the first I had rushed to the nearest tree; but I was soon fain to leave it and seek the only spot that seemed to afford refuge, the deep Doric doorway of the marble tomb. There, crouching against the massive bronze door, I gained a certain amount of protection from the beating of the hailstones, for now they only drove against me as they ricocheted from the ground and the side of the marble.

As I leaned against the door, it moved slightly and opened inwards. The shelter of even a tomb was welcome in that pitiless tempest, and I was about to enter it when there came a flash of forked-lightning that lit up the whole expanse of the heavens. In the instant, as I am a living man, I saw, as my eyes were turned into the darkness of the tomb, a beautiful woman, with rounded cheecks and red lips, seemingly sleeping on a bier. As the thunder broke overhead, I was grasped as by the hand of a giant and hurled out into the storm. The whole thing was so sudden that, before I could realize the shock, moral as well as physical, I found the hailstones beating me down. At the same time I had a strange, dominating feeling that I was not alone. I looked towards the tomb. Just then there came another blinding flash, which seemed to strike the iron stake that surmounted the tomb and to pour through to the earth, blasting and crumbling the marble, as in a burst of flame. The dead woman rose for a moment of agony, while she was lapped in the flame, and her bitter scream of pain was drowned in the thunder-crash. The last thing I heard was this mingling of dreadful sound, as again I was seized in the giant-grasp and dragged away, while the hailstones beat on me, and the air around seemed reverberant with the howling of wolves. The last sight that I remembered was a vague, white, moving mass, as if all the graves around me had sent out the phantoms of their sheeted dead, and that they were closing in on me through the white cloudiness of the driving hail.

Gradually there came a sort of vague beginning of consciousness; then a sense of weariness that was dreadful. For a time I remembered nothing; but slowly my senses returned. My feet seemed positively racked with pain, yet I could not move them.

They seemed to be numbed. There was an icy feeling at the back of my neck and all down my spine, and my ears, like my feet, were dead, yet in torment; but there was in my breast a sense of warmth which was, by comparison, delicious. It was as a nightmare—a physical nightmare, if one may use such an expression; for some heavy weight on my chest made it difficult for me to breathe.

This period of semi-lethargy seemed to remain a long time, and as it faded away I must have slept or swooned. Then came a sort of loathing, like the first stage of seasickness, and a wild desire to be free from something—I knew not what. A vast stillness enveloped me, as though all the world were asleep or dead—only broken by the low panting as of some animal close to me. I felt a warm rasping at my throat, then came a consciousness of the awful truth, which chilled me to the heart and sent the blood surging up through my brain. Some great animal was lying on me and now licking my throat. I feared to stir, for some instinct of prudence bade me lie still; but the brute seemed to realize that there was now some change in me, for it raised its head. Through my eyelashes I saw above me the two great flaming eyes of a gigantic wolf. Its sharp white teeth gleamed in the gaping red mouth, and I could feel its hot breath fierce and acrid upon me.

For another spell of time I remembered no more. Then I became conscious of a low growl, followed by a yelp, renewed again and again. Then, seemingly very far away, I heard a "Holloa! holloa!" as of many voices calling in unison. Cautiously I raised my head and looked in the direction whence the sound came; but the cemetery blocked my view. The wolf still continued to yelp in a strange way, and a red glare began to move round the grove of cypresses, as though following the sound. As the voices drew closer, the wolf yelped faster and louder. I feared to make either sound or motion. Nearer came the red glow, over the white pall which stretched into the darkness around me. Then all at once from beyond the trees there came at a trot a troop of horsemen bearing torches. The wolf rose from my breast and made for the cemetery. I saw one of the horsemen (soldiers by their caps and their long military cloaks) raise his carbine and take aim. A companion knocked up his arm, and I heard the ball whizz over my head. He had evidently taken my body for that of the wolf. Another sighted the animal as it slunk away, and a shot followed. Then, at a gallop, the troop rode forward—some towards me, others following the wolf as it disappeared amongst the snow-clad cypresses.

As they drew nearer I tried to move, but was powerless, although I could see and hear all that went on around me. Two or three of the soldiers jumped from their horses and knelt beside me. One of them raised my head, and placed his hand over my heart.

"Good news, comrades!" he cried. "His heart still beats!"

Then some brandy was poured down my throat; it put vigor into me, and I was able to open my eyes fully and look around. Lights and shadows were moving among the trees, and I heard men call to one another. They drew together, uttering frightened exclamations; and the lights flashed as the others came pouring out of the cemetery pell-mell, like men possessed. When the further ones came close to us, those who were around me asked them eagerly:

"Well, have you found him?"

The reply rang out hurriedly:

"No! no! Come away quick—quick! This is no place to stay, and on this of all nights!"

"What was it?" was the question, asked in all manner of keys. The answer came variously and all indefinitely as though the men were moved by some common impulse to speak, yet were restrained by some common fear from giving their thoughts.

"It—it—indeed!" gibbered one, whose wits had plainly given out for the moment.

"A wolf—and yet not a wolf!" another put in shudderingly.

"No use trying for him without the sacred bullet," a third remarked in a more ordinary manner.

"Serve us right for coming out on this night! Truly we have earned our thousand marks!" were the ejaculations of a fourth.

"There was blood on the broken marble," another said after a pause—"the lightning never brought that there. And for him—is he safe? Look at his throat! See, comrades, the wolf has been lying on him and keeping his blood warm."

The officer looked at my throat and replied:

"He is all right; the skin is not pierced. What does it all mean? We should never have found him but for the yelping of the wolf."

"What became of it?" asked the man who was holding up my head, and who seemed the least panic-stricken of the party, for his hands were steady and without tremor. On his sleeve was the chevron of a petty officer.

"It went to its home," answered the man, whose long face was pallid, and who actually shook with terror as he glanced around him fearfully. "There are graves enough there in which it may lie. Come, comrades—come quickly! Let us leave this cursed spot."

The officer raised me to a sitting posture, as he uttered a word of command; then several men placed me upon a horse. He sprang to the saddle behind me, took me in his arms, gave the word to advance; and, turning our faces away from the cypresses, we rode away in swift, military order.

As yet my tongue refused its office, and I was perforce silent. I must have fallen asleep; for the next hing I remembered was finding myself standing up, supported by a soldier on each side of me. It was almost broad daylight, and to the north a red streak of sunlight was reflected, like a path of blood, over the waste of snow. The officer was telling the men to say nothing of what they had seen, except that they found an English stranger, guarded by a large dog.

"Dog! that was no dog," cut in the man who had exhibited such fear. "I think I know a wolf when I see one."

The young officer answered calmly: "I said a dog."

"Dog!" reiterated the other ironically. It was evident that his courage was rising with the sun; and, pointing to me, he said, "Look at his throat. Is that the work of a dog, master?"

Instinctively I raised my hand to my throat, and as I touched it I cried out in pain. The men crowded round to look, some stooping down from their saddles; and again there came the calm voice of the young officer:

"A dog, as I said. If aught else were said we should only be laughed at."

I was then mounted behind a trooper, and we rode on into the suburbs of Munich. Here we came across a stray carriage, into which I was lifted, and it was driven off to the Quatre Saisons—the young officer accompanying me, whilst a trooper followed with his horse, and the others rode off to their barracks.

When we arrived, Herr Delbrück rushed so quickly down the steps to meet me, that it was apparent he had been watching within. Taking me by both hands he solicitously led me in. The officer saluted me and was turning to withdraw, when I recognized his purpose, and insisted that he should come to my rooms. Over a glass of wine I warmly thanked him and his brave comrades for saving me. He replied simply that he was more than glad, and that Herr Delbrück had at the first taken steps to make all the searching party pleased; at which ambiguous utterance the maître d'hôtel smiled, while the officer pleaded duty and withdrew.

"But Herr Delbrück," I enquired, "how and why was it that the soldiers searched for me?"

He shrugged his shoulders, as if in depreciation of his own deed, as he replied:

"I was so fortunate as to obtain leave from the commander of the regiment in which I served, to ask for volunteers."

"But how did you know I was lost?" I asked.

"The driver came hither with the remains of his carriage, which had been upset when the horses ran away."

"But surely you would not send a search party of soldiers merely on this account?"

"Oh, no!" he answered; "but even before the coachman arrived, I had this telegram from the Boyar whose guest you are," and he took from his pocket a telegram which he handed to me, and I read:

Bistritz.

Be careful of my guest—his safety is most precious to me. Should aught happen to him, or if he be missed, spare nothing to find him and ensure his safety. He is English and therefore adventurous. There are often dangers from snow and wolves and night. Lose not a moment if you suspect harm to him. I answer your zeal with my fortune. —*Dracula.*

As I held the telegram in my hand, the room seemed to whirl around me; and, if the attentive maître d'hôtel had not caught me, I think I should have fallen. There was something so strange in all this, something so weird and impossible to imagine, that there grew on me a sense of my being in some way the sport of opposite forces —the mere vague idea of which seemed in a way to paralyze me. I was certainly under some form of mysterious protection. From a distant country had come, in the very nick of time, a message that took me out of the danger of the snow-sleep and the jaws of the wolf.

GABRIEL-ERNEST
by SAKI (H.H. MUNRO)

The short stories of Saki are unparalleled (except perhaps by those of John Collier) in the literature of the macabre and the bizarre. Though his style is urbane and wittily satirical, it often masks some of the deadliest of notions— like a velvet cushion in which is hidden a wicked knife blade. Who can fail to feel a frisson *of horror at the final revelations in "Sredni Vashtar," "The Open Window," "The Music on the Hill," "The Hounds of Fate"? Who can forget these brief tales once they have been read?*

"Gabriel-Ernest" is another such amusing, ironic, and lethal story—indisputably one of the classics of werewolf fiction. I felt the little chill, the frisson, *the first time I read it; I rather imagine you will too.*

The man who signed his work as Saki, Hector Hugh Munro, was born in Burma in 1870 and educated in England. He served with the Indian Imperial Police in Burma in 1893; three years later he returned to London to pursue his writing career. His stories and articles regularly appeared in such publications as the Bystander, *the* Westminster Gazette, *and the* Morning Post, *and were later collected in* The Westminster Alice *(1902),* The Chronicles of Clovis *(1911),* Beasts and Super-Beasts *(1914), and other books. When World War I broke out in Europe he enlisted in the British Army and saw action in France, where in 1916 he was killed by a sniper's bullet in Delville Wood.*

"There is a wild beast in your woods," said the artist Cunningham, as he was being driven to the station. It was the only remark he had made during the drive, but as Van Cheele had talked incessantly his companion's silence had not been noticeable.

"A stray fox or two and some resident weasels. Nothing more formidable," said Van Cheele. The artist said nothing.

"What did you mean about a wild beast?" said Van Cheele later, when they were on the platform.

"Nothing. My imagination. Here is the train," said Cunningham.

That afternoon Van Cheele went for one of his frequent rambles through his woodland property. He had a stuffed bittern in his study, and knew the names of quite a number of wild flowers, so his aunt had possibly some justification in describing him as a great naturalist. At any rate, he was a great walker. It was his custom to take mental notes of everything he saw during his walks, not so much for the purpose of assisting contemporary science as to provide topics for conversation afterwards. When the bluebells began to show themselves in flower he made a point of informing everyone of the fact; the season of the year might have warned his hearers of the likelihood of such an occurrence, but at least they felt that he was being absolutely frank with them.

What Van Cheele saw on this particular afternoon was, however, something far removed from his ordinary range of experience. On a shelf of smooth stone overhanging a deep pool in the hollow of an oak coppice a boy of about sixteen lay asprawl, drying his wet brown limbs luxuriously in the sun. His wet hair, parted by a recent dive, lay close to his head, and his light-brown eyes, so light that there was an almost tigerish gleam in them, were turned towards Van Cheele with a certain lazy watchfulness. It was an unexpected apparition, and Van Cheele found himself engaged in the novel process of thinking before he spoke. Where on earth could this wild-looking boy hail from? The miller's wife had lost a child some two months ago, supposed to have been swept away by the mill-race, but that had been a mere baby, not a half-grown lad.

"What are you doing there?" he demanded.

"Obviously, sunning myself," replied the boy.

"Where do you live?"

"Here, in these woods."

"You can't live in the woods," said Van Cheele.

"They are very nice woods," said the boy, with a touch of patronage in his voice.

"But where do you sleep at night?"

"I don't sleep at night; that's my busiest time."

Van Cheele began to have an irritated feeling that he was grappling with a problem that was eluding him.

"What do you feed on?" he asked.

"Flesh," said the boy, and he pronounced the word with slow relish, as though he were tasting it.

"Flesh! What flesh?"

"Since it interests you, rabbits, wild-fowl, hares, poultry, lambs in their season, children when I can get any; they're usually too well locked in at night, when I do most of my hunting. It's quite two months since I tasted child-flesh."

Ignoring the chaffing nature of the last remark, Van Cheele tried to draw the boy on the subject of possible poaching operations.

"You're talking rather through your hat when you speak of feeding on hares." (Considering the nature of the boy's toilet, the simile was hardly an apt one.) "Our hillside hares aren't easily caught."

"At night I hunt on four feet," was the somewhat cryptic response.

"I suppose you mean that you hunt with a dog?" hazarded Van Cheele.

The boy rolled slowly over on to his back, and laughed a weird low laugh, that was pleasantly like a chuckle and disagreeably like a snarl.

"I don't fancy any dog would be very anxious for my company, especially at night."

Van Cheele began to feel that there was something positively uncanny about the strange-eyed, strange-tongued youngster.

"I can't have you staying in these woods," he declared authoritatively.

"I fancy you'd rather have me here than in your house," said the boy.

The prospect of this wild, nude animal in Van Cheele's primly ordered house was certainly an alarming one.

"If you don't go, I shall have to make you," said Van Cheele.

The boy turned like a flash, plunged into the pool, and in a moment had flung his wet and glistening body halfway up the bank where Van Cheele was standing. In an otter the movement would not have been remarkable; in a boy Van Cheele found it sufficiently startling. His foot slipped as he made an involuntary backward movement, and he found himself almost prostrate on the slippery weed-grown bank, with those tigerish yellow eyes not very far from his own. Almost instinctively he half-raised his hand to his throat. The boy laughed again, a laugh in which the snarl had nearly driven out the chuckle, and then, with another of his astonishing lightning movements, plunged out of view into a yielding tangle of weed and fern.

"What an extraordinary wild animal!" said Van Cheele as he picked himself up. And then he recalled Cunningham's remark, "There is a wild beast in your woods."

Walking slowly homeward, Van Cheele began to turn over in his mind various local occurrences which might be traceable to the existence of this astonishing young savage.

Something had been thinning the game in the woods lately, poultry had been missing from the farms, hares were growing unaccountably scarcer, and complaints had reached him of lambs being carried off bodily from the hills. Was it possible that this wild boy was really hunting the countryside in company with some clever poacher dog? He had spoken of hunting "four-footed" by night, but then, again, he had hinted strangely at no dog caring to come near him, "especially at night." It was certainly puzzling. And then, as Van Cheele ran his mind over the various depredations that had been committed during the last month or two, he came suddenly to a dead stop, alike in his walk and his speculations. The child missing from the mill two months ago—the accepted theory was that it had tumbled into the mill-race and been swept away; but the mother had always declared she had heard a shriek on the hill side of the house, in the opposite direction from the water. It was unthinkable, of course, but he wished that the boy had not made that uncanny remark about child-flesh eaten two months ago. Such dreadful things should not be said even in fun.

Van Cheele, contrary to his usual wont, did not feel disposed to be communicative about his discovery in the wood. His position as a parish councillor and justice of the peace seemed somehow compromised by the fact that he was harboring a personality of such doubtful repute on his property; there was even a possibility that a heavy bill of damages for raided lambs and poultry might be laid at his door. At dinner that night he was quite unusually silent.

"Where's your voice gone to?" said his aunt. "One would think you had seen a wolf."

Van Cheele, who was not familiar with the old saying, thought the remark rather foolish; if he *had* seen a wolf on his property his tongue would have been extraordinarily busy with the subject.

At breakfast next morning Van Cheele was conscious that his feeling of uneasiness regarding yesterday's episode had not wholly disappeared, and he resolved to go by train to the neighboring cathedral town, hunt up Cunningham, and learn from him what he had really seen that had prompted the remark about a wild beast in the woods. With this resolution taken, his usual cheerfulness partially returned, and he hummed a bright little melody as he sauntered to the morning room for his customary cigarette. As he entered the room the melody made way abruptly for a pious invocation. Gracefully asprawl on the ottoman, in an attitude of almost exaggerated repose, was the boy of the woods. He was drier than when Van Cheele had last seen him, but no other alteration was noticeable in his toilet.

"How dare you come here?" asked Van Cheele furiously.

"You told me I was not to stay in the woods," said the boy calmly.

"But not to come here. Supposing my aunt should see you!"

And with a view to minimizing that catastrophe Van Cheele hastily obscured as much of his unwelcome guest as possible under the folds of a *Morning Post.* At that moment his aunt entered the room.

"This is a poor boy who has lost his way—and lost his memory. He doesn't know who he is or where he comes from," explained Van Cheele desperately, glancing apprehensively at the waif's face to see whether he was going to add inconvenient candor to his other savage propensities.

Miss Van Cheele was enormously interested.

"Perhaps his underlinen is marked," she suggested.

"He seems to have lost most of that, too," said Van Cheele, making frantic little grabs at the *Morning Post* to keep it in its place.

A naked, homeless child appealed to Miss Van Cheele as warmly as a stray kitten or derelict puppy would have done.

"We must do all we can for him," she decided, and in a very short time a messenger, dispatched to the rectory, where a page-boy was kept, had returned with a suit of pantry clothes, and the necessary accessories of shirt, shoes, collar, etc. Clothed, clean and groomed, the boy lost none of his uncanniness in Van Cheele's eyes, but his aunt found him sweet.

"We must call him something till we know who he really is," she said. "Gabriel-Ernest, I think; those are nice suitable names."

Van Cheele agreed, but he privately doubted whether they were being grafted on to a nice suitable child. His misgivings were not diminished by the fact that his staid and elderly spaniel had bolted out of the house at the first incoming of the boy, and now obstinately remained shivering and yapping at the farther end of the orchard, while the canary, usually as vocally industrious as Van Cheele himself, had put itself on an allowance of frightened cheeps. More than ever he was resolved to consult Cunningham without loss of time.

As he drove off to the station his aunt was arranging that Gabriel-Ernest should help her to entertain the infant members of her Sunday-school class at tea that afternoon.

Cunningham was not at first disposed to be communicative.

"My mother died of some brain trouble," he explained, "so you will understand why I am averse to dwelling on anything of an impossibly fantastic nature that I may see or think that I have seen."

"But what *did* you see?" persisted Van Cheele.

"What I thought I saw was something so extraordinary that no really sane man could dignify it with the credit of having actually happened. I was standing, the last evening I was with you, half-hidden in the hedgegrowth by the orchard gate, watching the dying glow of the sunset. Suddenly I became aware of a naked boy, a bather from some neighboring pool, I took him to be, who was standing out on the bare hillside also watching the sunset. His pose was so suggestive of some wild faun of Pagan myth that I instantly wanted to engage him as a model, and in another moment I think I should have hailed him. But just then the sun dipped out of view, and all the orange and pink slid out of the landscape, leaving it cold and gray. And at the same moment an astounding thing happened —the boy vanished too!"

"What! Vanished away into nothing?" asked Van Cheele excitedly.

"No; that is the dreadful part of it," answered the artist; "on the open hillside where the boy had been standing a second ago, stood a large wolf, blackish in color, with gleaming fangs and cruel, yellow eyes. You may think—"

But Van Cheele did not stop for anything as futile as thought. Already he was tearing at top speed towards the station. He dismissed the idea of a telegram. "Gabriel-Ernest is a werewolf" was a hopelessly inadequate effort at conveying the situation, and his aunt would think it was a code message to which he had omitted to give her the key. His one hope was that he might reach home before sundown. The cab which he chartered at the other end of the railway journey bore him with what seemed exasperating slowness along the country roads, which were pink and mauve with the flush of the sinking sun. His aunt was putting away some unfinished jams and cake when he arrived.

"Where is Gabriel-Ernest?" he almost screamed.

"He is taking the little Toop child home," said his aunt. "It was getting so late, I thought it wasn't safe to let it go back alone. What a lovely sunset, isn't it?"

But Van Cheele, although not oblivious of the glow in the western sky, did not stay to discuss its beauties. At a speed for which he was scarcely geared he raced along the narrow lane that led to the home of the Toops. On one side ran the swift current of the mill-stream, on the other rose the stretch of bare hillside. A dwindling rim of red sun showed still on the skyline, and the next turning must bring him in view of the ill-assorted couple he was pursuing. Then the color went suddenly out of things, and a gray light settled itself with a quick shiver over the landscape. Van Cheele heard a shrill wail of fear, and stopped running.

Nothing was ever seen again of the Toops' child or Gabriel-Ernest, but the latter's discarded garments were found lying in the road, so it was assumed that the child had fallen into the water, and that the boy had stripped and jumped in, in a vain endeavor to save it. Van Cheele and some workmen who were nearby at the time testified to having heard a child scream loudly just near the spot where the clothes were found. Mrs. Toop, who had eleven other children, was decently resigned to her bereavement, but Miss Van Cheele sincerely mourned her lost foundling. It was on her initiative that a memorial brass was put up in the parish church to "Gabriel-Ernest, an unknown boy, who bravely sacrificed his life for another."

Van Cheele gave way to his aunt in most things, but he flatly refused to subscribe to the Gabriel-Ernest memorial.

Part Two:

CONTEMPORARY TALES AND VARIATIONS

THERE SHALL BE
NO DARKNESS
by JAMES BLISH

Of all the shorter works on the werewolf theme, "There Shall Be No Darkness" is my personal favorite. Set on a Scottish estate circa 1950, it utilizes the classic mystery and fantasy ploy of a group of disparate people isolated by the elements and in mortal danger of their lives—in this case, of course, from a werewolf in their midst. Its many other virtues include excellent characterization, liberal amounts of mood and atmosphere, steadily mounting suspense, and a clever surprise or two.

But what makes it especially exceptional is the fact that it outlines each and every segment of werewolf lore and offers sound scientific explanations for these phenomena. In no other story will you find such fascinating detail work on the subject of lycanthropy. (It must be noted that Blish does make a couple of small errors; the werewolf, unlike the vampire, is able to see his reflection in a mirror, for instance. But these are minor and do not harm plausibility or scientific efficacy.)

James Blish, who died in 1975 at the age of fifty-four, wrote little fantasy during his career. It was as a writer and outspoken critic in the field of science fiction that he achieved his considerable reputation. He is perhaps most popularly known as the author of the Star Trek *novelizations; among the science-fiction cognoscenti, however, it is his "Cities in Flight" series and such critical works as* Issues at Hand *and* More Issues at Hand *(both under the name William Atheling) which are most respected.*

87

I

It was about 10:00 P.M. when Paul Foote decided that there was a monster at Newcliffe's house party.

Foote was tight at the time—tighter than he liked to be ever. He sprawled in a too-easy chair in the front room, slanted on the end of his spine, his forearms resting on the high arms of the chair. A half-empty glass depended laxly from his right hand. A darker spot on one gray trouser leg showed where some of the drink had gone. Through half-shut eyes he watched Jarmoskowski at the piano.

The pianist was playing, finally, his transcription of the Wolf's-Glen scene from von Weber's *Der Freischuetz*. Though it was a tremendous technical showpiece, Jarmoskowski never used it in concert, but only at social gatherings. He played it with an odd, detached amusement which only made more astounding the way the notes came swarming out of Newcliffe's big Baldwin; the rest of the gathering had been waiting for it all evening.

For Foote, who was a painter with a tin ear, it wasn't music at all. It was an enormous, ominous noise, muted occasionally to allow the repetition of a cantrap whose implications were secret.

The room was stuffy and was only half as large as it had been during the afternoon, and Foote was afraid that he was the only living man in it except for Jan Jarmoskowski. The rest of the party were wax figures, pretending to be humans in an aesthetic trance.

Of Jarmoskowski's vitality there could be no question. He was not handsome, but there was in him a pure brute force that had its own beauty—that and the beauty of precision with which the force was controlled. When his big hairy hands came down it seemed that the piano should fall into flinders. But the impact of fingers upon keys was calculated to the single dyne.

It was odd to see such delicacy behind such a face. Jarmoskowski's hair grew too long on his rounded head, despite the fact that he had avoided carefully any suggestion of Musician's Haircut. His brows were straight, rectangular, so shaggy that they seemed to meet over his high-bridged nose.

From where Foote sat he noticed for the first time the odd way the Pole's ears were placed—tilted forward as if in animal attention, so that the vestigial "point" really was in the uppermost position. They were cocked directly toward the keyboard, reminding Foote irresistibly of the dog on the His Master's Voice trademark.

Where had he seen that head before? In Matthias Gruenewald, perhaps—in that panel on the Isenheim Altar that showed the Temptation of St. Anthony. Or had it been in one of the illustrations in the *Red Grimoire,* those dingy, primitive woodcuts which Chris Lundgren called "Rorschah tests of the medieval mind"?

On a side-table next to the chair the painter's cigarette burned in an onyx ash tray which bore also a tiny dancer frozen in twisted metal. From the unlit end of the cigarette a small tendril of white smoke flowed downward and oozed out into a clinging pool, an ameboid blur against the dark mahogany. The river of sound subsided suddenly and the cantrap was spoken, the three even, stony syllables and the answering wail. The pool of smoke leapt up in the middle exactly as if something had been dropped into it. Then the piano was howling again under Jarmoskowski's fingers, and the tiny smoke-spout twisted in the corner of Foote's vision, becoming more and more something like the metal dancer. His mouth dry, Foote shifted to the outer edge of the chair.

The transcription ended with three sharp chords, a "concert ending" contrived to suggest the three plucked notes of the cantrap. The smoke-figurine toppled and slumped as if stabbed; it poured over the edge of the table and disintegrated swiftly on the air. Jarmoskowski paused, touched his fingertips together reflectively, and then began a work more purely his own: the *Galliard Fantasque.*

The wax figures did not stir, but a soft eerie sigh of recognition came from their frozen lips. Through the window behind the pianist a newly risen moon showed another petrified vista, the snowy expanse of Newcliffe's Scottish estate.

There was another person in the room, but Foote could not tell who it was. When he turned his unfocused eyes to count, his mind went back on him and he never managed to reach a total; but somehow there was the impression of another presence that had not been of the party before. Someone Tom and Caroline hadn't invited was sitting in. Not Doris, nor the Laborite Palmer, either; they were too simple. By the same token, Bennington, the American critic, was much too tubbily comfortable to have standing as a menace. The visiting psychiatrist, Lundgren, Foote had known well in Sweden, and Hermann Ehrenberg was only another refugee novelist and didn't count; for that matter, no novelist was worth a snap in a painter's universe, so that crossed out Alec James, too.

His glance moved of itself back to the composer. Jarmoskowski was not the presence. He had been there before. But he had something to do with it. There was an eleventh presence now, and it had something to do with Jarmoskowski.

What was it?

For it was there—there was no doubt about that. The energy which the rest of Foote's senses ordinarily would have consumed was flowing into his instincts now, because his senses were numbed. Acutely, poignantly, his instincts told him of the monster. It hovered around the piano, sat next to Jarmoskowski as he caressed the musical beast's teeth, blended with the long body and the serpentine fingers.

Foote had never had the horrors from drinking before, and he knew he did not have them now. A part of his mind which was not drunk and could never be drunk had recognized real horror somewhere in the room; and the whole of his mind, its barriers of skepticism tumbled, believed and trembled within itself.

The batlike circling of the frantic notes was stilled abruptly. Foote blinked, startled.

"Already?" he said stupidly.

"Already?" Jarmoskowski echoed. "But that's a long piece, Paul. Your fascination speaks well for my writing."

His eyes turned directly upon the painter; they were almost completely suffused, though Jarmoskowski never drank. Foote tried frantically to remember whether or not his eyes had been red during the afternoon, and whether it was possible for any man's eyes to be as red at any time as this man's were now.

"The writing?" he said, condensing the far-flung diffusion of his brain. Newcliffe's highballs were damn strong. "Hardly the writing, Jan. Such fingers as those could put fascination into 'Three Blind Mice.' "

He snickered inside at the parade of emotions which marched across Jarmoskowski's face: startlement at a compliment from Foote —for the painter had a reputation for a savage tongue, and the inexplicable antagonism which had arisen between the two since the pianist had first arrived had given Foote plenty of opportunity to justify it—then puzzled reflection—and then at last veiled anger as the hidden slur bared its fangs in his mind. Nevertheless the man could laugh at it.

"They are long, aren't they?" he said to the rest of the group, unrolling the fingers like the party noisemakers which turn from snail to snake when blown through. "But it's a mistake to suppose that they assist my playing, I assure you. Mostly they stumble over each other. Especially over this one."

He held up his hands for inspection. On both, the index fingers and the middle fingers were exactly the same length.

"I suppose Lundgren would call me a mutation," Jarmoskowski said. "It's a nuisance at the piano. I have to work out my own fingerings for everything, even the simplest pieces."

Doris Gilmore, once a student of Jarmoskowski's in Prague, and still obviously, painfully in love with him, shook coppery hair back from her shoulders and held up her own hands.

"My fingers are so stubby," she said ruefully. "Hardly pianist's hands at all."

"On the contrary—the hands of a master pianist," Jarmoskowski said. He smiled, scratching his palms abstractedly, and Foote found himself in a universe of brilliant, perfectly even teeth. No, not perfectly even. The polished rows were bounded almost mathematically by slightly longer canines. They reminded him of that idiotic Poe story—was it *Berenice?* Obviously Jarmoskowski would not die a natural death. He would be killed by a dentist for possession of those teeth.

"Three fourths of the greatest pianists I know have hands like truck drivers," Jarmoskowski was saying. "Surgeons too, as Lundgren will tell you. Long fingers tend to be clumsy."

"You seem to manage to make tremendous music, all the same," Newcliffe said, getting up.

"Thank you, Tom." Jarmoskowski seemed to take his host's rising as a signal that he was not going to be required to play any more. He lifted his feet from the pedals and swung them around to the end of the bench. Several of the others rose also. Foote struggled up onto numb feet from the infernal depths of the armchair. Setting his glass on the side-table a good distance away from the onyx ash tray, he picked his way cautiously over to Christian Lundgren.

"Chris, I'm a fan of yours," he said, controlling his tongue with difficulty. "Now I'm sorry. I read your paper, the one you read to the Stockholm Endo-crin-ological Congress. Aren't Jarmoskowski's hands—"

"Yes, they are," the psychiatrist said, looking at Foote with sharp, troubled eyes. Suddenly Foote was aware of Lundgren's chain of thought; he knew the scientist very well. The gray, craggy man was assessing Foote's drunkenness, and wondering whether or not he would have forgotten the whole affair in the morning.

Lundgren made a gesture of dismissal. "I saw them too," he said, his tone flat. "A mutation, probably, as he himself suggested. Not every woman with a white streak through her hair is a witch; I give Jan the same reservation."

"That's not all, Chris."

"It is all I need to consider, since I live in the twentieth century. I am going to bed and forget all about it. Which you may take for advice as well as for information, Paul, if you will."

He stalked out of the room, leaving Foote standing alone, wondering whether to be reassured or more alarmed than before. Lundgren should know, and certainly the platinum path which parted Doris Gilmore's absurdly red hair indicated nothing about Doris but that her coiffure was too chic for her young, placid face. But Jarmoskowski was not so simple; if he was despite Lundgren just what he seemed—

The party appeared to be surviving quite nicely without Foote, or Lundgren either. Conversations were starting up about the big room. Jarmoskowski and Doris shared the piano bench and were talking in low tones, punctuated now and then by brilliant bits of passage work; evidently the Pole was showing her better ways of handling the Hindemith sonata she had played before dinner. James and Ehrenberg were dissecting each other's most recent books with civilized savagery before a fascinated Newcliffe. Blandly innocent Caroline Newcliffe was talking animatedly to Bennington and Palmer about nothing at all. Nobody missed Lundgren, and it seemed even less likely that Foote would be missed.

He walked with wobbly nonchalance into the dining room, where the butler was still clearing the table.

" 'Scuse me," he said. "Little experiment, if y'don't mind. Return it in the morning." He snatched a knife from the table, looked for the door which led directly from the dining room into the foyer, propelled himself through it. The hallway was dim, but intelligible; so was the talk in the next room.

As he passed the French door, he saw Bennington's figure through the ninon marquisette, now standing by the piano watching the progress of the lesson. The critic's voice stopped him dead as he was sliding the knife into his jacket. Foote was an incurable eavesdropper.

"Hoofy's taken his head to bed," Bennington was remarking. "I'm rather relieved. I thought he was going to be more unpleasant than he was."

"What was the point of that fuss about the silverware, at dinner?" the girl said. "Is he noted for that sort of thing?"

"Somewhat. He's really quite a brilliant artist, but being years ahead of one's time is frequently hard on the temper."

"He had me worried," Jarmoskowski confessed. "He kept looking at me as if I had forgotten to play the repeats."

Bennington chuckled. "In the presence of another inarguable artist he seems to become very malignant. You were being flattered, Jan."

Foote's attention was attracted by a prodigious yawn from Palmer. The Laborite was showing his preliminary signals of boredom, and at any moment now would break unceremoniously for his bed. Reluctantly Foote resumed his arrested departure; still the conversations babbled on indifferently behind him. The corners of his mouth pulled down, he passed the stairway and on down the hall.

As he swung closed the door of his bedroom, he paused a moment to listen to Jarmoskowski's technical exhibition on the keys, the only sound from the living room which was still audible at this distance. Then he shut the door all the way with a convulsive shrug. Let them say about Foote what they liked, even if it sometimes had to be the truth; but nevertheless it might be that at midnight Jarmoskowski would give another sort of exhibition.

If he did, Foote would be glad to have the knife.

2

At 11:30, Jarmoskowski stood alone on the terrace of Newcliffe's country house. Although there was no wind, the night was frozen with a piercing cold—but he did not seem to notice it. He stood motionless, like a black statue, with only the long streamers of his breathing, like twin jets of steam from the nostrils of a dragon, to show that he was alive.

Through the haze of watered silk which curtained Foote's window, Jarmoskowski was an heroic pillar of black stone—a pillar above a fumarole.

The front of the house was evidently entirely dark: there was no light on the pianist's back or shoulders. He was silhouetted against the snow, which gleamed dully in the moonlight. The shadow of the heavy tower which was the house's axis looked like a donjon-keep. Thin slits of embrasures, Foote remembered, watched the landscape with a dark vacuity, and each of the crowning merlons wore a helmet of snow.

He could feel the house huddling against the malice of the white Scottish night. A sense of age invested it. The curtains smelled of dust and spices. It seemed impossible that anyone but Foote and Jarmoskowski could be alive in it.

After a long moment, Foote moved the curtain very slightly and drew it back. His face was drenched in reflected moonlight and he stepped back into the dark again, leaving the curtains parted.

If Jarmoskowski saw the furtive movement he gave no sign. He remained engrossed in the acerb beauty of the night. Almost the

whole of Newcliffe's estate was visible from where he stood. Even
the black border of the forest, beyond the golf course to the right,
could be seen through the dry frigid air. A few isolated trees stood
nearer the house, casting sharply etched shadows on the snow,
shadows that flowed and changed shape with the slow movement of
the moon.

Jarmoskowski sighed and scratched his left palm. His lips moved
soundlessly.

A cloud floated across the moon, its shadow preceding it, gliding
in a rush of ink athwart the house. The gentle ripples of the snow
field reared ahead of the wave, like breakers, falling back, engulfed,
then surging again much closer. A thin singing of wind rose briefly,
whirling crystalline showers of snow from the terrace flagstones.

The wind died as the umbra engulfed the house. For a long
instant, the darkness and silence persisted. Then, from somewhere
near the stables and greenhouses behind the house, a dog raised his
voice in a faint sustained throbbing howl. Others joined in.

Jarmoskowski's teeth gleamed in the occluded moonlight. He
stood a moment longer; then his head turned with a quick jerk and
his eyes flashed a feral scarlet at the dark window where Foote
hovered. Foote released the curtains hastily. Even through them he
could see the pianist's phosphorescent smile.

The dog keened again. Jarmoskowski went back into the house.
Foote scurried to his door and cocked one eye around the jamb.

Some men, as has somewhere been remarked, cannot pass a bar;
some cannot pass a woman; some cannot pass a rare stamp or a
good fire. Foote could not help spying, but in this one case he knew
that one thing could be said for him: *this* time he wanted to be in
the wrong.

There was a single small light burning in the corridor. Jarmoskowski's room was at the end of the hall, next to Foote's. As the
pianist walked reflectively toward it, the door of the room directly
across from Foote's swung open and Doris Gilmore came out, clad
in a quilted sapphire housecoat with a high Russian collar. The
effect was marred a little by the towel over her arm and the toothbrush in her hand, but nevertheless she looked startlingly pretty.

"Oh!" she said. Jarmoskowski turned toward her, and then neither of them said anything for a while.

Foote ground his teeth. Was the girl, too, to be a witness to the thing he expected from Jarmoskowski? That would be beyond all decency. And it must be nearly midnight now.

The two still had not moved. Trembling, Foote edged out into the hall and slid behind Jarmoskowski's back along the wall to Jarmoskowski's room. By the grace of God, the door was open.

In a quieter voice, Doris said, "Oh, it's you, Jan. You startled me."

"So I see. I'm most sorry," Jarmoskowski's voice said. Foote again canted his head until he could see them both. "It appears that we are the night owls of the party."

"I think the rest are tight. Especially that horrible painter. I've been reading the magazines Tom left by my bed, and I finally decided I'd better try to sleep, too. What have you been up to?"

"I was out on the terrace, getting a breath. I like the winter night —it bites."

"The dogs are restless, too," she said. "Did you hear them? I suppose Brucey started them off."

Jarmoskowski smiled. "Very likely. Why does a full moon make a dog feel so sorry for himself?"

"Maybe there's a banshee about."

"I doubt it," Jarmoskowski said. "This house isn't old enough to have any family psychopomps; it's massive, but largely imitation. And as far as I know, none of Tom's or Caroline's relatives have had the privilege of dying in it."

"Don't. You talk as if you believed it." She wrapped the housecoat tighter about her waist; Foote guessed that she was repressing a shiver.

"I came from a country where belief in such things is common. In Poland most skeptics are imported."

"I wish you'd pretend to be an exception," she said. "You're giving me the creeps, Jan."

He nodded seriously. "That's—fair enough," he said gently.

There was another silence, while they looked at each other anew in the same dim light. Then Jarmoskowski stepped forward and took her hands in his.

Foote felt a long-belated flicker of embarrassment. Nothing could be more normal than this, and nothing interested him less. He was an eavesdropper, not a voyeur. If he were wrong after all, he'd speedily find himself in a position for which no apology would be possible.

The girl was looking up at Jarmoskowski, smiling uncertainly. Her smile was so touching as to make Foote writhe inside his skin. "Jan," she said.

"No . . . Doris, wait," Jarmoskowski said indistinctly. "Wait just a moment. It has been a long time since Prague."

"I see," she said. She tried to release her hands.

Jarmoskowski said sharply: "You don't see. I was eighteen then. You were—what was it?—eleven, I think. In those days I was proud of your school-girl crush, but of course infinitely too old for you. I am not so old any more, and when I saw this afternoon how lovely you have become the years went away like dandelion fluff—no, no, hear me out, please! There is much more. I love you now, Doris, as I can see you love me; but—"

In the brief pause Foote could hear the sharp indrawn breaths that Doris was trying to control. He felt like crawling. He had no business—

"But we must wait a little, Doris. I know something that concerns you that you do not know yourself. And I must warn you of something in Jan Jarmoskowski that neither of us could even have dreamed in the old days."

"Warn—me?"

"Yes." Jarmoskowski paused again. Then he said: "You will find it hard to believe. But if you can, we may be happy. Doris, I cannot be a skeptic. I am—"

He stopped. He had looked down abstractedly at her hands, as if searching for precisely the right English words. Then, slowly, he turned her hands over until they rested palms up on his. An expression of absolute shock transformed his face, and Foote saw his grip tighten spasmodically.

In that tetanic silence Foote heard his judgment of Jarmoskowski confirmed. It gave him no pleasure. He was frightened.

For an instant Jarmoskowski shut his eyes. The muscles along his jaw stood out with the violence with which he was clenching his teeth. Then, deliberately, he folded Doris' hands together, and his curious fingers made a fist about them. When his eyes opened again they were as red as flame in the weak light.

Doris jerked her hands free and crossed them over her breasts. "Jan—Jan, what is it? What's the matter?"

His face, that should have been flying into flinders under the force of the knowledge behind it, came under control muscle by muscle.

"Nothing," he said. "There's really no point in what I was going to say. I have been foolish; please pardon me. Nice to have seen you again, Doris. Good night."

He brushed past her and stalked on down the corridor. Doris turned to look after him, her cheeks beginning to glisten, one freed hand clutching her toothbrush.

Jarmoskowski wrenched the unresisting doorknob of his room and threw the door shut behind him. Foote only barely managed to dodge out of his way.

Behind the house, a dog howled and went silent again.

3

In Jarmoskowski's room the moonlight played in through the open window upon a carefully turned-down bed. The cold air had penetrated every cranny. He ran both hands through his hair and went directly across the carpet to the table beside his bed. As he crossed the path of colorless light his shadow was oddly foreshortened, so that it looked as if he were walking on all fours. There was a lamp on the side-table and he reached for it.

Then he stopped dead still, his hand halfway to the switch. He seemed to be listening. Finally, he turned and looked back across the room, directly at the spot behind the door where Foote was standing.

It was the blackest spot of all, for it had its back to the moon; but Jarmoskowski said immediately, "Hello, Paul. Aren't you up rather late?"

Foote did not reply for a while. His senses were still alcohol-numbed, and he was further poisoned by the sheer outrageous impossibility of the thing he knew to be true. He stood silently in the darkness, watching the Pole's barely visible figure beside the fresh bed, and the sound of his own breathing was loud in his ears.

The broad flat streamer of moonlight lay between them like a metallic river.

"I'm going to bed shortly," he said at last. His voice sounded flat and dead and faraway, as if it belonged to someone else entirely. "I just came to issue a little warning."

"Well, well," said Jarmoskowski pleasantly. "Warnings seem to be all the vogue this evening. Do you customarily pay your social calls with a knife in your hand?"

"That's the warning, Jarmoskowski. The knife. I'm sleeping with it. It's made of silver."

"You must be drunker than usual," said the composer. "Why don't you just go to bed—with the knife, if you fancy it? We can talk again in the morning."

"Don't give me that," Foote snapped savagely. "You can't fool me. I know you for what you are."

"All right, you know me. Is it a riddle? I'll bite, as Bennington would say."

"Yes, you'd bite," Foote said, and his voice shook a little despite himself. "Should I really give it a name, Jarmoskowski? Where you were born it was *vrolok*, wasn't it? And in France it was *loup-garou*. In the Carpathians it was *stregoica* or *strega*, or sometimes *vlkolak*. In—"

"Your command of languages is greater than your common sense," Jarmoskowski said. "And *stregoica* and *strega* are different in sex, and neither of them is equivalent to *loup-garou*. But all the same you interest me. Isn't it a little out of season for all such things? Wolfsbane does not bloom in the dead of winter. And perhaps the things you give so many fluent names are also out of season in 1952."

"The dogs hate you," Foote said softly. "That was a fine display Brucey put on this afternoon, when Tom brought him in from his run and he found you here. I doubt that you've forgotten it. I think you've seen a dog behave like that before, walking sidewise through a room where you were, growling, watching you with every step until Tom or some other owner dragged him out. He's howling now.

"And that shock you got from the table silverware at dinner—and your excuse about rubber-soled shoes. I looked under the table, if you recall, and your shoes turned out to be leather-soled. But it was a pretty feeble excuse anyhow, for anybody knows that you can't get an electric shock from an ungrounded piece of tableware, no matter how long you've been scuffing rubber. Silver's deadly, isn't it, Jarmoskowski?

"And those fingers—the index fingers as long as the middle ones —you were clever about those. You were careful to call everybody's attention to them. It's supposed to be the obvious that everybody misses. But Jarmoskowski, that 'Purloined Letter' mechanism has been ground through too often already in detective stories. It didn't fool Lundgren, it didn't fool me."

"Ah, so," Jarmoskowski said. "Quite a catalogue."

"There's more. How does it happen that your eyes were gray all afternoon, and turned red as soon as the moon rose? And the palms of your hands—there was some hair growing there, but you shaved it off, didn't you, Jarmoskowski? I've been watching you scratch them. Everything about you, the way you look, the way you talk, every move you make—it all screams out your nature in a dozen languages to anyone who knows the signs."

After a long silence, Jarmoskowski said, "I see. You've been most attentive, Paul—I see you are what people call the suspicious drunk. But I appreciate your warning, Paul. Let us suppose that what you say of me is true. What then? Are you prepared to broadcast it to the rest of the house? Would you like to be known until the day you die as 'The Boy Who Cried—' "

"I don't intend to say anything unless you make it necessary. I want you to know that I know, in case you've seen a pentagram on anyone's palm tonight."

Jarmoskowski smiled. "Have you thought that, knowing that you know, I could have no further choice? That the first word you said to me about it all might brand *your* palm with the pentagram?"

Foote had not thought about it. He had spent far too much time convincing himself that it had all come out of the bottle. He heard the silver knife clatter against the floor before he was aware that he had dropped it; his eyes throbbed with the effort to see through the dimness the hands he was holding before them.

From the other side of his moonlit room, Jarmoskowski's voice drifted, dry, distant, and amused. "So—you hadn't thought. That's too bad. *Better never* than late, Paul."

The dim figure of Jarmoskowski began to sink down, rippling a little in the reflected moonlight. At first it seemed only as if he were sitting down upon the bed; but the foreshortening proceeded without any real movement, and the pianist's body was twisting, too, and his clothing with it, his shirt-bosom dimming to an indistinct blaze upon his broadening chest, his shoulders hunching, his pointed jaw already squared into a blunt muzzle, his curled pads ticking as they struck the bare floor and moved deliberately toward Foote. His tail was thrust straight out behind him, and the ruff of coarse hair along his back stirred gently. He sniffed.

Somehow Foote got his legs to move. He found the doorknob and threw himself out of Jarmoskowski's room into the corridor.

A bare second after he had slammed the door, something struck it a massive blow from inside. The paneling split sharply. He held it shut by the knob with all the strength in his body. He could see almost nothing; his eyes seemed to have rolled all the way back into his head.

A dim white shape drifted down upon him through the dark corridor, and a fresh spasm of fear sent rivers of sweat down his back, his sides, his cheeks. But it was only the girl.

"Paul! What on Earth! What's the *matter?*"

"Quick!" he said, choking. "Get something silver—something heavy made out of silver—quick, *quick!*"

Despite her astonishment, the frantic urgency in his voice drove her away. She darted back into her room. Kalpas of eternity went by after that while he listened for sounds inside Jarmoskowski's room. Once he thought he heard a low rumble, but he was not sure. The sealike hissing and sighing of his blood, rushing through the channels of the middle ear, seemed very loud to him. He couldn't imagine why it was not arousing the whole countryside. He clung to the doorknob and panted.

Then the girl was back, bearing a silver candlestick nearly three feet in length—a weapon that was almost too good, for his fright-weakened muscles had some difficulty in lifting it. He shifted his grip on the knob to the left hand alone, and hefted the candlestick awkwardly with his right.

"All right," he said, in what he hoped was a grim voice. "Now let him come."

"What in heaven's name is this all about?" Doris said. "You're waking everybody in the house with this racket. Look—even the dog's come in to see—"

"*The dog!*"

He swung around, releasing the doorknob. Not ten paces from them, an enormous coal-black animal, nearly five feet in length, grinned at them with polished fangs. As soon as it saw Foote move it snarled. Its eyes gleamed red under the single bulb.

It sprang.

Foote heaved the candlestick high and brought it down—but the animal was not there. Somehow the leap was never completed. There was a brief flash of movement at the open end of the corridor, then darkness and silence.

"He saw the candlestick," Foote panted. "Must have jumped out the window and come around through the front door. Then he saw the silver and beat it."

"Paul!" Doris cried. "What—how did you know that thing would jump? It was so big! And what has silver—"

He chuckled, surprising even himself. He had a mental picture of what the truth was going to sound like to Doris. "That," he said, "was a wolf and a whopping one. Even the usual kind isn't very friendly and—"

Footsteps sounded on the floor above, and the voice of Newcliffe, grumbling loudly, came down the stairs. Newcliffe liked his evenings noisy and his nights quiet. The whole house now seemed to have heard the commotion, for in a moment a number of half-clad figures were elbowing out into the corridor, wanting to know what was up or plaintively requesting less noise.

Abruptly the lights went on, revealing blinking faces and pajama-clad forms struggling into robes. Newcliffe came down the stairs. Caroline was with him, impeccable even in disarray, her face openly and honestly ignorant and unashamedly beautiful. She was no lion-hunter but she loved parties. Evidently she was pleased that the party was starting again.

"What's all this?" Newcliffe demanded in a gravelly voice. "Foote, are you the center of this whirlpool? Why all the noise?"

"Werewolf," Foote said, as painfully conscious as he had expected to be of how meaningless the word would sound. "We've got a werewolf here. And somebody's marked out for him."

How else could you put it? Let it stand.

There was a chorus of "What's" as the group jostled about him. "Eh? What was it? . . . Werewolf, I thought he said . . . What's this all about? . . . Somebody's seen a wolf . . . Is that new? . . . What an uproar!"

"Paul," Lundgren's voice cut through. "Details, please."

"Jarmoskowski's a werewolf," Foote said grimly, making his tone as emotionless and factual as he could. "I suspected it earlier tonight and went into his room and accused him of it. He changed shape, right on the spot while I was watching."

The sweat started out afresh at the recollection of that half-seen mutation. "He came around into the hall and went for us. I scared him off with a silver candlestick for a club." He realized that he still held the candlestick and brandished it as proof. "Doris saw the wolf —she'll vouch for that."

"I saw a big doglike thing, all right," Doris admitted. "And it did jump at us. It was black and had a lot of teeth. But—Paul, was that supposed to be Jan? Why, that's ridiculous."

"It certainly is," Newcliffe said feelingly. "Getting us all up for a practical joke. Probably one of the dogs is loose."

"Do you have any all-black dogs five feet long?" Foote demanded desperately. "And where's Jarmoskowski now? Why isn't he here? Answer me that!"

Bennington gave a skeptical grunt from the background and opened Jarmoskowski's door. The party tried to jam itself as a unit into the room. Foote forced his way through the clot.

"See? He isn't here, either. And the bed's not been slept in. Doris —" He paused for an instant, realizing what he was about to admit, then plunged ahead. The stakes were now too big to hesitate over social conventions. "Doris, you saw him go in here. Did you see him come out again?"

The girl looked startled. "No, but I was in my room—"

"All right. Here. Look at this." Foote led the way over to the window and pointed out. "See? The prints on the snow?"

One by one the others leaned out. There was no arguing it. A set of animal prints, like large dog-tracks, led away from a spot just beneath Jarmoskowski's window—a spot where the disturbed snow indicated the landing of some heavy body.

"Follow them around," Foote said. "They lead around to the front door, and away again—I hope."

"Have you traced them?" James asked.

"I didn't have to. I saw the thing, James."

"The tracks could be coincidence," Caroline suggested. "Maybe Jan just went for a walk."

"Barefoot? There are his shoes."

Bennington vaulted over the windowsill with an agility astonishing in so round a man, and plowed away with slippered feet along the line of tracks. A little while later he entered the room behind their backs.

"Paul's right," he said, above the hubbub of excited conversation. "The tracks go around to the terrace to the front door, then away again and around the side of the house toward the golf course." He rolled up his wet pajama cuffs awkwardly. A little of the weight came off Foote's heart; at least the beast was not still in the house, then—

"This is crazy," Newcliffe declared angrily. "We're like a lot of little children, panicked by darkness. There's no such thing as a werewolf."

"I wouldn't place any wagers on that," Ehrenberg said. "Millions of people have believed in the werewolf for hundreds of years. One multiplies the years by the people and the answer is a big figure, nicht wahr?"

Newcliffe turned sharply to Lundgren. "Chris, I can depend upon you at least to have your wits about you."

The psychiatrist smiled wanly. "You didn't read my Stockholm paper, did you, Tom? I mean my paper on psychoses of Middle Ages populations. Much of it dealt with lycanthropy—werewolfism."

"You mean—you believe this idiot story?"

"I spotted Jarmoskowski early in the evening," Lundgren said. "He must have shaved the hair on his palms, but he has all the other signs—eyes bloodshot with moonrise, first and second fingers of equal length, pointed ears, merged eyebrows, domed prefrontal bones, elongated upper cuspids. In short, the typical hyperpineal type—a lycanthrope."

"Why didn't you say something?"

"I have a natural horror of being laughed at," Lundgren said dryly. "And *I didn't want to draw Jarmoskowski's attention to me.* These endocrine-imbalance cases have a way of making enemies very easily."

Foote grinned ruefully. If he had thought of that part of it before he had confronted Jarmoskowski, he would have kept his big mouth shut. It was deflating to know how ignoble one's motives could be in the face of the most demanding situations.

"Lycanthropy is no longer common," Lundgren droned, "and so seldom mentioned except in out-of-the-way journals. It is the little-known aberration of a little-known ductless gland; beyond that we know only what we knew in 1400, and that is that it appears to enable the victim to control his shape."

"I'm still leery of this whole business," Bennington growled, from somewhere deep in his teddy-bear chest. "I've known Jan for years. Nice fella—helped me out of a bad hole once, without owing me any favors at all. And I think there's enough discord in this house so that I won't add to it much if I say I wouldn't trust Paul Foote as far as I could throw him. By God, Paul, if this does turn out to be some practical joke of yours—"

"Ask Lundgren," Foote said.

There was dead silence, disturbed only by heavy breathing. Lundgren was known to almost all of them as the world's ultimate authority on hormone-created insanity. Nobody seemed to want to ask him.

"Paul's right," Lundgren said at last. "You must take it or leave it. Jarmoskowski is a lycanthrope. A hyperpineal. No other gland could affect the blood vessels of the eyes like that or make such a reorganization of the soma possible. Jarmoskowski is inarguably a werewolf."

Bennington sagged, the light of righteous incredulity dying from his eyes. "I'll be damned!" he muttered. "It can't be. It can't be."

"We've got to get him tonight," Foote said. "He's seen the penta-gram on somebody's palm—somebody in the party."

"What's that?" asked James.

"It's a five-pointed star inscribed in a circle, a very old magical symbol. You find it in all the old mystical books, right back to the so-called fourth and fifth Books of Moses. The werewolf sees it on the palm of his next victim."

There was a gasping little scream from Doris. "So that's it!" she cried. "Dear God, I'm the one! He saw something on my hand tonight while we were talking in the hall. He was awfully startled and went away with hardly another word. He said he was going to warn me about something and then he—"

"Steady," Bennington said, in a soft voice that had all the penetrating power of a thunderclap. "There's safety in numbers. We're all here." Nevertheless, he could not keep himself from glancing surreptitiously over his shoulder.

"It's a common illusion in lycanthropic seizures," Lundgren agreed. "Or hallucination, I should say. But Paul, you're wrong about its significance to the lycanthrope; I believe you must have gotten that idea from some movie. The pentagram means something quite different. Doris, let me ask you a question."

"Why—certainly, Dr. Lundgren. What is it?"

"What were you doing with that piece of modelling clay this evening?"

To Foote, and evidently to the rest of the party, the question was meaningless. Doris, however, looked down at the floor and scuffed one slippered toe back and forth over the carpet.

"Answer me, please," Lundgren said patiently. "I watched you manipulating it while Jan was playing, and it seemed to me to be an odd thing for a woman to have in her handbag. What were you doing with it?"

"I—was trying to scare Paul Foote," she said, in so low a voice that she could scarcely be heard at all.

"How? Believe me, Doris, this is most important. How?"

"There was a little cloud of smoke coming out of his cigarette. I was—trying to make it take—"

"Yes. Go on."

"—take the shape of a statuette near it," Foote said flatly. He could feel droplets of ice on his forehead. The girl looked at him sideways; then she nodded and looked back at the floor. "The music helped," she murmured.

"Very good," Lundgren said. "Doris, I'm not trying to put you on the spot. Have you had much success at this sort of game?"

"Lately," she said, not quite so reluctantly. "It doesn't always work. But sometimes it does."

"Chris, what does this mean?" Foote demanded.

"It means that we have an important ally here, if only we can find out how to make use of her," Lundgren said. "This girl is what the Middle Ages would have called a witch. Nowadays we'd probably say she's been given a liberal helping of extrasensory powers, but I must confess that never seems to me to explain much that the old term didn't explain.

"That is the significance of the pentagram, and Jarmoskowski knows it very well. The werewolf hunts best and ranges most widely when he has a witch for an accomplice, as a mate when they are both in human form, as a marker or stalker when the werewolf is in the animal form. The appearance of the pentagram identifies to the lycanthrope the witch he believes appointed for him."

"That's hardly good news," Doris said faintly.

"But it is. In all these ancient psychopathic relationships there is a natural—or, if you like, a supernatural—balance. The werewolf adopts such a partner with the belief—for him of course it is a certain foreknowledge—that the witch inevitably will betray him. That is what so shocked Jarmoskowski; but his changing to the wolf form shows that he has taken the gambit. He knows as well as we do, probably better, that as a witch Doris is only a beginner, unaware of most of her own powers. He is gambling very coolly on our being unable to use her against him. It is my belief that he is most wrong."

"So we still don't know who Jan's chosen as a victim," James said in earnest, squeaky tones. "That settles it. We've got to trail the— the beast and kill him. We must kill him before he kills one of us —if not Doris, then somebody else. Even if he misses us, it would be just as bad to have him roaming the countryside."

"What are you going to kill him with?" Lundgren asked matter-of-factly.

"Eh?"

"I said, what are you going to kill him with? With that pineal hormone in his blood he can laugh at any ordinary bullet. And since there are no chapels dedicated to St. Hubert around here, you won't be able to scare him to death with a church-blessed bullet."

"Silver will do," Foote said.

"Yes, silver will do. It poisons the pinearin-catalysis. But are you going to hunt a full-grown wolf armed with table silver and candlesticks? Or is somebody here metallurgist enough to cast a decent silver bullet?"

Foote sighed. With the burden of proof lifted from him, and completely sobered up by shock, he felt a little more like his old self, despite the pall which hung over him and the others.

"Like I always tell my friends," he said, "there's never a dull moment at a Newcliffe house party."

4

The clock struck 1:30. Foote picked up one of Newcliffe's rifles and hefted it. It felt—useless. He said, "How are you coming?"

The group by the kitchen range shook their heads in comical unison. One of the gas burners had been jury-rigged as a giant Bunsen burner, and they were trying to melt down over it some soft unalloyed silver articles, mostly of Mexican manufacture.

They were using a small earthenware bowl, also Mexican, for a crucible. It was lidded with the bottom of a flower pot, the hole in which had been plugged with shredded asbestos yanked forcibly out of the insulation of the garret; garden clay gave the stuff a dubious cohesiveness. The awkward flame leapt uncertainly and sent fantastic shadows flickering over their intent faces.

"We've got it melted, all right," Bennington said, lifting the lid cautiously with a pair of kitchen tongs and peering under it. "But what do we do with it now? Drop it from the top of the tower?"

"You can't kill a wolf with buckshot unless you're damned lucky," Newcliffe pointed out. Now that the problem had been reduced temporarily from a hypernatural one to a matter of ordinary hunting, he was in his element. "And I haven't got a decent shotgun here anyhow. But we ought to be able to whack together a mold. The bullet should be soft enough so that it won't stick in the rifling of my guns."

He opened the door to the cellar stairs and disappeared down them, carrying in one hand several ordinary rifle cartridges. Faintly, the dogs renewed their howling. Doris began to tremble. Foote put his arm around her.

"It's all right," he said. "We'll get him. You're safe enough."

She swallowed. "I know," she agreed in a small voice. "But every time I think of the way he looked at my hands, and how red his eyes were— You don't suppose he's prowling around the house? That that's what the dogs are howling about?"

"I don't know," Foote said carefully. "But dogs are funny that way. They can sense things at great distances. I suppose a man with pinearin in his blood would have a strong odor to them. But he probably knows that we're after his scalp, so he won't be hanging around if he's smart."

She managed a tremulous smile. "All right," she said. "I'll try not to be hysterical." He gave her an awkward reassuring pat, feeling a little absurd.

"Do you suppose we can use the dogs?" Ehrenberg wanted to know.

"Certainly," said Lundgren. "Dogs have always been our greatest allies against the abnormal. You saw what a rage Jarmoskowski's very presence put Brucey in this afternoon. He must have smelled the incipient seizure. Ah, Tom—what did you manage?"

Newcliffe set a wooden transplanting box on the kitchen table. "I pried the slug out of one shell for each gun," he said, "and used one of them to make impressions in the clay here. The cold has made the stuff pretty hard, so the impressions should be passable molds. Bring the silver over here."

Bennington lifted his improvised crucible from the burner, which immediately shot up a tall, ragged blue flame. James carefully turned it off.

"All right, pour," Newcliffe said. "Chris, you don't suppose it might help to chant a blessing or something?"

"Not unless Jarmoskowski overheard it—probably not even then, since we have no priest among us."

"Very well. Pour, Bennington, before the goo hardens."

Bennington decanted sluggishly molten silver into each depression in the clay, and Newcliffe cleaned away the oozy residue from the casts before it had time to thicken. At any other time the whole scene would have been funny—now it was grotesque, as if it had been composed by a Holbein. Newcliffe picked up the box and carried it back down to the cellar, where the emasculated cartridges awaited their new slugs.

"Who's going to carry these things, now?" Foote asked. "There are six rifles. James, how about you?"

"I couldn't hit an elephant's rump at three paces. Tom's an expert shot. So is Bennington here, with a shotgun anyhow; he holds skeet-shooting medals.

"I can use a rifle," Bennington said diffidently.

"So can I," said Palmer curtly. "Not that I've got much sympathy for this business. This is just the kind of thing you'd expect to happen in this place."

"You had better shelve your politics for a while," James said, turning an unexpectedly hard face to the Laborite. "Lycanthropy as a disease isn't going to limit its activities to the House of Lords. Suppose a werewolf got loose in the Welsh coal fields?"

"I've done some shooting," Foote said. "During the show at Dunkirk I even hit something."

"I," Lundgren said, "am an honorary member of the Swiss Militia."

Nobody laughed. Even Palmer was aware that Lundgren in his own oblique way was bragging, and that he had something to brag about. Newcliffe appeared abruptly from the cellar.

"I pried 'em loose, cooled 'em with snow and rolled 'em smooth with a file. They're probably badly crystallized, but we needn't let that worry us. At worst it'll just make 'em go dum-dum on us—no one here prepared to argue that that would be inhumane, I hope?"

He put one cartridge into the chamber of each rifle in turn and shot the bolts home. "There's no sense in loading these any more thoroughly—ordinary bullets are no good anyhow, Chris says. Just make your first shots count. Who's elected?"

Foote, Palmer, Lundgren and Bennington each took a rifle. Newcliffe took the fifth and handed the last one to his wife.

"I say, wait a minute," James objected. "Do you think that's wise, Tom? I mean, taking Caroline along?"

"Why, certainly," Newcliffe said, looking surprised. "She shoots like a fiend—she's snatched prizes away from me a couple of times. I thought *everybody* was going along."

"That isn't right," Foote said. "Especially not Doris, since the wolf—that is, I don't think she ought to go."

"Are you going to subtract a marksman from the hunting party to protect her? Or are you going to leave her here by herself?"

"Oh no!" Doris cried. "Not here! I've got to go! I don't want to wait all alone in this house. He might come back, and there'd be nobody here. I couldn't stand it."

"There is no telling what Jarmoskowski might learn from such an encounter," Lundgren added, "or, worse, what he might teach Doris without her being aware of it. For the rest of us—forgive me, Doris, I must be brutal—it would go harder with us if he did not kill her than if he did. Let us keep our small store of magic with us, not leave it here for Jan."

"That would seem to settle the matter," Newcliffe said grimly. "Let's get under way. It's after two now."

He put on his heavy coat and went out with the heavy-eyed groom to rouse out the dogs. The rest of the company fetched their own heavy clothes. Doris and Caroline climbed into ski suits. They assembled again, one by one, in the living room.

Lundgren's eyes swung on a vase of irislike flowers on top of the closed piano. "Hello, what are these?" he said.

"Monkshood," Caroline informed him. "We grow it in the greenhouse. It's pretty, isn't it? Though the gardener says it's poisonous."

"Chris," Foote said. "That isn't—wolfsbane, is it?"

The psychiatrist shook his head. "I'm no botanist. I can't tell one aconite from another. But it doesn't matter; hyperpineals are allergic to the whole group. The pollen, you see. As in hay fever, your hyperpineal case breathes the pollen, anaphylaxis sets in, and—"

"The last twist of the knife," James murmured.

A clamoring of dogs outside announced that Newcliffe was ready. With somber faces the party filed out onto the terrace. For some reason all of them avoided stepping on the wolf's prints in the snow. Their mien was that of condemned prisoners on the way to the tumbrels. Lundgren took one of the sprigs of flowers from the vase.

The moon had long ago passed its zenith and was almost halfway down the sky, projecting the Bastille-like shadow of the house a long way out onto the grounds; but there was still plenty of light, and the house itself was glowing from cellar to tower room. Lundgren located Brucey in the milling, yapping pack and abruptly thrust the sprig of flowers under his muzzle. The animal sniffed once, then crouched back and snarled softly.

"Wolfsbane," Lundgren said. "Dogs don't dislike the other aconites—basis of the legend, no doubt. Better fire your gardener, Caroline. In the end he may be the one to blame for all this happening in the dead of winter. Lycanthropy normally is an autumn affliction."

James said:

> "Even a man who says his prayers
> Before he sleeps each night
> May turn to a wolf when the wolfsbane blooms
> And the moon is high and bright."

"Stop it, you give me the horrors," Foote snapped angrily.

"Well, the dog knows now," said Newcliffe. "Good. It would have been hard for them to pick up the trail from hard snow, but Brucey can lead them. Let's go."

The tracks of the wolf were clear and sharp in the ridged drifts. The snow had formed a hard crust from which fine, powdery showers of tiny ice crystals were whipped by a fitful wind. The tracks led around the side of the house, as Bennington had reported, and out across the golf course. The little group plodded grimly along beside them. The spoor was cold for the dogs, but every so often they would pick up a faint trace and go bounding ahead, yanking their master after them. For the most part, however, the party had to depend upon its eyes.

A heavy mass of clouds had gathered in the west over the Firth of Lorne. The moon dipped lower. Foote's shadow, knobby and attenuated, marched on before him, and the crusted snow crunched and crackled beneath his feet. The night seemed unnaturally still and watchful, and the party moved in tense silence except for an occasional growl or subdued bark from the dogs.

Once the marks of the werewolf doubled back a short distance, then doubled again, as if the monster had turned for a moment to look back at the house before resuming his prowling. For the most part, however, the trail led directly toward the dark boundary of the woods.

As the brush began to rise around them they stopped by mutual consent and peered warily ahead, rifles lifted halfway, muzzles weaving nervously as the dogs' heads shifted this way and that. Far out across the countryside behind them, the great cloud-shadow continued its sailing. The brilliantly lit house stood out against the gloom as if it were on fire.

"Should have turned those out," Newcliffe muttered, looking back at it. "Outlines us."

The dogs strained at their leashes. In the black west there was a barely audible muttering, as of winter thunder. Brucey pointed a quivering nose at the woods and snarled.

"He's in there, all right."

"We'd better step on it," Bennington said, whispering. "Going to be plenty dark in about five minutes. Looks like a storm."

Still they hesitated, looking at the noncommittal darkness of the forest. Then Newcliffe waved his gun hand and his dog hand in the conventional deploy-as-skirmishers signal and plowed forward. The rest spread out in a loosely spaced line and followed him. Foote's finger trembled over his trigger.

The forest was shrouded and very still. Occasionally a branch groaned as someone pushed against it, or twigs snapped with sharp, tiny musical explosions. Foote could see almost nothing. The underbrush tangled his legs; his feet broke jarringly through the crust of snow, or were supported by it when he least expected support. Each time his shoulder struck an unseen trunk gouts of snow fell on him.

After a while the twisted, leafless trees began to remind him of something; after a brief mental search he found it. It was a Doré engraving of the woods of Hell, from an illustrated Dante which had frightened him green as a child: the woods where each tree was a sinner in which harpies nested, and where the branches bled when they were broken off. The concept still frightened him a little—it made the forest by Newcliffe's golf course seem almost cozy.

The dogs strained and panted, weaving, no longer growling, silent with a vicious intentness. A hand touched Foote's arm and he jumped; but it was only Doris.

"They've picked up something, all right," Bennington's whisper said. "Turn 'em loose, Tom?"

Newcliffe pulled the animals to a taut halt and bent over them, snapping the leashes free. One by one, without a sound, they shot ahead and vanished.

Over the forest the oncoming storm clouds cruised across the moon. Total blackness engulfed them. The beam of a powerful flashlight splashed from Newcliffe's free hand, flooding a path of tracks on the brush-littered snow. The rest of the night drew in closer about the blue-white glare.

"Hate to do this," Newcliffe said. "It gives us away. But he knows we're— Hello, it's snowing."

"Let's go then," Foote said. "The tracks will be blotted out shortly."

A many-voiced, clamorous baying, like tenor bugles, rang suddenly through the woods. It was a wild and beautiful sound! Foote, who had never heard it before, thought for an instant that his heart had stopped. Certainly he would never have associated so pure a choiring with anything as prosaic as dogs.

"That's it!" Newcliffe shouted. "Listen to them! That's the vie-whalloo. Go get him, Brucey!"

They crashed ahead. The belling cry seemed to ring all around them.

"What a racket!" Bennington panted. "They'll raise the whole countryside."

They plowed blindly through the snow-filled woods. Then, without any interval, they broke through into a small clearing. Snowflakes flocculated the air. Something dashed between Foote's legs, snapping savagely, and he tripped and fell into a drift.

A voice shouted something indistinguishable. Foote's mouth was full of snow. He jerked his head up—and looked straight into the red rage-glowing eyes of the wolf.

It was standing on the other side of the clearing, facing him, the dogs leaping about it, snapping furiously at its legs. It made no sound at all, but stood with its forefeet planted, its head lowered below its enormous shoulders, its lips drawn back in a travesty of Jarmoskowski's smile. A white streamer of breath trailed horizontally from its long muzzle, like the tail of a malign comet.

It was more powerful than all of them, and it knew it. For an instant it hardly moved, except to stir lazily the heavy brush of tail across its haunches. Then one of the dogs came too close.

The heavy head lashed sidewise. The dog yelped and danced back. The dogs already had learned caution: one of them already lay writhing on the ground, a black pool spreading from it, staining the snow.

"Shoot, in God's name!" James screamed.

Newcliffe clapped his rifle to his shoulder with one hand, then lowered it indecisively. "I can't," he said. "The dogs are in the way—"

"To hell with the dogs—this is no fox hunt! Shoot, Tom, you're the only one of us that's clear—"

It was Palmer who shot first. He had no reason to be chary of Newcliffe's expensive dogs. Almost at the same time the dogs gave Foote a small hole to shoot through, and he took it.

The double flat crack of the two rifles echoed through the woods and snow puffed up in a little explosion behind the wolf's left hind pad. The other shot—whose had come closest could never be known—struck a frozen tree trunk and went squealing away. The wolf settled deliberately into a crouch.

A concerted groan had gone up from the party; above it Newcliffe's voice thundered, ordering his dogs back. Bennington aimed with inexorable care.

The werewolf did not wait. With a screaming snarl it launched itself through the ring of dogs and charged.

Foote jumped in front of Doris, throwing one arm across his own throat. The world dissolved into rolling pandemonium, filled with shouts, screams, snarls, and the frantic hatred of dogs. The snow flew thick. Newcliffe's flashlight fell and tumbled away, coming to rest at last on the snow on its base, regarding the treetops with an idiot stare.

Then there was the sound of a heavy body moving swiftly away. The noise died gradually.

"Anybody hurt?" James' voice asked. There was a general chorus of "no's."

"That's not good enough," Bennington puffed. "How does a

dead man answer No? Let's have a nose-count."

Newcliffe retrieved his flashlight and played it about, but the snowstorm had reached blizzard proportions, and the light showed nothing but shadows and cold confetti. "Caroline?" he said anxiously.

"Yes, dear. Soaked, but here."

"Doris? Good. Paul, where are you—oh, I see you, I think. Ehrenberg? And Palmer? So; there you have it, Bennington. We didn't invite anybody else to this party—except—"

"He got away," Bennington said ironically. "Didn't like the entertainment. And the snow will cover his tracks this time. Better call your dogs back, Tom."

"They're back," Newcliffe said. He sounded a little tired, for the first time since the beginning of the trouble. "When I call them off, they come off."

He walked heavily forward to the body of the injured animal, which was still twitching feebly, as if trying to answer his summons. He squatted down on his hams and bent his shoulders, stroking the restlessly rolling head.

"So—so," he said softly. "So, Brucey. Easy—easy. So, Brucey—so."

Still murmuring, he brought his rifle into position with one arm. The dog's tail beat once against the snow.

The rifle leapt noisily against Newcliffe's shoulder.

Newcliffe arose slowly, and looked away.

"It looks like we lose round one," he said tonelessly.

5

It seemed to become daylight very quickly. The butler went phlegmatically around the house, snapping off the lights. If he knew what was going on he gave no sign of it.

Newcliffe was on the phone to London. "Cappy? Tom here—listen and get this straight, it's damned important. Get Consolidated Warfare—no, no, not the Zurich office, they've offices in the city—and place an order for a case of .30 caliber rifle cartridges—listen to me, dammit, I'm not through yet—with *silver slugs*. Yes, that's right—silver—and it had better be the pure stuff, too. No, not sterling, that's too hard for my purposes. Tell them I want them flown up, and that they've got to arrive here tomorrow . . . I don't care if it is impossible. Make it worth their while; I'll cover it. And I want it direct to the house here. On Loch Rannoch 20 kilometers due west of Blair Atholl . . . Of course you know the house but how will CWS's pilot unless you tell them? Now read it back to me."

"Garlic," Lundgren was saying to Caroline. She wrote it dutifully on her marketing list. "How many windows does this house have? All right, buy one clove for each, and get a half-dozen tins of ground rosemary, also."

He turned to Foote. "We must cover every possibility," he said somberly. "As soon as Tom gets off the line I will try to raise the local priest and get him out here with a drayload of silver crucifixes. Understand, Paul, there is a strong physiological basis beneath all that medieval mumbo-jumbo.

"The herbs, for example, are anti-spasmodics—they act rather as ephedrine does, in hay fever, to reduce the violence of the seizure. It's possible that Jan may not be able to maintain the wolf shape if he gets a heavy enough sniff.

"As for the religious trappings, their effects are perhaps solely psychological—and perhaps not, I have no opinion in the matter. It's possible that they won't bother Jan if he happens to be a skeptic in such matters, but I suspect that he's—" Lundgren's usually excellent English abruptly gave out on him. The word he wanted obviously was not in his vocabulary. *"Aberglaeubig,"* he said. *"Criandre."*

"Superstitious?" Foote suggested, smiling grimly.

"Is that it? Yes. Yes, certainly. Who has better reason, may I ask?"

"But how does he maintain the wolf shape at all, Chris?"

"Oh, that's the easiest part. You know how water takes the shape of the vessel it sits in? Well, protoplasm is a liquid. This pineal hormone lowers the surface tension of the cells; and at the same time it short-circuits the sympathetic nervous system directly through to the cerebral cortex by increasing the efficiency of the cerebrospinal fluid as an electrolyte beyond the limits in which it's supposed to function—"

"Whoa there, I'm lost already."

"I'll go over it with you later, I have several books in my luggage which have bearing on the problem which I think you should see. In any event, the result is a plastic, malleable body, within limits. A wolf is the easiest form because the skeletons are so similar. Not much pinearin can do to bone, you see. An ape would be easier still, but lycanthropes don't assume shapes outside their own ecology. A were-ape would be logical in Africa, but not here. Also, of course, apes don't eat people; there is the really horrible part of this disease."

"And vampires?"

"Vampires," Lundgren said pontifically, "are people we put in padded cells. It's impossible to change the bony structure *that* much. They just think they are bats. But yes, that too is advanced hyperpinealism.

"In the last stages it is quite something to see. As the pinearin blood level increases, the cellular surface tension is lowered so much that the cells literally begin to boil away. At the end there is just a—a mess. The process is arrested when the vascular systems no longer can circulate the hormone, but of course the victim dies long before that stage is reached."

Foote swallowed. "And there's no cure?"

"None yet. Palliatives only. Someday, perhaps, there will be a cure—but until then— Believe me, we will be doing Jan a favor."

"Also," Newcliffe was saying, "drive over and pick me up six automatic rifles. No, not Brownings, they're too hard to handle. Get American T-47's. All right, they're secret—what else are we paying CWS a retainer for? What? Well, you might call it a siege. All right, Cappy. No, I won't be in this week. Pay everybody off and send them home until further notice. No, that doesn't include you. All right. Yes, that sounds all right."

"It's a good thing," Foote said, "that Newcliffe has money."

"It's a good thing," Lundgren said, "that he has me—and you. We'll see how twentieth-century methods can cope with this Middle Ages madness."

Newcliffe hung up, and Lundgren took immediate possession of the phone.

"As soon as my man gets back from the village," Newcliffe said, "I'm going to set out traps. Jan may be able to detect hidden metal

—I've known dogs that could do it by smell in wet weather—but it's worth a try.''

"What's to prevent his just going away?" Doris asked hopefully. The shadows of exhaustion and fear around her eyes touched Foote obscurely; she looked totally unlike the blank-faced, eager youngster who had bounded into the party in ski clothes so long ago.

"I'm afraid you are," he said gently. "As I understand it, he believes he's bound by the pentagram." At the telephone, where Lundgren evidently was listening to a different speaker with each ear, there was an energetic nod. "In the old books, the figure is supposed to be a sure trap for demons and such, if you can lure or conjure them into it. And once the werewolf has seen his appointed partner marked with it, he feels compelled to remain until he has made the alliance good."

"Doesn't it—make you afraid of me?" Doris said, her voice trembling.

He touched her hand. "Don't be foolish. There's no need for us to swallow all of a myth just because we've found that part of it is so. The pentagram we have to accept; but I for one reserve judgment on the witchcraft."

Lundgren said "Excuse me," and put one hand over the mouthpiece. "Only lasts seven days," he said.

"The compulsion? Then we'll have to get him before then."

"Well, maybe we'll sleep tonight anyhow," Doris said dubiously.

"We're not going to do much sleeping until we get him," Newcliffe announced. "I could boil him in molten lead just for killing Brucey."

"Brucey!" Palmer snorted. "Don't you think of anything but your damned prize dogs, even when all our lives are forfeit?" Newcliffe turned on him, but Bennington grasped his arm.

"That's enough," the American said evenly. "Both of you. We certainly don't dare quarrel among ourselves with this thing hanging over us. I know your nerves are shot. We're all in the same state. But dissension among us would make things just that much easier for Jan."

"Bravo," Lundgren said. He hung up the phone and rejoined them. "I didn't have much difficulty in selling the good Father the idea," he said. "He was stunned, but not at all incredulous. Unfortunately, he has only crucifixes enough for our ground-floor windows, at least in silver; gold, he says, is much more popular. By the way, he wants a picture of Jan, in case he should turn up in the village."

"There are no existing photographs of Jarmoskowski," Newcliffe said positively. "He never allowed any to be taken. It was a headache to his concert manager."

"That's understandable," Lundgren said. "With his cell radiogens under constant stimulation, any picture of him would turn out overexposed anyhow—probably a total blank. And that in turn would expose Jan."

"Well, that's too bad, but it's not irreparable," Foote said. He was glad to be of some use again. He opened Caroline's secretary and took out a sheet of stationery and a pencil. In ten minutes he had produced a head of Jarmoskowski in three-quarter profile, as he had seen him at the piano that last night so many centuries ago. Lundgren studied it.

"To the life," he said. "Tom can send this over by messenger. You draw well, Paul."

Bennington laughed. "You're not telling him anything he doesn't know," he said. Nevertheless, Foote thought, there was considerably less animosity in the critic's manner.

"What now?" James asked.

"We wait," Newcliffe said. "Palmer's gun was ruined by that one hand-made slug, and Foote's isn't in much better shape. The one thing we can't afford is to have our weapons taken out of action. If I know Consolidated, they'll have the machine-made bullets here tomorrow, and then we'll have some hope of getting him. Right now we'll just have to lie doggo and hope that our defenses are effective —he's shown that he's more than a match for us in open country."

The rest looked at each other uneasily. Some little understanding of what it would be like to wait through helpless, inactive days and dog-haunted nights already showed on their faces. But before the concurrence of both master hunters—Newcliffe and Lundgren— they were forced to yield.

The conference broke up in silence.

When Foote came into the small study with one of the books Lundgren had given him, he was surprised and somewhat disappointed to find that both Caroline and Doris had preceded him. Doris was sitting on a hassock near the grate, with the fire warming her face, and a great sheaf of red-gold hair pouring down her back. Caroline, seated just behind her, was brushing it out with even strokes.

"I'm sorry," he said. "I didn't know you were in here. I had a little reading to do and this looked like the best place for it—"

"Why, of course, Paul," Caroline said. "Don't let us distract you in the least. We came in here for the fire."

"Well, if you're sure it's all right—"

"Of course it's all right," Doris said. "If our talking won't annoy you—"

"No, no." He found the desk with the gooseneck lamp on it, turned on the lamp, and put down the heavy book in the pool of light. Caroline's arm resumed its monotonous, rhythmic movement over Doris' bent head. Both of them made a wonderful study: Caroline no longer the long-faced hounds-and-horses Englishwoman in jodhpurs, but now the exactly opposite type, tall, clear-skinned, capable of carrying a bare-shouldered evening gown with enchanting naturalness, yet in both avatars clearly the wife of the same man; Doris transformed from the bouncing youngster to the preternaturally still virgin waiting beside the lake, her youth not so much emphasized as epiphanized by the maternal shape stroking her head.

But for once in his life he had something to do that he considered more pressing than making a sketch for an abstraction. He turned his back on them and sat down, paging through the book to the chapter Lundgren had mentioned. He would have preferred studying it with Lundgren at his side, but the psychiatrist, wiry though he was, felt his years as the hour grew late, and was now presumably asleep.

The book was hard going. It was essentially a summary of out-of-the-way psychoses associated with peasant populations, and it had been written by some American who assumed an intolerably patronizing attitude toward the beliefs he was discussing, and who was further handicapped by a lack of basic familiarity with the English language. Foote suspected that sooner or later someone like

Lundgren was going to have to do the whole job over again from scratch.

Behind him the murmuring of the two women's voices blended with the sighing of the fire in the grate. It was a warm, musical sound, so soothing that Foote found himself nodding at the end of virtually every one of the book's badly constructed paragraphs, and forced to reread nearly every other sentence.

"I do believe you've conquered Tom completely," Caroline was saying. The brush went crackle . . . crackle . . . through the girl's hair. "He hates women who talk. About anything. That's hard on him, for he loves artists of all sorts, and so many of them are women, aren't they?"

. . . Within a few years I was able to show to a startled world that between sympathetic magic and the sympatheticomimetic rituals of childhood there are a distinct relationship, directly connectable to the benighted fantasies of Balkan superstition of which I have just given so graphic a series of instances. Shortly thereafter, with the aid of Drs. Egk and Bergenweiser, I was able to demonstrate . . .

"So many of them are pianists, anyhow," Doris said.

"Sometimes I wish I'd taken to the harp, or maybe the bassoon."

"Well, now, I sometimes feel that way about being a woman. There really is a great deal of competition abroad in the world. Your hair is lovely. That white part is so fashionable now that it's a pleasure to see one that's natural."

"Thank you, Caroline. You've been very brave and kind. I feel better already."

"I've never known a woman," Caroline said, "who didn't feel better with the tangles out of her hair. Does this affair really disturb you greatly?"

. . . in order to make it clear that this total misconception of the real world can have no REAL consequences except in the mind of the ignorant. To explain the accounts of the deceived observers we must first of all assume . . .

"Shouldn't it? I wouldn't have taken it seriously for a moment a few days ago, but—well, we did go out to hunt for Jan, and there really doesn't seem to be much doubt about it. It is frightening."

"Of course it is," Caroline said. "Still I wouldn't dream of losing my sleep over it. I remember when Brucey had the colic when he was five weeks old; London was being bombed at the same time by those flying things. Tom carried on terribly, and the house was full of refugees, which simply made everything more difficult. And Jan is really very sweet and he's been most effective in the World Federation movement, really one of the best speakers we've ever had; I can't imagine that he would hurt anyone. I know what Tom would do if he discovered he could turn himself into a wolf. He'd turn himself in to the authorities; he's really very serious-minded, and fills every weekend with these artists until one wonders if anybody else in the world is sane. But Jan has a sense of humor. He'll be back tomorrow laughing at us."

Foote turned a page in the book, but he had given up everything but the pretense of reading it.

"Chris takes it very seriously," Doris said.

"Of course, he's a specialist. There now, that should feel better. And there's Paul, studying his eyes out; I'd forgotten you were there. What have you found?"

"Nothing much," Foote said, turning to look at them. "I really need Chris to understand what I'm reading. I haven't the training to extract meaning out of this kind of study. I'll tackle it with him tomorrow."

Caroline sighed. "Men are so single-minded. Isn't it wonderful how essential Chris turned out to be? I'd never have dreamed that he'd be the hero of the party."

Doris got up. "If you're through with me, Caroline, I'm very tired. Good night, and thank you. Good night, Paul."

"Good night," Foote said.

"Quite through," Caroline said. "Good night, dear."

Then it was deep night again. The snowstorm had passed, leaving fresh drifts, and the moon was gradually being uncovered. The clouds blew across the house toward the North Sea on a heavy wind which hummed under the gutters, rattled windows, ground together the limbs of trees.

The sounds stirred the atmosphere of the house, which was hot and stuffy because of the closed windows and reeking with garlic. It was not difficult to hear in them other noises less welcome. In the empty room next to Foote's there was the imagined coming and going of thin ghosts to go with them, and the crouched expectancy

of a turned-down bed which awaited a curiously deformed guest—
a guest who might depress its sheets regardless of the tiny glint of
the crucifix upon the pillow.

The boundary between the real and the unreal had been let down
in Foote's mind, and between the comings and goings of the cloud-
shadows and the dark errands of the ghosts there was no longer any
way of making a selection. He had entered the cobwebby border-
land between the human and the animal, where nothing is ever
more than half true, and only as much as half true for the one
moment.

After a while he felt afloat on the stagnant air, ready to drift all
the way across the threshold at the slightest motion. Above him,
other sleepers turned restlessly, or groaned and started up with a
creak of springs. Something was seeping through the darkness
among them. The wind followed it, keeping a tally of the doors that
it passed.

One.

Two.

Three. Closer now.

Four. The fourth sleeper struggled a little; Foote could hear a
muffled squeaking of floorboards above his head.

Five.

Six. Who was six? Who's next? When?

Seven—

Oh my God, I'm next . . . I'm next . . .

He curled into a ball, trembling. The wind died away and there
was silence, tremendous and unquiet. After a long while he un-
curled, swearing at himself; but not aloud, for he was afraid to hear
his own voice. Cut that out, now, Foote, you bloody fool. You're like
a kid hiding from the trolls. You're perfectly safe. Lundgren says so.

Mamma says so.

How the hell does Lundgren know?

He's an expert. He wrote a paper. Go ahead, be a kid. Remember
your childhood faith in the printed word? All right, then. Go to
sleep, will you?

There goes that damned counting again.

But after a while his worn-down nerves would be excited no
longer. He slept a little, but fitfully, falling in his dreams through

such deep pits that he awoke fighting the covers and gasping for the vitiated, garlic-heavy air. There was a foulness in his mouth and his heart pounded. He threw off the blankets and sat up, lighting a cigarette with shaking hands and trying not to see the shadows the match-flame threw.

He was no longer waiting for the night to end. He had forgotten that there had ever been such a thing as daylight. He was waiting only to hear the low, inevitable snuffling that would tell him he had a visitor.

But when he looked out the window, he saw dawn brightening over the forest. After staring incredulously at it for a long while, he snubbed out his cigarette in the socket of the candlestick—which he had been carrying about the house as if it had grown to him—and fell straight back. With a sigh he was instantly in profound and dreamless sleep.

When he finally came to consciousness he was being shaken, and Bennington's voice was in his ears. "Get up, man," the critic was saying. "No, you needn't reach for the candlestick—everything's okay thus far."

Foote grinned and reached for his trousers. "It's a pleasure to see a friendly expression on your face, Bennington," he said.

Bennington looked a little abashed. "I misjudged you," he admitted. "I guess it takes a crisis to bring out what's really in a man so that blunt brains like mine can see it. You don't mind if I continue to dislike your latest abstractions, I trust?"

"That's your function: to be a gadfly," Foote said cheerfully. "Now, what's happened?"

"Newcliffe got up early and made the rounds of the traps. We got a good-sized rabbit out of one of them and made Hassenp-feffer—very good—you'll see. The other one was empty, but there was blood on it and on the snow around it. Lundgren's still asleep, but we've saved scrapings for him; still there doesn't seem to be much doubt about it—there's a bit of flesh with coarse black hair on it—"

James poked his head around the doorjamb, then came in. "Hope it cripples him," he said, dexterously snaffling a cigarette from Foote's shirt pocket. "Pardon me. All the servants have deserted us but the butler, and nobody will bring cigarettes up from the village."

"My, my," Foote said. "You're a chipper pair of chaps. Nice sunrise, wasn't it?"

"Wasn't it, though."

In the kitchen they were joined by Ehrenberg, his normally ruddy complexion pale and shrunken from sleeplessness.

"Greetings, Hermann. How you look! And how would you like your egg?"

"*Himmel, Asch und Zwirn,* how can you sound so cheerful? You must be part ghoul."

"You must be part angel—nobody human could be so deadly serious so long, even at the foot of the scaffold."

"Bennington, if you burn my breakfast I'll turn you out of doors without a shilling. Hello, Doris; can you cook?"

"I'll make some coffee for you." Newcliffe entered as she spoke, a pipe between his teeth. "How about you, Tom?"

"Very nice, I'm sure," Newcliffe said: "Look—what do you make of this?" He produced a wad of architect's oiled tracing cloth from his jacket pocket and carefully unwrapped it. In it were a few bloody fragments. Doris choked and backed away.

"I got these off the trap this morning—you saw me do it, Bennington—and they had hair on 'em then. Now look at 'em."

Foote poked at the scraps with the point of his pencil. "Human," he said.

"That's what I thought."

"Well, isn't that to be expected? It was light when you opened the trap, evidently, but the sun hadn't come up. The werewolf assumes human form in full daylight—these probably changed just a few moments after you wrapped them up. As for the hair—this piece here looks to me like a bloodstained sample of Jarmoskowski's shirt cuff."

"We've nipped him, all right," Bennington agreed.

"By the way," Newcliffe added, "we've just had our first desertion. Palmer left this morning."

"No loss," James said. "But I know how he feels. When this affair is over, I'm going to take a month off at Brighton and let the world go to hell."

"What? In the winter?"

"I don't care. I'll watch the tides come in and out in the W.C."

"Just be sure to live to get there," Ehrenberg said gloomily.

"Hermann, you are a black cloud and a thunderclap of doom."

There was a sound outside. It sounded like the world's biggest tea kettle. Something flitted through the sky, wheeled and came back. Foote went to the nearest window.

"Look at that," he said, shading his eyes. "An Avro jet—and he's trying to land here. He must be out of his mind."

The plane circled silently, engines cut. It lost flying speed and glided in over the golf course, struck, and rolled at breakneck speed directly for the forest. At the last minute the pilot ground-looped the ship expertly, and the snow fountained under its wheels.

"By heaven, I'll bet that's Newcliffe's bullets!"

They pounded through the foyer and out onto the terrace. Newcliffe, without bothering to don coat or hat, plowed away toward the plane. A few minutes later, he and the pilot came puffing into the front room, carrying a small wooden case between them. Then they went back and got another, larger but obviously not so heavy.

Newcliffe pried the first crate open. Then he sighed. "Look at 'em," he said. "Shiny brass cartridges, and dull silver heads, machined for perfect accuracy—there's a study in beauty for you artist chaps. Where'd you leave from?"

"Croydon," said the pilot. "If you don't mind, Mr. Newcliffe, the company said I was to collect from you. That's six hundred pounds for the weapons, two-fifty for the ammo and a hundred fifty for me, just a thousand in all."

"Fair enough. Hold on, I'll write you a check."

Foote whistled. It was obvious—not that there had ever been any doubt about it—that Tom Newcliffe did not paint for a living.

The pilot took the check, and shortly thereafter the teakettle began to whistle again. From the larger crate Newcliffe was handing out brand-new rifles, queer ungainly things with muzzle brakes and disproportionately large stocks.

"Now let him come," he said grimly. "Don't worry about wasting shots. There's a full case of clips. As soon as you see him, blaze away like mad. Use it like a hose if you have to. This is a high-velocity weapon: if you hit him square anywhere—even if it's only his hand —you'll kill him from shock. If you get him in the body, there won't be enough of that area left for him to reform, no matter what his powers."

"Somebody go wake Chris," Bennington said. "He should have lessons, too. Doris, go knock on his door like a good girl."

Doris nodded and went upstairs. "Now this stud here," Newcliffe said, "is the fire-control button. You put it in this position and the gun will fire one shot and reload itself, like the Garand. Put it here and you have to reload it yourself, like a bolt-action rifle. Put it here and it goes into automatic operation, firing every shell in the clip, one after the other and in a hurry."

"Thunder!" James said admiringly. "We could stand off an army."

"Wait a minute—there seem to be two missing."

"Those are all you unpacked," Foote pointed out.

"Yes, but there were two older models of my own. I never used 'em because it didn't seem sporting to hunt with such cannon. But I got 'em out last night on account of this trouble."

"Oh," Bennington said with an air of sudden enlightenment. "I thought that thing I had looked odd. I slept with one last night. I think Lundgren has the other."

"Where is Lundgren? Doris should have had him up by now. Go see, Bennington, and fetch back that rifle while you're at it."

"Isn't there a lot of recoil?" Foote asked.

"Not a great deal; that's what the muzzle brake is for. But it would be best to be careful when you have the stud on fully automatic. Hold the machine at your hip, rather than at your shoulder—what's *that!*"

"Bennington's voice," Foote said, his jaw muscles suddenly almost unmanageable. "Something must be wrong with Doris." The group stampeded for the stairs.

They found Doris at Bennington's feet in front of Lundgren's open door. She was perfectly safe; she had only fainted. The critic was in the process of being very sick. On Lundgren's bed something was lying.

The throat had been ripped out, and the face and all the soft parts of the body were gone. The right leg had been gnawed in one place all the way to the bone, which gleamed white and polished in the reassuring sunlight.

6

Foote stood in the living room by the piano in the full glare of all the electric lights. He hefted the T-47 and surveyed the remainder of the party, which was standing in a puzzled group before him.

"No," he said, "I don't like that. I don't want you all bunched together. String out in a line, please, against the far wall, so that I can see everybody."

He grinned briefly. "Got the drop on you, didn't I? Not a rifle in sight. Of course, there's the big candlestick behind you, Tom—aha, I saw you sneak your hopeful look at it—but I know from experience that it's too heavy to throw. I can shoot quicker than you can club me, too." His voice grew ugly. *"And I will,* if you make it necessary. So I would advise everybody—including the women—not to make any sudden movements."

"What's this all about, Paul?" Bennington demanded angrily. "As if things weren't bad enough—"

"You'll see directly. Get into line with the rest, Bennington. *Quick!"* He moved the gun suggestively. "And remember what I said about moving too suddenly. It may be dark outside, but I didn't turn on all the lights for nothing."

Quietly the line formed. The eyes that looked at Foote were narrowed with suspicion of madness, or something worse.

"Good. Now we can talk comfortably. You see, after what happened to Chris I'm not taking any chances. That was partly his fault, and partly mine. But the gods allow no one to err twice in matters of this kind. He paid for his second error—a price I don't intend to pay, or to see anyone else here pay."

"Would you honor us with an explanation of this error?" Newcliffe said icily.

"Yes. I don't blame you for being angry, Tom, since I'm your guest. But you see I'm forced to treat you all alike for the moment. I was fond of Lundgren."

There was silence for a moment, then a thin indrawing of breath from Bennington. "All alike?" he whispered raggedly. "My God, Paul. Tell us what you mean."

"You know already, I see, Bennington. I mean that Lundgren was not killed by Jarmoskowski. He was killed by someone else. Another werewolf—yes, we have two now. One of them is standing in this room at this moment."

A concerted gasp went up.

"Surprised?" Foote said, coldly, and deliberately. "But it's true. The error for which Chris paid so dearly, an error which I made too, was this: we forgot to examine everyone for injuries after the encounter with Jan. We forgot one of the cardinal laws of lycanthropy.

"A man who survives being bitten by a werewolf himself becomes a werewolf. That's how the disease is passed on. The pinearin in the wolf's saliva evidently gets into the bloodstream, stimulates the victim's own pineal gland, and—"

"But nobody was bitten, Paul," Doris said in a suspiciously reasonable voice.

"Somebody was, even if only lightly. None of you but Chris and myself could have known about the bite-infection. Evidently somebody got a few small scratches, didn't think them worth mentioning, put iodine on them and forgot about them—until it was too late."

There were slow movements in the line—heads turning surreptitiously, eyes swinging to neighbors left and right.

"Paul, this is merely a hypothesis," Ehrenberg said. "There is no reason to suppose that it is so, just because it sounds likely."

"But there is. Jarmoskowski can't get in here."

"Unproven," Ehrenberg said.

"I'll prove it. Once the seizure occurred, Chris was the logical first victim. The expert, hence the most dangerous enemy. I wish I had thought of this before lunch. I might have seen which one of you was uninterested in his lunch. In any event, if I'm right, Chris' safeguards against letting Jarmoskowski in also keep you from getting out. If you think you'll ever leave this room again, you're bloody wrong—"

He gritted his teeth and brought himself back into control. "All right," he said. "This is the end of the line. Everybody hold up both hands in plain view."

Almost instantly there was a ravening wolf in the room.

Only Foote, who could see at one glance the order of the people in the staggered line, could know who it was. His drummed-up courage, based solely on terror, went flooding out of him on a tide of sick pity; he dropped the rifle and began to weep convulsively. The beast lunged for his throat like a reddish projectile.

Newcliffe's hand darted back and grasped the candlestick. He leapt forward with swift clumsy grace and brought it down, whistling, against the werewolf's side. Ribs burst with a sharp splintering sound. The wolf spun, its haunches hitting the floor. Newcliffe hit it again. It fell, screaming like a great dog run down by a car, its fangs slashing the air.

Three times, with scientific viciousness, Newcliffe heaved the candlestick back and struck at its head. Then it cried out in an almost-familiar voice, and died.

Slowly the cells of its body groped back toward their natural positions. Even its fur moved, becoming more matted, more regular —more fabriclike.

The crawling metamorphosis was never completed; but the hairy-haunched thing with the crushed skull which sprawled at Newcliffe's feet was recognizable.

It had been Caroline Newcliffe.

Tears coursed along Foote's palms, dropped from under them, fell to the carpet. After a while he dropped his hands. Blurrily he saw a frozen tableau of wax figures in the yellow lamplight. Bennington's face was gray with illness, but rigidly expressionless, like a granite statue. James' back was against the wall; he watched the anomalous corpse as if waiting for some new movement. Ehrenberg had turned away, his pudgy fists clenched.

As for Newcliffe, he had no expression at all. He merely stood where he was, the bloody candlestick hanging straight down from a limp hand.

His eyes were quite empty.

After a moment Doris walked over to Newcliffe and touched his shoulder compassionately. The contact seemed to let something out of him. He shrank visibly into himself, shoulders slumping, his whole body withering to a dry husk.

The candlestick thumped against the floor, rocked wildly on its base, toppled across the body. As it struck, Foote's cigarette butt, which had somehow remained in its socket all day, tumbled out and rolled crazily along the carpet.

"Tom," Doris said softly. "Come away now. There's nothing you can do."

"It was the blood," his empty voice said. "She had a cut. On her hand. Handled the scrapings from the trap. My trap. I did it to her. Just a breadknife cut from making canapés. I did it."

"No you didn't, Tom. You're not to blame. Let's get some rest."

She took his hand. He followed her obediently, stumbling a little as his spattered shoes scuffed over the thick carpet, his breath expelling from his lungs with a soft whisper. The French doors closed behind them.

Bennington bolted for the kitchen sink.

Foote sat down on the piano bench, his worn face taut with dried tears. Like any nonmusician he was drawn almost by reflex to pick at the dusty keys. Ehrenberg remained standing where he was, so motionless as to absent himself from the room altogether, but the lightly struck notes aroused James. He crossed the room, skirting the body widely, and looked down at Foote.

"You did well," the novelist said shakily. "Don't condemn yourself, Paul. What you did was just and proper—and merciful in the long run."

Foote nodded. He felt—nothing. Nothing at all.

"The body?" James said.

"Yes. I suppose so." He got up from the bench. Together they lifted the ugly shape; it was awkward to handle. Ehrenberg remained dumb, blind and deaf. They maneuvered their way through the house and on out to the greenhouse.

"We should leave her here," Foote said, the inside of his mouth suddenly sharp and sour. "Here's where the wolfsbane bloomed that started the whole business."

"Poetic justice of sorts, I suppose," James said. "But I don't think it's wise. Tom has a tool shed at the other end that isn't steam-heated. It should be cold enough there."

Gently they lowered the body to the cement floor, laid down gunnysacks and rolled it onto them. There seemed to be nothing available to cover it. "In the morning," Foote said, "we can have someone come for her."

"How about legal trouble?" James said, frowning. "Here's a woman whose skull has been crushed with a blunt instrument—"

"I think we can get Lundgren's priest to help us there, and with Lundgren, too," Foote said somberly. "They have authority to make death certificates in Scotland. Besides, Alec—is that a woman? Inarguably it isn't Caroline."

James looked sidewise at the felted, muscular haunches. "No. It's —legally it's nothing. I see your point."

Together they went back into the house. "Jarmoskowski?" James said.

"Not tonight, I imagine. We're all too tired and sick. And we do seem to be safe enough in here. Chris saw to that."

Ehrenberg had gone. James looked around the big empty room. "Another night. What a damnable business. Well, good night, Paul."

He went out. Foote remained in the empty room a few minutes longer, looking thoughtfully at the splotch of blood on the priceless Persian carpet. Then he felt of his face and throat, looked at his hands, arms and legs, and explored his chest under his shirt.

Not a scratch. Tom had been very fast.

He was exhausted, but he could not bring himself to go to bed. With Lundgren dead, the problem was his; he knew exactly how little he knew about it still, but he knew as well how much less the rest of the party knew. Hegemony of the house was his now—and the next death would be his responsibility.

He went around the room, making sure that all the windows were tightly closed and the crucifixes in place, turning out the lights as he went. The garlic was getting rancid—it smelled like mercaptan —but as far as he knew it was still effective. He clicked out all but the last light, picked up his rifle and went out into the hall.

Doris' room door was open and there was no light coming out of it. Evidently she was still upstairs tending Newcliffe. He stood for a few moments battling with indecision, then toiled up the staircase.

He found her in Caroline's room, her head bowed upon her arm among the scattered, expensive vials and flasks which had been Caroline's armamentarium. The room was surprisingly froufrou; even the telephone had a doll over it. This, evidently, had been the one room in the house which Caroline had felt was completely hers, where her outdoorsy, estate-managing daytime personality had been ousted by her nocturnal femininity.

And what, in turn, had ousted that? Had the womanly Caroline been crowded, trying not to weep, into some remote and impotent corner of her brain as the monster grew in her? What did go on in the mind of a werewolf?

Last night, for instance, when she had brushed Doris' hair, she had seemed completely and only herself, the Caroline Newcliffe with the beautiful face and the empty noggin, toward whom Foote had so long felt a deep affection mixed with no respect whatsoever. But she had already been taken. It made his throat ache to realize that in her matronly hovering over the girl there had already been some of the tenseness of the stalker.

Men are so single-minded. Isn't it wonderful how essential Chris turned out to be?

At that moment she had shifted her target from Doris to Chris, moved by nothing more than Foote's remark about being unable to progress very far without the psychiatrist. Earlier this evening he had said that Chris had been the most logical target because he was the expert—yet that had not really occurred to Caroline except as an afterthought. It was wolf-reasoning; Caroline's own mind had seen danger first in single-mindedness.

And it had been Caroline's mind, not the wolf's, which had dictated the original fix on Doris. The girl, after all, was the only other woman in the party, thanks to Tom's lion-hunting and his dislike of the Modern Girl; and Caroline had mentioned that Tom seemed drawn to Doris. Which was wolf, which human? Or had they become blended, like two innocuous substances combining to form a poison? Caroline had once been incapable of jealousy—but when the evil had begun to seethe in her bloodstream she had been no longer entirely Caroline . . .

He sighed. Doris had seemed to be asleep on the vanity, but she stirred at the small sound, and the first step he took across the threshold brought her bolt upright. Her eyes were reddened and strange.

"I'm sorry," he said. "I was looking for you. I have to talk to you, Doris; I've been putting it off for quite a while, but I can't do that any longer. May I?"

"Yes, of course, Paul," she said wearily. "I've been very rude to you. It's a little late for an apology, but I am sorry."

He smiled. "Perhaps I had it coming. How is Tom?"

"He's—not well. He doesn't know where he is or what he's doing. He ate a little and went to sleep, but he breathes very strangely." She began to knead her hands in her lap. "What did you want?"

"Doris—what about this witchcraft business? Lundgren seemed to think it might help us. God knows we need help. Have you any idea why Chris thought it was important? Beyond what he told us, that is?"

She shook her head. "Paul, it seemed a little silly to me then, and I still don't understand it. I can do a few small tricks, that's all, like the one I did to you with the smoke. I never thought much about them; they came more or less naturally, and I thought of them just as a sort of sleight-of-hand. I've seen stage conjurers do much more mystifying things."

"But by trickery—not by going right around natural law."

"What do I know about natural law?" she said reasonably. "It seems natural to me that if you want to make something plastic behave, you mold something else that's plastic nearby. To make smoke move, you move clay, or something else that's like smoke. Isn't that natural?"

"Not very," he said wryly. "It's a law of magic, if that's any comfort to either of us. But it's supposed to be a false law."

"I've made it work," she said, shrugging.

He leaned forward. "I know that. That's why I'm here. If you can do that, there should be other things that you can do, things that can help us. What I want to do is to review with you what Chris thought of your talents, and see whether or not anything occurs to you that we can use."

She put her hands to her checks, and then put them back in her lap again. "I'll try," she said.

"Good for you. Chris said he thought witches in the old days were persons with extrasensory perception and allied gifts. I think he believed also that the magic rituals that were used in witchcraft were just manipulative in intention—symbolic objects needed by the witch to focus her extrasensory powers. If he was right, the 'laws' of magic really were illusions, and what was in operation was something much deeper."

"I think I follow that," Doris said. "Where does it lead?"

"I don't know. But I can at least try you on a catalogue. Have you ever had a prophetic dream, Doris? Or read palms? Or cast horoscopes? Or even had the notion that you could look into the future?"

She shook her head decidedly.

"All right, we'll rule that out. Ever felt that you knew what someone else was thinking?"

"Well, by guesswork—"

"No, no," Foote said. "Have you ever felt certain that you knew —"

"Never."

"How about sensing the positions of objects in another room or in another city—no. Well, have you ever been in the vicinity of an unexplained fire? A fire that just seemed to happen because you were there?"

"No, Paul, I've never seen a single fire outside of a fireplace."

"Ever moved anything larger and harder to handle than a column of smoke?"

Doris frowned. "Many times," she said. "But just little things. There was a soprano with a rusty voice that I had to accompany once. She was overbearing and a terrible stage hog. I tied her shoe-bows together so that she fell when she took her first bow, but it was awfully hard work; I was all in a sweat."

Foote suppressed an involuntary groan. "How did you do it?"

"I'm not quite sure. I don't think I could have done it at all if we hadn't wound up the concert with *Das Buch der Haengenden Gaerten.*" She smiled wanly. "If you don't know Schoenberg's crazy counterpoint that wouldn't mean anything to you."

"It tells me what I need to know, I'm afraid. There really isn't much left for me to do but ask you whether or not you've ever transformed a woman into a white mouse, or ridden through the air on a broomstick. Doris, doesn't *anything* occur to you? Chris never talked without having something to talk about; when he said that you could help us, he meant it. But he's dead now, and we can't ask him for the particulars. It's up to you."

She burst into tears. Foote got clumsily to his feet, but after that he had no idea what to do.

"Doris—"

"I don't know," she wailed. "I'm not a witch! I don't want to be a witch! I don't know anything, anything at all, and I'm so tired and so frightened and please go away, please—"

He turned helplessly to go, then started to turn back again. At the same instant, the sound of her weeping was extinguished in the roar of an automatic rifle, somewhere over their heads, exhausting its magazine in a passionate rush.

Foote shot out of the room and back down the stairs. The ground floor still seemed to be deserted under the one light. Aloft there was another end-stopped snarl of gunfire; then Bennington came bouncing down the stairs.

"Watch out tonight," he panted as soon as he saw Foote. "He's around. I saw him come out of the woods in wolf form. I emptied the clip, but he's a hard target against those trees. I sprayed another ten rounds around where I saw him go back in, but I'm sure I didn't hit him. The rifle just isn't my weapon."

"Where were you shooting from?"

"The top of the tower." His face was very stern. "Went up for a breath and a last look around, and there he was. I hope he comes back tonight. I want to be the one who kills him."

"You're not alone."

"Thank God for that. Well, good night. Keep your eyes peeled."

Foote stood in the dark for a while after Bennington had left. Bennington had given him something to think about. While he waited, Doris picked her way down the stairs and passed him without seeing him. She was carrying a small, bulky object; since he had already put the light out, he could not see what it was. But she went directly to her room.

I want to be the one who kills him.

Even the mild Bennington could say that now; but Foote, who understood the feeling behind it all too well, was startled to find that he could not share it.

How could one hate these afflicted people? Why was it so hard for equal-minded men like Bennington to remember that lycanthropy was a disease like any other, and that it struck its victims only in accordance with its own etiology, without regard for their merits as persons? Bennington had the reputation of being what the Americans called a liberal, all the way to his bones; presumably he could not find it in his heart to hate an alcoholic or an addict. He knew also—he had been the first to point it out—that Jarmoskowski as a human being had been compassionate and kindly, as well as brilliant; and that Caroline, like the poor devil in Andreyev's *The Red Laugh,* had been noble-hearted and gentle and had wished no one evil. Yet he was full of hatred now.

He was afraid, of course, just as Foote was. Foote wondered if it had occurred to him that God might be on the side of the werewolves.

The blasphemy of an exhausted mind; but he had been unable to put the idea from him. Suppose Jarmoskowski should conquer his compulsion and lie out of sight until the seven days were over. Then he could disappear; Scotland was large and sparsely populated. It would not be necessary for him to kill all his victims thereafter—only those he actually needed for food. A nip here, a scratch there—

And then from wherever he hunted, the circle of lycanthropy would grow and widen and engulf—

Perhaps God had decided that proper humans had made a muddle of running the world; had decided to give the *nosferatu,* the undead, a chance at it. Perhaps the human race was on the threshold of that darkness into which he had looked throughout last night.

He ground his teeth and made a noise of exasperation. Shock and exhaustion would drive him as crazy as Newcliffe if he kept this up. He put his hands to his forehead, wiped them on his thighs, and went into the little study.

The grate was cold, and he had no materials for firing it up again. All the same, the room was warmer than his bed would be at this hour. He sat down at the small desk and began to go through Lundgren's book again.

Cases of stigmata. Accounts of Sabbats straight out of Krafft-Ebing. The dancing madness. Theory of familiars. Conjuration and exorcism. The besom as hermaphroditic symbol. Fraser's Laws. Goetha as an international community. Observations of Lucien Levy-Bruehl. The case of Bertrand. Political commentary in *Dracula.* Necromancy vs. necrophilia. Nordau on magic and modern man. Basic rituals of the Anti-Church. Fetishism and the theory of talismans . . .

Round and round and round, and the mixture as before. Without Chris there was simply no hope of integrating all this material. Nothing would avail them now but the rifles with the silver bullets in them; their reservoir of knowledge of the thing they fought had been destroyed.

Foote looked tiredly at the ship's clock on the mantel over the cold grate. The fruitless expedition through the book had taken him nearly two hours. He would no longer be able to avoid going to bed. He rose stiffly, took up the automatic rifle, put out the light, and went out into the cold hall.

As he passed Doris' room, he saw that the door was now just barely ajar. Inside, two voices murmured.

Foote was an incurable eavesdropper. He stopped and listened.

7

It was years later before Foote found out exactly what had happened at the beginning. Doris, physically exhausted by her hideous day, emotionally drained by tending the childlike Newcliffe, feeding him from a blunt spoon, parrying his chant about traps and breadknives, and herding him into bed, had fallen asleep almost immediately. It was a sleep dreamless except for a vague, dull undercurrent of despair. When the light tapping against the windowpanes finally reached through to her, she had no idea how long she had been lying there.

She struggled to a sitting position and forced her eyelids up. Across the room the moonlight, gleaming in patches against the rotting snow outside, glared through the window. Silhouetted against it was a tall human figure. She could not see its face, but there was no mistaking the red glint of its eyes. She clutched for her rifle and brought it awkwardly into line.

Jarmoskowski did not dodge. He moved his forearms out a little way from his body, palms forward in a gesture that looked almost supplicating, and waited. Indecisively she lowered the gun again. What was he asking for?

As she dropped the muzzle she saw that the fire-control stud was at *automatic.* She shifted it carefully to *repeat.* She was afraid of the recoil Newcliffe had mentioned; she could feel surer of her target if she could throw one shot at a time at it.

Jarmoskowski tapped again and motioned with his finger. Reasoning that he would come in of his own accord if he were able, she took time out to get into her housecoat. Then, holding her finger against the trigger, she went to the window. All its sections were closed tightly, and a crucifix, suspended from a silk thread, hung exactly in the center of it. She touched it, then opened one of the small panes directly above Jarmoskowski's head.

"Hello, Doris," he said softly. "You look a little like a clerk behind that window. May I make a small deposit, miss?"

"Hello." She was more uncertain than afraid. Was this really happening, or was it just the recurrent nightmare? "What do you want? I should shoot you. Can you tell me why I shouldn't?"

"Yes, I can. Otherwise I wouldn't have risked exposing myself. That's a nasty-looking weapon."

"There are ten silver bullets in it."

"I know that too. I had some fired at me earlier tonight. And I would be a good target for you, so I have no hope of escape—my nostrils are full of rosemary." He smiled ruefully. "And Lundgren and Caroline are dead, and I am responsible. I deserve to die; that is why I am here."

"You'll get your wish, Jan," she said. "But you have some other reason, I know. I'll back my wits against yours. I want to ask you questions."

"Ask."

"You have your evening clothes on. Paul said they changed with you. How is that possible?"

"But a wolf has clothes," Jarmoskowski said. "He is not naked like a man. And surely Chris must have spoken of the effect of the pineal upon the cell radiogens. These little bodies act upon any organic matter, wool, cotton, linen, it hardly matters. When I change, my clothes change with me. I can hardly say how, for it is in the blood —the chromosomes—like musicianship, Doris. Either you can or you can't. If you can—they change."

"Jan—are there many like you? Chris seemed to think—"

Jarmoskowski's smile became a little mocking. "Go into a great railroad station some day—Waterloo, or a Metro station, or Grand Central in New York; get up above the crowd on a balcony or stairway and look down at it in a mirror. We do not show in a silvered mirror. Or if you are in America, find one of the street photographers they have there who take 'three action pictures of yourself' against your will and try to sell them to you; ask him what percentage of his shots show nothing but background."

His voice darkened gradually to a somber diapason. "Lundgren was right throughout. This werewolfery is now nothing but a disease. It is not prosurvival. Long ago there must have been a number of mutations which brought the pineal gland into use; but none of them survived but the werewolves, and the werewolves are madmen —like me. We are dying out.

"Someday there will be another mutation, the pineal will come into better use, and all men will be able to modify their forms without this terrible cannibalism as a penalty. But for us, the lycanthropes, the failures of evolution, nothing is left.

"It is not good for a man to wander from country to country, knowing that he is a monster to his fellow-men and cursed eternally by his God—if he can claim a God. I went through Europe, playing the piano and giving pleasure, writing music for others to play, meeting people, making friends—and always, sooner or later, there were whisperings and strange looks and dawning horror.

"And whether I was hunted down for the beast I was, or whether there was only a gradually growing revulsion, they drove me out. Hatred, silver bullets, crucifixes—they are all the same in the end.

"Sometimes, I could spend several months without incident in some one place, and my life would take on a veneer of normality. I could attend to my music, and have people around me that I liked, and be—human. Then the wolfsbane bloomed and the pollen freighted the air, and when the moon shone down on that flower my blood surged with the thing I carry within me—

"And then I made apologies to my friends and went north to Sweden, where Lundgren was and where spring came much later. I loved him, and I think he missed the truth about me until night before last; I was careful.

"Once or twice I did *not* go north, and then the people who had been my friends would be hammering silver behind my back and waiting for me in dark corners. After years of this few places in Europe would have me. With my reputation as a composer and a pianist spread darker rumors, none of them near the truth, but near enough.

"Towns I had never visited closed their gates to me without a word. Concert halls were booked up too many months in advance for me to use them, inns and hotels were filled indefinitely, people were too busy to talk to me, to listen to my playing, to write me any letters.

"I have been in love. That—I will not describe.

"Eventually I went to America. There no one believes in were-wolves. I sought scientific help—which I had never sought from Lundgren, because I was afraid I would do him some harm. But overseas I thought someone would know enough to deal with what I had become. I would say, 'I was bitten during a hunt on Graf Hrutkai's estate, and the next fall I had my first seizure—'

"But it was not so. No matter where I go, the primitive hatred of my kind lies at the heart of the human as it lies at the heart of the dog. There was no help for me.

"I am here to ask for an end to it."

Slow tears rolled over Doris' cheeks. The voice faded away indefinitely. It did not seem to end at all, but rather to retreat into some limbo where men could not hear it. Jarmoskowski stood silently in the moonlight, his eyes burning bloodily, a somber sullen scarlet.

Doris said, "Jan—Jan, I am sorry, I am so sorry. What can I do?"

"Shoot."

"I—can't!"

"Please, Doris."

The girl was crying uncontrollably. "Jan, don't. I can't. You know I can't. Go away, *please* go away."

Jarmoskowski said, "Then come with me, Doris. Open the window and come with me."

"Where?"

"Does it matter? You have denied me the death I ask. Would you deny me this last desperate hope for love, would you deny your own love, your own last and deepest desire? That would be a vile cruelty. It is too late now, too late for you to pretend revulsion. Come with me."

He held out his hands.

"Say goodbye," he said. "Goodbye to these self-righteous humans. I will give you of my blood and we will range the world, wild and uncontrollable, the last of our race. They will remember us, I promise you."

"Jan—"

"I am here. Come now."

Like a somnambulist, she swung the panes out. Jarmoskowski did not move, but looked first at her, then at the crucifix. She lifted one end of the thread and let the little thing tinkle to the floor.

"After us, there shall be no darkness comparable to our darkness," Jarmoskowski said. "Let them rest—let the world rest."

He sprang into the room with so sudden, so feral a motion that he seemed hardly to have moved at all. From the doorway an automatic rifle yammered with demoniac ferocity. The impact of the silver slugs hurled Jarmoskowski back against the side of the window. Foote lowered the smoking muzzle and took one step into the room.

"Too late, Jan," he said stonily.

Doris wailed like a little girl awakened from a dream. Jarmoskowski's lips moved, but there was not enough left of his lungs. The effort to speak brought a bloody froth to his mouth. He stood for an instant, stretched out a hand toward the girl. Then the long fingers clenched convulsively and the long body folded.

He smiled, put aside that last of all his purposes, and died.

"Why did he come in?" Foote whispered. "I could never have gotten a clear shot at him if he'd stayed outside."

He swung on the sobbing girl. "Doris, you must tell me, if you know. With his hearing, he should have heard me breathing. But he stayed—and he came in, right into my line of fire. *Why?*"

The girl did not answer; but stiffly, as if she had all at once become old, she went to her bedside light and turned it on. Standing beneath it was a grotesque figurine which Foote had difficulty in recognizing as Caroline's telephone doll. All the frills had been stripped off it, and a heavy black line had been penciled across its innocuous forehead in imitation of Jarmoskowski's eyebrows. Fastened to one of its wrists with a rubber band was one of the fragments of skin Newcliffe had scraped out of his trap; and completely around the doll, on the surface of the table, a pentagram had been drawn in lipstick.

The nascent witch had turned from white magic to black. Doris had rediscovered the malign art of poppetry, and had destroyed her demon lover.

Compassionately, Foote turned to her; and very slowly, as if responding to the gravitational tug of a still-distant planet, the muzzle of his rifle swung, too. Together, the man and the machine, they waited for her.

Both would have to be patient.

NIGHTSHAPES
by BARRY N. MALZBERG

It is a writing axiom that a professional blessed with sufficient talent and dexterity can take a conventional plot or set of conventional components and make of them something fresh and unique. Barry N. Malzberg is just such a writer and "Nightshapes" is just such a tale.

In the hands of someone less gifted, this story, with its familiar lycanthropic elements, journal format, and "mad scientist," would have been "just another werewolf story," hardly a candidate for this anthology. What it is, though, is a grim, powerful account of love, obsession, and horror that turns on a completely innovative plot twist. And its final three hundred words are as dark as anything you're likely to read in macabre fiction.

In his somewhat controversial twelve-year career (writers with unusual and idiosyncratic approaches to fiction are always controversial), Barry N. Malzberg has published an impressive number of works in a variety of fields: more than seventy novels, six collections, five coedited anthologies, and some 250 short stories, essays, and book reviews. Among his novels are Beyond Apollo, *which received the John W. Campbell Memorial Award as the best science-fiction novel of 1972,* Herovit's World (1973), Guernica Night (1974), *and* Chorale (1978); *he has also coauthored a number of stories and three suspense novels with your faithful editor.*

1 August

Small flecks of blood in her pelt when she returned this evening, the Change a hot and deadly flicker in the dry spaces of the room, the odor sharp, whimpers as she shrugged back into her own form. Then clambering against me in the night, her teeth hot and sharp, the net of her hands drawing me in, drawing me in, and at the end a cry lupine and fierce, my own cry muffled in that desperate exchange of the blood. And now she lies open to the night and circumstance and I sit here and look at her, her body curled in the tentativeness of sleep, the submissiveness of darkness . . . and I do not know, I do not know. She is not the monster, I am the monster. If I were not the monster I would find the cure for her, grant her peace, that most precious gift. I understand this now but to understand is nothing. Nothing. The commission is unspeakable.

2 August

The researches disclose few explanations, the foaming beakers in the shoddy laboratory below stairs yield the most uncertain of formulae. I struggle nonetheless. I must help her.

At one time it all appeared simple, a simplicity: the mystery would open its darkest of hearts and one by one the methods of rationality would provide rational method. I was a fool, of course. I have always been a fool and I understand that too, now. Something about her in her present condition is attractive to me; it is not the wife with whom I am lying on these nights but the wolf, it is not the wife but the wolf whom I penetrate, the image of the beast at the center of all ecstasy. I admit this now; I must always have known it, it must have been the wolf that drove me on or long since I would have made myself free.

I think that I have gone mad.

Nonetheless I believe I have, at long last, devised a potion.

I will administer it to her tomorrow night.

3 August

"I'm going out, Eric," she said to me, "I'm going to walk on the fields." Actually they are not fields but rolling empty moors beyond this village in which our house and those of a few stolid neighbors cluster. She is, however, of a romantic turn of mind. Werewolves of necessity must be romantic; it is only this which protects them from the truest apprehension of their being. I allow her these expressions, then. "I wouldn't wait up, Eric, I will be out quite late. I need to think, and I'm restless."

"Yes, Clara," I said. Clara, clearness, clarity. She takes me to be a fool unaware of her condition, her contempt is absolute, but I do not care. For if she knew the degree of my apprehension, what might she do? She might turn upon me. Better to feed her the potion which unsuspecting she drank in her tea at that moment. "Yes, Clara, Clarinda, do as you must." I affected a scholarly bumble, a researcher's detachment, a mild, stunned old man puttering around the ruins of his ambition. "I will not wait up for you."

"I would ask you to walk with me," she said, "but I know what the cold does to your feet, your digestion. Besides, I walk more quickly than you and you might lose your footing."

She is twenty-four, young, graceful, pretty by all conventional standards: What would she want with a man such as me? My own motivations are less mysterious; familiar needs extrude through this uncomfortable shroud of age. But why would Clara, Clarice, Clarinda desire a man with blanket drawn up to his knees, fervidly drinking tea in hot gulps on a cool and penetrating night?

She took another sip from her cup; it clattered against the saucer. Will the potion help her? It is my only hope.

"On the way in," I said, "you might check to see that the fire is still lit. I will be long asleep by then."

"Of course," she said. She came to kiss me with cool and deadly lips, smoothed the blanket over my frail lap. Her features are of unusual delicacy, her bosom soft and fragrant, the taunting secrets which have been revealed to me one by one infinitely tantalizing, leading me to consummation that can never have issue. Of what matter should it be that she is a werewolf ? At that moment, feeling her hands light upon me, I came close or closer to the acceptance of my condition.

It is not bad to be here alone with her on the edge of the moors, even though the terrain is already splattered with the blood of another victim. The graves surrounding London know the bodies of more than even I could suspect; they swaddle knowledge that will never be mine. It was necessary for us to leave London in absurd haste and for the flimsiest of excuses. I cannot stand civilization, clutter, we must move, I must have space, she said to me, and I abandoned my position at the university, my domicile, the rounds of my life to move to this place with her.

Some would call this the damp clutch of passion, but I would assay it as sanity. The police would have come sooner or later, and I would have been implicated. Therefore my researches and at last the potion, the potion that must grant her a cure.

"I will return, Eric," she said and left the room, left the fire, the door clattering behind her, then silence. I wondered if the Change would come upon her immediately, as it so often does, or whether the potion would block it. Or whether, more likely, there would be a retarding action and she would retain human custody until she was beyond the village. Once I would have peered through the window to find the truth, but now I have all the truth with which I can deal in the premises of my consciousness.

I do not want to know.

She will do as she must, just as will I, and when she returns we will huddle in the night and from that jumbled mass on the bed will come the cry. The cry that rends me from myself, my own change, the mantle of change descended, and lupine I will scream within her.

In the darkness.

4 August

These notes commenced at month's beginning, when the potion was nearly perfected, to attempt some order: If I could place on this chaos some sense of progression, string the beads of the days one by one upon the long, raveled line of life, then I might have some grasp of what was happening. I thought. But it was a bad idea. I am a vain man and endlessly these entries refract upon myself: my pain, my researches, my potion and its administration. Not her pain but mine. I am a useless man, useless and frivolous to the core. The word, perhaps, is silly. I am a silly man, Eric the silly, but his Clara, Clarice, Clarinda matters. She matters.

For she crept in again with blood upon her jaws.

Lying in the bed, my eyes alert to the terrible light of that first dawn, I saw her slip within, a gray shape, ears pricked, tail at an angle. And on her jaws, the blood. I feigned sleep, that sodden unconsciousness with which aspect I have always confronted her, leading her to the feeling (it is justified) that she has married a fool who will protect her forever and will never know what she is; but I was intent on her every gesture. Slow murmurous whimpers came from her throat. To be a werewolf is to hurt. The freedom of her nightshape cannot console. Weeping, she came to the bed.

I waited for the scent and aura of the Change, but it did not come. She poised, ears down. Why was she not Changing?

The potion?

Was that its effect, a retarded change? Had it worked against rather than toward her humanity?

Outside, a distant cry. And another and another. It is quiet in the village at dawn but it was not quiet now: Her latest victim had been found. Soft growls and the whimpers from within her. I knew her fear then, shared it, and in that moment saw that if the villagers were to come here, if we were somehow to be discovered, it would not be Clarice, Clarinda but we two with whom they would have to deal.

The distant cries faded.

The Change came upon her convulsively.

It came in that next instant and this creature—not my wife, not a wolf—lay stunned on the floor and wept. I dared not stretch a hand in entreaty or comfort; were she to see me it would end for us at once and I would never possess her again. *Had* the potion affected her in some way? Would it yet lead to a cure?

After a time she came to bed.

I touched her then and felt the terrible desire raging, and in her way she accommodated me as she always has. On one corner of her mouth, still a small spot of blood, a gangrenous red eye winking as if to lure me home. I lay across her, sunlight in the room. We slept.

And awoke and began the new day. It was an old man, a wanderer on the moors, who died last night. I have heard a fragmentary report from the postman. I dare not go amongst the villagers to inquire further; unusual interest would only draw attention.

5 August

I have reread these entries.

The only way I can make sense of them now is to see them as done by a man enthralled. And although this is part of it, enchantment is not all. There is something else about me, something about my obsession I cannot reach. The formulae are strong and the answer lies within them; I must believe that. For only when the Change has come to Clara for the last time will I be able to understand the change that has taken place in me.

Yet I still do not know if the potion has worked or not. I must understand the truth; if I have not helped her I cannot . . . to improve the formulae is beyond my means. Also I am much agitated. The last murder was unspeakable. Its details cannot be communicated in the journal of Eric the silly; I have no taste for horror, nor can I convey it. I was made for idiosyncrasy: brandy and badminton, conundrums in the eventide, little tales for infants as conceived by my equally frivolous colleague Dodson.

I still do not know.

6 August

"You must not go out tonight," I said to her this evening, when she was already pacing and I could sense the need inside her. Yet her aspect was merry. "You must stay here."

"Eric," she said with that strange and solemn gaiety, "you mustn't tell me what to do."

"There was another murder three nights ago. This is no time for a young woman to walk alone on the moors."

"You know the conditions, Eric," she said. "They were made quite clear at the outset, when I agreed to marry, that you would never interfere with me nor I with you. What we do alone must never be questioned." She was smiling. Her eyes were joyous. Was it the potion, which I had again administered in her tea? Or was it anticipation of the night's hunt which made her seem so happy?

"You must not go out," I said again. Fear gave me the force of determination. "Not until the murders are solved."

"I am not afraid, Eric." She walked to the door.

I followed her. Seized her wrist. "I have been searching for a cure," I said. "I know your pain and I can help you find its release."

Her eyes shone with that solemn gaiety. "What are you trying to say?" she said. "Eric, what are you saying?"

"The truth." Grief lent me strength. "We can no longer conceal the truth from each other. Clarice, Clarinda, I have known, I have always known—"

"Known what?"

"About your affliction," I said. "About the Change."

She broke away from me. Still that strange gaiety. "You've given me something, haven't you. Something from your laboratory."

"Yes. But I—"

"Then you understand everything," she said, "but you understand nothing." She spread her fingers and looked into her palm, gazed into it with an expression of delight. "After such cunning, to show such ignoble stupidity!" She opened the door, little bubbles of laughter coming from her throat. I reached toward her. "No," she said, "don't stop me, you won't like it if you do."

And she was gone.

She was gone and I let her go, I sat here to write these words. But I cannot remain alone any longer, I cannot wait again for her to come home at the dawn light. I must follow her. I must know what I have done.

7 August

She is dead she
Is dead she is dead she

Is dead she is dead she was out there on the moors I saw her framed against the moon, I saw the light shining off her pelt and heard the laughter, oh the laughter, and she reached for her throat, I could not comprehend but she reached for her throat and now

I understand what she saw in her palm and what it is I have done, I understand everything: the nature of my own change and what I secretly desired from the first. I wanted to be what she was, a sleek gray shape running free with her in the night, and I yearn now to take the potion and wait for the Change, sit here upon my haunches in the dying blood of the day waiting for the pentagram to appear in my palm, the pentagram that would mark me as my own victim, waiting for the Change that can never come I

Want to be a werewolf so I can die like my Clara, Clarice, Clarinda, she

Tore her throat she

Tore out her own throat in the moonlight but

The moonlight has passed and the day has passed and the potion made her free, it worked as I could never have dreamed. I was not silly but a genius, a man of spirit but the spirit destroyed her and destroyed me, I was undone by my spirit and

And I needed her

I needed her, I needed the blood

Striking once and striking twice and striking thrice and the villagers are striking on the door, screaming, but I will say this, I will say this as they come with the torches that will burn me away, I will say I am not silly. I was a mind of iron, a will of fire. Silly no more silly no more, nor Eric that great Fool, but my Clara my Cordelia driven here and there alone upon the heath until that great wheel of self turned inward, her claws reaching, and only Blinded Gloucester left to show the way through that serene, that gay and mocking, that rigorous and deadly fire

The fire of the shapes of the night.

ThE hOUND
by FRITZ LEIBER

The basic premise of "The Hound" (which first appeared in the best of the fantasy pulp magazines, Weird Tales, *in 1942) is unique among werewolf stories. Its setting is a large modern city, rather than the usual rural locale, and it postulates that the supernatural beings which inhabit such a city would be different from those of the past—a "horde of demons" spawned by the fears and superstitions of present-day urban dwellers.*

As one of the characters in the story explains: "Why, they'd haunt us, terrorize us, try to rule us. Our fears would be their fodder. A parasite-host relationship. Supernatural symbiosis . . . Yes, I think there'd be werewolves among our demons, but they wouldn't be much like the old ones. No nice clean fur, white teeth, and shining eyes. Instead you'd get some nasty hound that wouldn't surprise you if you saw it nosing at a garbage pail or crawling out from under a truck. Frighten and terrorize you, yes. But surprise, no. It would fit into the environment. Look as if it belonged in a city and smell the same. Because of the twisted emotions that would be its food, your emotions and mine. A matter of diet . . ."

A chilling concept. And a chilling and suspenseful tale of terror woven around it—especially if you happen to live in just such a city yourself.

Fritz Leiber is widely recognized as a master of the contemporary horror-fantasy story, as evidenced by his receipt of a Life Achievement Award given at the Second World Fantasy Convention held in 1976. His novel of modern witchcraft, Conjure Wife *(1953), is one of a handful of classics in macabre fiction; it is still in print today, as is his superior collection,* Night's Black

Agents, *originally published by Arkham House in 1948. He is also a promi-nent writer of science fiction, and has won several Nebula and Hugo awards for his novels and short stories in this field.*

 David Lashley huddled the skimpy blankets around him and dully watched the cold light of morning seep through the window and stiffen in his room. He could not recall the exact nature of the terror against which he had fought his way to wakefulness, except that it had been in some way gigantic and had brought back to him the fear-ridden helplessness of childhood. It had lurked near him all night and finally it had crouched over him and thrust down toward his face.

The radiator whined dismally with the first push of steam from the basement, and he shivered in response. He thought that his shivering was an ironically humorous recognition of the fact that his room was never warm except when he was out of it. But there was more to it than that. The penetrating whine had touched something in his mind without being quite able to dislodge it into consciousness. The mounting rumble of city traffic, together with the hoarse panting of a locomotive in the railroad yards, mingled themselves with the nearer sound, intensifying its disturbing tug at hidden fears. For a few moments he lay inert, listening. There was an unpleasant stench too in the room, he noticed, but that was nothing to be surprised at. He had experienced more than once the strange olfactory illusions that are part of the aftermath of flu. Then he heard his mother moving around laboriously in the kitchen, and that stung him into action.

"Have you another cold?" she asked, watching him anxiously as he hurriedly spooned in a boiled egg before its heat should be entirely lost in the chilly plate. "Are you sure?" she persisted. "I heard someone sniffling all night."

"Perhaps father—" he began.

She shook her head. "No, he's all right. His side was giving him a lot of pain yesterday evening, but he slept quietly enough. That's why I thought it must be you, David. I got up twice to see, but"—her voice became a little doleful—"I know you don't like me to come poking into your room at all hours."

"That's not true!" he contradicted. She looked so frail and little and worn, standing there in front of the stove with one of father's shapeless bathrobes hugged around her, so like a sick sparrow trying to appear chipper, that a futile irritation, an indignation that he couldn't help her more, welled up within him, choking his voice a little. "It's that I don't want you getting up all the time and missing your sleep. You have enough to do taking care of father all day long. And I've told you a dozen times that you mustn't make breakfast for me. You know the doctor says you need all the rest you can get."

"Oh, *I'm* all right," she answered quickly, "but I was sure you'd caught another cold. All night long I kept hearing it—a sniffling and a snuffling—"

Coffee spilled over into the saucer as David set down the half-raised cup. His mother's words had reawakened the elusive memory, and now that it had come back he did not want to look it in the face.

"It's late, I'll have to rush," he said.

She accompanied him to the door, so accustomed to his hastiness that she saw in it nothing unusual. Her wan voice followed him down the dark apartment stair: "I hope a rat hasn't died in the walls. Did you notice the nasty smell?"

And then he was out of the door and had lost himself and his memories in the early morning rush of the city. Tires singing on asphalt. Cold engines coughing, then starting with a roar. Heels clicking on the sidewalk, hurrying, trotting, converging on streetcar intersections and elevated stations. Low heels, high heels, heels of stenographers bound downtown, and of war workers headed for the outlying factories. Shouts of newsboys and glimpses of headlines: "AIR BLITZ ON . . . BATTLESHIP SUNK . . . BLACKOUT EXPECTED HERE . . . DRIVEN BACK."

But sitting in the stuffy solemnity of the streetcar, it was impossible to keep from thinking of it any longer. Besides, the stale medicinal smell of the yellow woodwork immediately brought back the memory of that other smell. David Lashley clenched his hands in his overcoat pockets and asked himself how it was possible for a grown man to be so suddenly overwhelmed by a fear from childhood. Yet in the same instant he knew with acute certainty that this was no childhood fear, this thing that had pursued him up the years, growing ever more vast and menacing, until, like the demon wolf Fenris at Ragnorak, its gaping jaws scraped heaven and earth, seeking to open wider. This thing that had dogged his footsteps, sometimes so far behind that he forgot its existence, but now so close that he could feel its cold sick breath on his neck. Werewolves? He had read up on such things at the library, fingering dusty books in uneasy fascination, but what he had read made them seem innocuous and without significance—dead superstitions—in comparison with this thing that was part and parcel of the great sprawling cities and chaotic peoples of the twentieth century, so much a part that he, David Lashley, winced at the endlessly varying howls and growls of traffic and industry—sounds at once animal and mechanical; shrank back with a start from the sight of headlights at night—those dazzling unwinking eyes; trembled uncontrollably if he heard the scuffling of rats in an alley or caught sight in the evenings of the shadowy forms of lean mongrel dogs looking for food in vacant lots. "Sniffling and snuffling," his mother had said. What better words could you want to describe the inquisitive, persistent pryings of the beast that had crouched outside the bedroom door all night in his dreams and then finally pushed through to plant its dirty paws on his chest. For a moment he saw, superimposed on the yellow ceiling and garish advertising placards of the streetcar, its malformed muzzle . . . the red eyes like thickly scummed molten metal . . . the jaws slavered with thick black oil . . .

Wildly he looked around at his fellow passengers, seeking to blot out that vision, but it seemed to have slipped down into all of them, infecting them, giving their features an ugly canine cast—the slack, receding jaw of an otherwise pretty blonde, the narrow head and wide-set eyes of an unshaven mechanic returning from the night shift. He sought refuge in the open newspaper of the man sitting beside him, studying it intently without regard for the impression of rudeness he was creating. But there was a wolf in the cartoon, and he quickly turned away to stare through the dusty pane at the stores sliding by. Gradually the sense of oppressive menace lifted a little. But the cartoon had established another contact in his brain—the memory of a cartoon from the First World War. What the wolf or hound in that earlier cartoon had represented—war, famine, or the ruthlessness of the enemy—he could not say, but it had haunted his dreams for weeks, crouched in corners, and waited for him at the head of the stairs. Later he had tried to explain to friends the horrors that may lie in the concrete symbolisms and personifications of a cartoon if interpreted naively by a child, but had been unable to get his idea across.

The conductor growled out the name of a downtown street, and once again he lost himself in the crowd, finding relief in the never-ceasing movement, the brushing of shoulders against his own. But as the time-clock emitted its delayed musical bong! and he turned to stick his card in the rack, the girl at the desk looked up and remarked, "Aren't you going to punch in for your dog, too?"

"My dog?"

"Well, it was there just a second ago. Came in right behind you, looking as if it owned you—I mean you owned it." She giggled briefly through her nose. "One of Mrs. Montmorency's mastiffs come to inspect conditions among the working class, I presume."

He continued to stare at her blankly. "A joke," she explained patiently, and returned to her work.

"I've got to get a grip on myself," he found himself muttering tritely as the elevator lowered him noiselessly to the basement.

He kept repeating it as he hurried to the locker room, left his coat and lunch, gave his hair a quick careful brushing, hurried again through the still-empty aisles, and slipped in behind the socks-and-handkerchiefs counter. "It's just nerves. I'm not crazy. But I've got to get a grip on myself."

"Of course you're crazy. Don't you know that talking to yourself and not noticing anybody is the first symptom of insanity?"

Gertrude Rees had stopped on her way over to neckties. Light brown hair, painstakingly waved and ordered, framed a serious not-too-pretty face.

"Sorry," he murmured. "I'm jittery." What else could you say? Even to Gertrude.

She grimaced sympathetically. Her hand slipped across the counter to squeeze his for a moment.

But even as he watched her walk away, his hands automatically setting out the display boxes, the new question was furiously hammering in his brain. What else could you say? What words could you use to explain it? Above all, to whom could you tell it? A dozen names printed themselves in his mind and were as quickly discarded.

One remained. Tom Goodsell. He would tell Tom. Tonight, after the first-aid class.

Shoppers were already filtering into the basement. "He wears size eleven, madam? Yes, we have some new patterns. These are silk and lisle." But their ever-increasing numbers gave him no sense of security. Crowding the aisles, they became shapes behind which something might hide. He was continually peering past them. A little child who wandered behind the counter and pushed at his knee, gave him a sudden fright.

Lunch came early for him. He arrived at the locker room in time to catch hold of Gertrude Rees as she retreated uncertainly from the dark doorway.

"Dog," she gasped. "Huge one. Gave me an awful start. Talk about jitters! Wonder where he could have come from? Watch out. He looked nasty."

But David, impelled by sudden recklessness born of fear and shock, was already inside and switching on the light.

"No dog in sight," he told her.

"You're crazy. It must be there." Her face, gingerly poked through the doorway, lengthened in surprise. "But I tell you I—Oh, I guess it must have pushed out through the other door."

He did not tell her that the other door was bolted.

"I suppose a customer brought it in," she rattled on nervously. "Some of them can't seem to shop unless they've got a pair of Russian wolfhounds. Though that kind usually keeps out of the bargain basement. I suppose we ought to find it before we eat lunch. It looked dangerous."

But he hardly heard her. He had just noticed that his locker was open and his overcoat dragged down on the floor. The brown paper bag containing his lunch had been torn open and the contents rummaged through, as if an animal had been nosing at it. As he stooped, he saw that there were greasy, black stains on the sandwiches, and a familiar stale stench rose to his nostrils.

That night he found Tom Goodsell in a nervous, expansive mood. The latter had been called up and would start for camp in a week. As they sipped coffee in the empty little restaurant, Tom poured out a flood of talk about old times. David would have been able to listen better, had not the uncertain, shadowy shapes outside the window been continually distracting his attention. Eventually he found an appropriate opportunity to turn the conversation down the channels which absorbed his mind.

"The supernatural beings of a modern city?" Tom answered, seeming to find nothing out of the way in the question. "Sure, they'd be different from the ghosts of yesterday. Each culture creates its own ghosts. Look, the Middle Ages built cathedrals, and pretty soon there were little gray shapes gliding around at night to talk with the gargoyles. Same thing ought to happen to us, with our skyscrapers and factories." He spoke eagerly, with all his old poetic flair, as if he'd just been meaning to discuss this very matter. He would talk about anything tonight. "I'll tell you how it works, Dave. We begin by denying all the old haunts and superstitions. Why shouldn't we? They belong to the era of cottage and castle. They can't take root in the new environment. Science goes materialistic, proving that there isn't anything in the universe except tiny bundles of energy. As if, for that matter, a tiny bundle of energy mightn't mean anything.

"But wait, that's just the beginning. We go on inventing and discovering and organizing. We cover the earth with huge structures. We pile them together in great heaps that make old Rome and Alexandria and Babylon seem almost toy-towns by comparison. The new environment, you see, is forming."

David stared at him with incredulous fascination, profoundly disturbed. This was not at all what he had expected or hoped for—this almost telepathic prying into his most hidden fears. He had wanted to talk about these things—yes—but in a skeptical reassuring way.

Instead, Tom sounded almost serious. David started to speak, but Tom held up his finger for silence, aping the gesture of a school-teacher.

"Meanwhile, what's happening inside each one of us? I'll tell you. All sorts of inhibited emotions are accumulating. Fear is accumulating. Horror is accumulating. A new kind of awe of the mysteries of the universe is accumulating. A psychological environment is forming, along with the physical one. Wait, let me finish. Our culture becomes ripe for infection. From somewhere. It's just like a bacteriologist's culture—I didn't intend the pun—when it gets to the right temperature and consistency for supporting a colony of germs. Similarly, our culture suddenly spawns a horde of demons. And, like germs, they have a peculiar affinity for our culture. They're unique. They fit in. You wouldn't find the same kind any other time or place.

"How would you know when the infection had taken place? Say, you're taking this pretty seriously, aren't you? Well, so am I, maybe. Why, they'd haunt us, terrorize us, try to rule us. Our fears would be their fodder. A parasite-host relationship. Supernatural symbiosis. Some of us—the sensitive ones—would notice them sooner than others. Some of us might see them without knowing what they were. Others might know about them without seeing them. Like me, eh?

"What was that? I didn't catch your remark. Oh, about werewolves. Well, that's a pretty special question, but tonight I'd take a crack at anything. Yes, I think there'd be werewolves among our demons, but they wouldn't be much like the old ones. No nice clean fur, white teeth and shining eyes. Oh, no. Instead you'd get some nasty hound that wouldn't surprise you if you saw it nosing at a garbage pail or crawling out from under a truck. Frighten and terrorize you, yes. But surprise, no. It would fit into the environment. Look as if it belonged in a city and smell the same. Because of the twisted emotions that would be its food, your emotions and mine. A matter of diet."

Tom Goodsell chuckled loudly and lit another cigarette. But David only stared at the scarred counter. He realized he couldn't tell Tom what had happened this morning—or this noon. Of course, Tom would immediately scoff and be skeptical. But that wouldn't get around the fact that Tom had already agreed—agreed in partial jest perhaps, but still agreed. And Tom himself confirmed this, when, in a more serious, friendlier voice, he said:

"Oh, I know I've talked a lot of rot tonight, but still, you know, the way things are, there's something to it. At least, I can't express my feelings any other way."

They shook hands at the corner, and David rode the surging streetcar home through a city whose every bolt and stone seemed subtly infected, whose every noise carried shuddering overtones. His mother was waiting up for him, and after he had wearily argued with her about getting more rest and seen her off to bed, he lay sleepless himself, all through the night, like a child in a strange house, listening to each tiny noise and watching intently each changing shape taken by the shadows.

That night nothing shouldered through the door or pressed its muzzle against the windowpane.

Yet he found that it cost him an effort to go down to the department store next morning, so conscious was he of the thing's presence in the faces and forms, the structures and machines around him. It was as if he were forcing himself into the heart of a monster. Detestation of the city grew within him. As yesterday, the crowded aisles seemed only hiding places, and he avoided the locker room. Gertrude Rees remarked sympathetically on his fatigued look, and he took the opportunity to invite her out that evening. Of course, he told himself while they sat watching the movie, she wasn't very close to him. None of the girls had been close to him—a not-very-competent young man tied down to the task of supporting parents whose little reserve of money had long ago dribbled away. He had dated them for a while, talked to them, told them his beliefs and ambitions, and then one by one they had drifted off to marry other men. But that did not change the fact that he needed the wholesomeness Gertrude could give him.

And as they walked home through the chilly night, he found himself talking inconsequentially and laughing at his own jokes. Then, as they turned to one another in the shadowy vestibule and she lifted her lips, he sensed her features altering queerly, lengthening. "A funny sort of light here," he thought as he took her in his arms. But the thin strip of fur on her collar grew matted and oily under his touch, her fingers grew hard and sharp against his back, he felt her teeth pushing out against her lips, and then a sharp, prickling sensation as of icy needles.

Blindly he pushed away from her, then saw—and the sight stopped him dead—that she had not changed at all or that whatever change had been was now gone.

"What's the matter, dear?" he heard her ask startledly. "What's happened? What's that you're mumbling? Changed, you say? What's changed? Infected with it? What do you mean? For heaven's sake, don't talk that way. You've done it to me, you say? Done what?" He felt her hand on his arm, a soft hand now. "No, you're not crazy. Don't think of such things. But you're neurotic and maybe a little batty. For heaven's sake, pull yourself together."

"I don't know what happened to me," he managed to say, in his right voice again. Then, because he had to say something more: "My nerves all jumped, like someone had snapped them."

He expected her to be angry, but she seemed only puzzledly sympathetic, as if she liked him but had become afraid of him, as if she sensed something wrong in him beyond her powers of under-standing or repair.

"Do take care of yourself," she said doubtfully. "We're all a little crazy now and then, I guess. My nerves get like wires too. Good night."

He watched her disappear up the stairs. Then he turned and ran.

At home his mother was waiting up again, close to the hall radiator to catch its dying warmth, the inevitable shapeless bathrobe wrapped about her. Because of a new thought that had come to the forefront of his brain, he avoided her embrace and, after a few brief words, hurried off toward his room. But she followed him down the hall.

"You're not looking at all well, David," she told him anxiously, whispering because father might be asleep. "Are you sure you're not getting flu again? Don't you think you should see the doctor tomorrow?" Then she went on quickly to another subject, using that nervously apologetic tone with which he was so familiar. "I shouldn't bother you with it, David, but you really must be more careful of the bedclothes, You'd laid something greasy on the cover-let and there were big, black stains."

He was pushing open the bedroom door. Her words halted his

hand only for an instant. How could you avoid the thing by going one place rather than another?

"And one thing more," she added, as he switched on the lights. "Will you try to get some cardboard tomorrow to black out the windows? They're out of it at the stores around here and the radio says we should be ready."

"Yes, I will. Good night, Mother."

"Oh, and something else," she persisted, lingering uneasily just beyond the door. "That really must be a dead rat in the walls. The smell keeps coming in waves. I spoke to the real estate agent, but he hasn't done anything about it. I wish you'd speak to him."

"Yes. Good night, Mother."

He waited until he heard her door softly close. He lit a cigarette and slumped down on the bed to try and think as clearly as he could about something to which everyday ideas could not be applied.

Question One (and he realized with an ironic twinge that it sounded melodramatic enough for a dime-novel): Was Gertrude Rees what might be called, for want of a better term, a werewolf? Answer: Almost certainly not, in any ordinary sense of the word. What had momentarily come to her had been something he had communicated to her. It had happened because of his presence. And either his own shock had interrupted the transformation or else Gertrude Rees had not proved a suitable vehicle of incarnation for the thing.

Question Two: Might he not communicate the thing to some other person? Answer: Yes. For a moment his thinking paused, as there swept before his mind's eye kaleidoscopic visions of the faces which might, without warning, begin to change in his presence: His mother, his father, Tom Goodsell, the prim-mouthed real estate agent, a customer at the store, a panhandler who would approach him on a rainy night.

Question Three: Was there any escape from the thing? Answer: No. And yet—there was one bare possibility. Escape from the city. The city had bred the thing; might it not be chained to the city? It hardly seemed to be a reasonable possibility; how could a supernatural entity be tied down to one locality? And yet—he stepped quickly to the window and, after a moment's hesitation, jerked it up. Sounds which had been temporarily blotted out by his thinking now poured past him in quadrupled volume, mixing together discordantly like instruments tuning up for some titanic symphony—the racking surge of streetcar and elevated, the coughing of a locomotive in the yards, the hum of tires on asphalt and the growl of engines, the mumbling of radio voices, the faint mournful note of distant horns. But now they were no longer separate sounds. They all issued from one cavernous throat—a single moan, infinitely penetrating, infinitely menacing. He slammed down the window and put his hands to his ears. He switched out the lights and threw himself on the bed, burying his head in the pillows. Still the sound came through. And it was then he realized that ultimately, whether he wanted to or not, the thing would drive him from the city. The moment would come when the sound would begin to penetrate too deeply, to reverberate too unendurably in his ears.

The sight of so many faces, trembling on the brink of an almost unimaginable change, would become too much for him. And he would leave whatever he was doing and go away.

That moment came a little after four o'clock next afternoon. He could not say what sensation it was that, adding its straw-weight to the rest, drove him to take the step. Perhaps it was a heaving movement in the rack of dresses two counters away; perhaps it was the snoutlike appearance momentarily taken by a crumpled piece of cloth. Whatever it was, he slipped from behind the counter without a word, leaving a customer to mutter indignantly, and walked up the stairs and out into the street, moving almost like a sleepwalker yet constantly edging from side to side to avoid any direct contact with the crowd engulfing him. Once in the street, he took the first car that came by, never noting its number, and found himself an empty place in the corner of the front platform.

With ominous slowness at first, then with increasing rapidity the heart of the city was left behind. A great gloomy bridge spanning an oily river was passed over, and the frowning cliffs of the buildings grew lower. Warehouses gave way to factories, factories to apartment buildings, apartment buildings to dwellings which were at first small and dirty white, then large and mansionlike but very much decayed, then new and monotonous in their uniformity. Peoples of different economic status and racial affiliation filed in and emptied out as the different strata of the city were passed through. Finally the vacant lots began to come, at first one by one, then in increasing numbers, until the houses were spaced out two or three to a block.

"End of the line," sang out the conductor, and without hesitation David swung down from the platform and walked on in the same direction that the streetcar had been going. He did not hurry. He did not lag. He moved as an automaton that had been wound up and set going, and will not stop until it runs down.

The sun was setting smokingly red in the west. He could not see it because of a tree-fringed rise ahead, but its last rays winked at him from the windowpanes of little houses blocks off to the right and left, as if flaming lights had been lit inside. As he moved they flashed on and off like signals. Two blocks further on the sidewalk ended, and he walked down the center of a muddy lane. After passing a final house, the lane also came to an end, giving way to a narrow dirt path between high weeds. The path led up the rise and through the fringe of trees. Emerging on the other side, he slowed his pace and finally stopped, so bewilderingly fantastic was the scene spread out before him. The sun had set, but high cloud-banks reflected its light, giving a spectral glow to the landscape.

Immediately before him stretched the equivalent of two or three empty blocks, but beyond that began a strange realm that seemed to have been plucked from another climate and another geological system and set down here outside the city. There were strange trees and shrubs, but, most striking of all, great uneven blocks of reddish stone which rose from the earth at unequal intervals and culminated in a massive central eminence fifty or sixty feet high.

As he gazed, the light drained from the landscape, as if a cloak had been flipped over the earth, and in the sudden twilight there rose from somewhere in the region ahead a faint howling, mournful and sinister, but in no way allied to the other howling that had haunted him day and night. Once again he moved forward, but now impulsively toward the source of the new sound.

A small gate in a high wire fence pushed open, giving him access to the realm of rocks. He found himself following a gravel path between thick shrubs and trees. At first it seemed quite dark, in contrast to the open land behind him. And with every step he took, the hollow howling grew closer. Finally the path turned abruptly around a shoulder of rock, and he found himself at the sound's source.

A ditch of rough stone about eight feet wide and of similar depth separated him from a space overgrown with short, brownish vegetation and closely surrounded on the other three sides by precipitous, rocky walls in which were the dark mouths of two or three caves. In the center of the open space were gathered a half dozen white-furred canine figures, their muzzles pointing toward the sky, giving voice to the mournful cry that had drawn him here.

It was only when he felt the low iron fence against his knees and made out the neat little sign reading, ARCTIC WOLVES, that he realized where he must be—in the famous zoological gardens which he had heard about but never visited, where the animals were kept in as nearly natural conditions as was feasible. Looking around, he noted the outlines of two or three low inconspicuous buildings, and some distance away he could see the form of a uniformed guard silhouetted against a patch of dark sky. Evidently he had come in after hours and through an auxiliary gate that should have been locked.

Swinging around again, he stared with casual curiosity at the wolves. The turn of events had the effect of making him feel stupid and bewildered, and for a long time he pondered dully as to why he should find these animals unalarming and even attractive.

Perhaps it was because they were so much a part of the wild, so little of the city. That great brute there, for instance, the biggest of the lot, who had come forward to the edge of the ditch to stare back at him. He seemed an incarnation of primitive strength. His fur so creamy white—well, perhaps not so white; it seemed darker than he had thought at first, streaked with black—or was that due to the fading light? But at least his eyes were clear and clean, shining faintly like jewels in the gathering dark. But no, they weren't clean; their reddish gleam was thickening, scumming over, until they looked more like two tiny peepholes in the walls of a choked furnace. And why hadn't he noticed before that the creature was obviously malformed? And why should the other wolves draw away from it and snarl as if afraid?

Then the brute licked its black tongue across its greasy jowls, and from its throat came a faint familiar growl that had in it nothing of the wild, and David Lashley knew that before him crouched the monster of his dreams, finally made flesh and blood.

With a choked scream he turned and fled blindly down the gravel path that led between thick shrubs to the little gate, fled in panic across empty blocks, stumbling over the uneven ground and twice falling. When he reached the fringe of trees he looked back, to see a low, lurching form emerge from the gate. Even at this distance he could tell that the eyes were those of no animal.

It was dark in the trees, and dark in the lane beyond. Ahead the street lamps glowed, and there were lights in the houses. A pang of helpless terror gripped him when he saw there was no streetcar waiting, until he realized—and the realization was like the onset of insanity—that nothing whatever in the city promised him refuge. This—everything that lay ahead—was the thing's hunting ground. It was driving him in toward its lair for the kill.

Then he ran, ran with the hopeless terror of a victim in the arena, of a rabbit loosed before greyhounds, ran until his sides were walls of pain and his gasping throat seemed aflame, and then still ran. Over mud, dirt and brick, and then onto the endless sidewalks. Past the neat suburban dwellings which in their uniformity seemed like monoliths lining some avenue of Egypt. The streets were almost empty, and those few people he passed stared at him as at a madman.

Brighter lights came into view, a corner with two or three stores. There he paused to look back. For a moment he saw nothing. Then it emerged from the shadows a block behind him, loping unevenly with long strides that carried it forward with a rush, its matted fur shining oilily under a street lamp. With a croaking sob he turned and ran on.

The thing's howling seemed suddenly to increase a thousandfold, becoming a pulsating wail, a screaming ululation that seemed to blanket the whole city with sound. And as that demoniac screeching continued, the lights in the houses began to go out one by one. Then the streetlights vanished in a rush, and an approaching streetcar was blotted out, and he knew that the sound did not come altogether or directly from the thing. This was the long-predicted blackout.

He ran on with arms outstretched, feeling rather than seeing the intersections as he approached them, misjudging his step at curbs, tripping and falling flat, picking himself up to stagger on half-stunned. His diaphragm contracted to a knot of pain that tied itself tighter and tighter. Breath rasped like a file in his throat. There seemed no light in the whole world, for the clouds had gathered thicker and thicker ever since sunset. No light, except those twin points of dirty red in the blackness behind.

A solid edge of darkness struck him down, inflicting pain on his shoulder and side. He scrambled up. Then a second solid obstacle in his path smashed him full in the face and chest. This time he did not rise. Dazed, tortured by exhaustion, motionless, he waited its approach.

First a padding of footsteps, with the faint scraping of claws on cement. Then a snuffing. Then a sickening stench. Then a glimpse of red eyes. And then the thing was upon him, its weight pinning him down, its jaws thrusting at his throat. Instinctively his hand went up, and his forearm was clamped by teeth whose icy sharpness stung through the layers of cloth, while a foul oily fluid splattered his face.

At that moment light flooded them, and he was aware of a mal-formed muzzle retreating into the blackness, and of weight lifted from him. Then silence and cessation of movement. Nothing, nothing at all—except the light flooding down. As consciousness and sanity teetered in his brain, his eyes found the source of light, a glaring white disk only a few feet away. A flashlight, but nothing visible in the blackness behind it. For what seemed an eternity, there was no change in the situation—himself supine and exposed upon the ground in the unwavering circle of light.

Then a voice from the darkness, the voice of a man paralyzed by supernatural fear. "God, God, God," over and over again. Each word dragged out with prodigious effort.

An unfamiliar sensation stirred in David, a feeling almost of security and relief.

"You—saw it then?" he heard issue from his own dry throat. "The hound? the—wolf?"

"Hound? Wolf?" The voice from behind the flashlight was hideously shaken. "It was nothing like that. It was—" Then the voice broke, became earthly once more. "Good grief, man, we must get you inside."

WOLVES DON'T CRY
by BRUCE ELLIOTT

"Wolves Don't Cry" first appeared in The Magazine of Fantasy and Science Fiction *in 1954; in his introduction to the story, Anthony Boucher, co-founder and then-editor of* F&SF, *said that it was a werewolf tale "at once moving, plausible . . . and completely unlike any other you have ever read." Indeed it is. For it is not about a man who turns into a wolf, but rather about a wolf who has turned into a "were-man"—the flip side of lycanthropy, the side we never consider.*

What would it be like for a creature of the forest to find himself trapped in human form and human society? How would he cope, what would he do? These are the questions which Bruce Elliott asks and then answers with a neat mixture of poignancy and underplayed satire. The result is a story which might just linger in your memory after you've finished reading it.

Elliott, whose primary vocation was as an editor with a number of men's magazines, published many fantasy, mystery, and science-fiction stories in the '50s and '60s, as well as a handful of paperback novels (one of which is the provocatively titled The Rivet in Grandfather's Neck). *A tragic accident claimed his life in New York City several years ago.*

The naked man behind the bars was sound asleep. In the cage next to him a bear rolled over on its back, and peered sleepily at the rising sun. Not far away a jackal paced springily back and forth as though essaying the impossible, trying to leave its own stench far behind.

Flies were gathered around the big bone that rested near the man's sleeping head. Little bits of decaying flesh attracted the insects and their hungry buzzing made the man stir uneasily. Accustomed to instant awakening, his eyes flickered and simultaneously his right hand darted out and smashed down at the irritating flies.

They left in a swarm, but the naked man stayed frozen in the position he had assumed. His eyes were on his hand.

He was still that way when the zoo attendant came close to the cage. The attendant, a pail of food in one hand, a pail of water in the other, said, "Hi Lobo, up and at 'em, the customers'll be here soon." Then he too froze.

Inside the naked man's head strange ideas were stirring. His paw, what had happened to it? Where was the stiff gray hair? The jet-black steel-strong nails? And what was the odd fifth thing that jutted out from his paw at right angles? He moved it experimentally. It rotated. He'd never been able to move his dew claw, and the fact that he could move this fifth extension was somehow more baffling than the other oddities that were puzzling him.

"You goddamn drunks!" the attendant raved. "Wasn't bad enough the night a flock of you came in here, and a girl bothered the bear and lost an arm for her trouble, no, that wasn't bad enough. Now you have to sleep in my cages! And where's Lobo? What have you done with him?"

The naked figure wished the two-legged would stop barking. It was enough trouble trying to figure out what had happened without the angry short barks of the two-legged who fed him, interfering with his thoughts.

Then there were many more of the two-leggeds and a lot of barking, and the naked one wished they'd all go away and let him think. Finally the cage was opened and the two-leggeds tried to make him come out of his cage. He retreated hurriedly on all fours to the back of his cage toward his den.

"Let him alone," the two-legged who fed him barked. "Let him go into Lobo's den. He'll be sorry!"

Inside the den, inside the hollowed-out rock that so cleverly approximated his home before he had been captured, he paced back and forth, finding it bafflingly uncomfortable to walk on his naked feet. His paws did not grip the ground the way they should and the rock hurt his new soft pads.

The two-legged ones were getting angry, he could smell the emotion as it poured from them, but even that was puzzling, for he had to flare his nostrils wide to get the scent, and it was blurred, not crisp and clear the way he ordinarily smelled things. Throwing back his head, he howled in frustration and anger. But the sound was wrong. It did not ululate as was its wont. Instead he found to his horror that he sounded like a cub, or a female.

What had happened to him?

Cutting one of his soft pads on a stone, he lifted his foot and licked at the blood.

His pounding heart almost stopped.

This was no wolf blood.

Then the two-legged ones came in after him and the fight was one that ordinarily he would have enjoyed, but now his heart was not in it. Dismay filled him, for the taste of his own blood had put fear in him. Fear unlike any he had ever known, even when he was trapped that time, and put in a box, and thrown onto a wheeled thing that had rocked back and forth, and smelled so badly of two-legged things.

This was a new fear, and a horrible one.

Their barking got louder when they found that he was alone in his den. Over and over they barked, not that he could understand them, "What have you done with Lobo? Where is he? Have you turned him loose?"

It was only after a long time, when the sun was riding high in the summer sky, that he was wrapped in a foul-smelling thing and put in a four-wheeled object and taken away from his den.

He would never have thought, when he was captured, that he would ever miss the new home that the two-leggeds had given him, but he found that he did, and most of all, as the four-wheeled thing rolled through the city streets, he found himself worrying about his mate in the next cage. What would she think when she found him gone, and she just about to have a litter? He knew that most males did not worry about their young, but wolves were different. No mother wolf ever had to worry, the way female bears did, about a male wolf eating his young. No indeed; wolves were different.

And being different, he found that worse than being tied up in a cloth and thrown in the back of a long, wheeled thing was the worry he felt about his mate, and her young-to-be.

But worse was to come: When he was carried out of the moving thing, the two-legged ones carried him into a big building and the smells that surged in on his outraged nostrils literally made him cringe. There was sickness, and stenches worse than he had ever smelled, and above and beyond all other smells the odor of death was heavy in the long white corridors through which he was carried.

Seeing around him as he did ordinarily in grays and blacks and whites, he found that the new sensations that crashed against his smarting eye balls were not to be explained by anything he knew. Not having the words for red, and green, and yellow, for pink and orange and all the other colors in a polychromatic world, not having any idea of what they were, just served to confuse him even more miserably.

He moaned.

The smells, the discomfort, the horror of being handled, were as nothing against the hurt his eyes were enduring.

Lying on a flat hard thing he found that it helped just to stare directly upwards. At least the flat covering ten feet above him was white, and he could cope with that.

The two-legged thing sitting next to him had a gentle bark, but that didn't help much.

The two-legged said patiently over and over again, "Who are you? Have you any idea? Do you know where you are? What day is this?"

After a while the barks became soothing, and nude no longer, wrapped now in a long wet sheet that held him cocoonlike in its embrace, he found that his eyes were closing. It was all too much for him.

He slept.

The next awakening was if anything worse than the first.

First he thought that he was back in his cage in the zoo, for directly ahead of him he could see bars. Heaving a sigh of vast relief, he wondered what had made an adult wolf have such an absurd dream. He could still remember his puppyhood when sleep had been made peculiar by a life unlike the one he enjoyed when awake. The twitchings, the growls, the sleepy murmurs—he had seen his own sons and daughters go through them and they had reminded him of his youth.

But now the bars were in front of him and all was well.

Except that he must have slept in a peculiar position. He was stiff, and when he went to roll over he fell off the hard thing he had been on and crashed to the floor.

Bars or no bars, this was not his cage.

That was what made the second awakening so difficult. For, once he had fallen off the hospital bed, he found that his limbs were encumbered by a long garment that flapped around him as he rolled to all fours and began to pace fearfully back and forth inside the narrow confines of the cell that he now inhabited.

Worse yet, when the sound of his fall reached the ears of a two-legged one, he found that some more two-legs hurried to his side and he was forced, literally forced into an odd garment that covered his lower limbs.

Then they made him sit on the end of his spine and it hurt cruelly, and they put a metal thing in his right paw, and wrapped the soft flesh of his paw around the metal object and holding both, they made him lift some kind of slop from a round thing on the flat surface in front of him.

That was bad, but the taste of the mush they forced into his mouth was grotesque.

Where was his meat? Where was his bone? How could he sharpen his fangs on such food as this? What were they trying to do? Make him lose his teeth?

He gagged and regurgitated the slops. That didn't do the slightest bit of good. The two-leggeds kept right on forcing the mush into his aching jaws. Finally, in despair, he kept some of it down.

Then they made him balance on his hind legs.

He'd often seen the bear in the next cage doing this trick and sneered at the big fat oaf for pandering to the two-leggeds by aping them. Now he found that it was harder than he would have thought. But finally, after the two-leggeds had worked with him for a long time, he found that he could, by much teetering, stand erect.

But he didn't like it.

His nose was too far from the floor, and with whatever it was wrong with his smelling, he found that he had trouble sniffing the ground under him. From this distance he could not track anything. Not even a rabbit. If one had run right by him, he thought, feeling terribly sorry for himself, he'd never be able to smell it, or if he did, be able to track it down, no matter how fat and juicy, for how could a wolf run on two legs?

They did many things to him in the new big zoo, and in time he found that, dislike it as much as he did, they could force him by painful expedients to do many of the tasks they set him.

That, of course, did not help him to understand why they wanted him to do such absurd things as encumber his legs with cloth that flapped and got in the way, or balance precariously on his hind legs, or any of the other absurdities they made him perform. But somehow he surmounted everything and in time even learned to bark a little the way they did. He found that he could bark *hello* and *I'm hungry* and, after months of effort, ask *why can't I go back to the zoo?*

But that didn't do much good, because all they ever barked back was *because you're a man.*

Now of many things he was unsure since that terrible morning, but of one thing he was sure: he *was* a wolf.

Other people knew it too.

He found this out on the day some outsiders were let into the place where he was being kept. He had been sitting, painful as it was, on the tip of his spine, in what he had found the two-leggeds called a chair, when some shes passed by.

His nostrils closed at the sweet smell that they had poured on themselves, but through it he could detect the real smell, the female smell, and his nostrils had flared, and he had run to the door of his cell, and his eyes had become red as he looked at them. Not so attractive as his mate, but at least they were covered with fur, not like the peeled ones that he sometimes saw dressed in stiff white crackling things.

The fur-covered ones had giggled just like ripening she-cubs, and his paws had ached to grasp them, and his jaws ached to bite into their fur-covered necks.

One of the fur-covered two-leggeds had giggled, "Look at that wolf!"

So some of the two-leggeds had perception and could tell that the ones who held him in this big strange zoo were wrong, that he was not a man, but a wolf.

Inflating his now puny lungs to the utmost, he had thrown back his head and roared out a challenge that in the old days, in the forest, would have sent a thrill of pleasure through every female for miles around. But instead of that bloodcurdling, stomach-wrenching roar, a little barking, choking sound came from his throat. If he had still had a tail it would have curled down under his belly as he slunk away.

The first time they let him see himself in what they called a mirror he had moaned like a cub. Where was his long snout, the bristling whiskers, the flat head, the pointed ears? What was this thing that stared with dilated eyes out of the flat shiny surface? White-faced, almost hairless save for a jet-black bar of eyebrows that made a straight line across his high round forehead, small-jawed, small-toothed—he knew with a sinking sensation in the pit of his stomach that even a year-old would not hesitate to challenge him in the mating fights.

Not only challenge him but beat him, for how could he fight with those little canines, those feeble white hairless paws?

Another thing that irritated him, as it would any wolf, was that they kept moving him around. He would no sooner get used to one den and make it his own but what they'd move him to another one.

The last one that contained him had no bars.

If he had been able to read his chart he would have known that he was considered on the way to recovery, that the authorities thought him almost "cured" of his aberration. The den with no bars was one that was used for limited liberty patients. They were on a kind of parole basis. But he had no idea of what the word meant and the first time he was released on his own cognizance, allowed to make a trip out into the "real" world, he put out of his mind the curious forms of "occupational therapy" with which the authorities were deviling him.

His daytime liberty was unreal and dragged by in a way that made him almost anxious to get back home to the new den.

He had all but made up his mind to do so, when the setting sun conjured up visions which he could not resist. In the dark he could get down on all fours!

Leaving the crowded city streets behind him he hurried out into the suburbs where the spring smells were making the night air exciting.

He had looked forward so to dropping on all fours and racing through the velvet spring night that when he did so, only to find that all the months of standing upright had made him too stiff to run, he could have howled. Then too the clumsy leather things on his back paws got in the way, and he would have ripped them off, but he remembered how soft his new pads were, and he was afraid of what would happen to them.

Forcing himself upright, keeping the curve in his back that he had found helped him to stand on his hind legs, he made his way cautiously along a flat thing that stretched off into the distance.

The four-wheeler that stopped near him would ordinarily have frightened him. But even his new weak nose could sniff through the rank acrid smells of the four-wheeler and find, under the too sweet something on the two-legged female, the real smell, so that when she said, "Hop in, I'll give you a lift," he did not run away. Instead he joined the she.

Her bark was nice, at first.

Later, while he was doing to her what her scent had told him she wanted done, her bark became shrill, and it hurt even his new dull ears. That, of course, did not stop him from doing what had to be done in the spring.

The sounds that still came from her got fainter as he tried to run off on his hind legs. It was not much faster than a walk, but he had to get some of the good feeling of the air against his face, of his lungs panting; he had to run.

Regret was in him that he would not be able to get food for the she and be near her when she whelped, for that was the way of a wolf; but he knew too that he would always know her by her scent, and if possible when her time came he would be at her side.

Not even the spring running was as it should be, for without the excitement of being on all fours, without the nimbleness that had been his, he found that he stumbled too much, there was no thrill.

Besides, around him, the manifold smells told him that many of the two-leggeds were all jammed together. The odor was like a miasma and not even the all-pervading stench that came from the four-wheelers could drown it out.

Coming to a halt, he sat on his haunches, and for the first time he wondered if he were really, as he knew he was, a wolf, for a salty wetness was making itself felt at the corners of his eyes.

Wolves don't cry.

But if he were not a wolf, what then was he? What *were* all the memories that crowded his sick brain?

Tears or no, he knew that he was a wolf. And being a wolf, he must rid himself of this soft pelt, this hairlessness that made him sick at his stomach just to touch it with his too soft pads.

This was his dream, to become again as he had been. To be what was his only reality, a wolf, with a wolf's life and a wolf's loves.

That was his first venture into the reality of the world at large. His second day and night of "limited liberty" sent him hurrying back to his den. Nothing in his wolf life had prepared him for what he found in the midnight streets of the big city. For he found that bears were not the only males from whom the shes had to protect their young . . .

And no animal of which he had ever heard could have moaned, as he heard a man moan, "If only pain didn't hurt so much . . ." and the strangled cries, the thrashing of limbs, the violence, and the sound of a whip. He had never known that humans used whips on themselves too . . .

The third time out, he tried to drug himself the way the two-leggeds did by going to a big place where, on a screen, black and white shadows went through imitations of reality. He didn't go to a show that advertised it was in full glorious color, for he found the other shadows in neutral grays and blacks and whites gave a picture of life the way his wolf eyes were used to looking at it.

It was in this big place where the shadows acted that he found that perhaps he was not unique. His eyes glued to the screen, he watched as a man slowly fell to all fours, threw his head back, bayed at the moon, and then, right before everyone, turned into a wolf!

A *werewolf,* the man was called in the shadow play. And if there were werewolves, he thought, as he sat frozen in the middle of all the seated two-leggeds, then of course there must be *weremen* (would that be the word?) . . . and he was one of them . . .

On the screen the melodrama came to its quick, bloody, foreordained end and the werewolf died when shot by a silver bullet . . . He saw the fur disappear from the skin, and the paws change into hands and feet.

All he had to do, he thought as he left the theater, his mind full of his dream, was to find out how to become a wolf again, without dying. Meanwhile, on every trip out without fail he went to the zoo. The keepers had become used to seeing him. They no longer objected when he threw little bits of meat into the cage to his pups. At first his she had snarled when he came near the bars, but after a while, although still puzzled, and even though she flattened her ears and sniffed constantly at him, she seemed to become resigned to having him stand as near the cage as he possibly could.

His pups were coming along nicely, almost full-grown. He was sorry, in a way, that they had to come to wolfhood behind bars, for now they'd never know the thrill of the spring running, but it was good to know they were safe, and had full bellies, and a den to call their own.

It was when his cubs were almost ready to leave their mother that he found the two-leggeds had a place of books. It was called a *library,* and he had been sent there by the woman in the hospital who was teaching him and some of the other aphasics how to read and write and speak.

Remembering the shadow play about the werewolf, he forced his puzzled eyes to read all that he could find on the baffling subject of lycanthropy.

In every time, in every clime, he found that there were references to two-leggeds who had become four-leggeds, wolves, tigers, panthers . . . but never a reference to an animal that had become a two-legged.

In the course of his reading he found directions whereby a two-legged could change himself. They were complicated and meaningless to him. They involved curious things like a belt made of human skin, with a certain odd number of nail heads arranged in a quaint pattern on the body of the belt. The buckle had to be made under peculiar circumstances, and there were many chants that had to be sung.

It was essential, he read in the crabbed old books, that the two-legged desirous of making the change go to a place where two roads intersected at a specific angle. Then, standing at th intersection, chanting the peculiar words, feeling the human skin belt, the two-legged was told to divest himself of all clothing, and then to relieve his bladder.

Only then, the old books said, could the change take place.

He found that his heart was beating madly when he finished the last of the old books.

For if a two-legged could become a four-legged, surely . . .

After due thought, which was painful, he decided that a human skin belt would be wrong for him. The man in the fur store looked at him oddly when he asked for a length of wolf fur long and narrow, capable of being made into a belt . . .

But he got the fur, and he made the pattern of nail heads, and he did the things the books had described.

It was lucky, he thought as he stood in the deserted zoo, that not far from the cages he had found two roads that cut into each other in just the manner that the books said they should.

Standing where they crossed, his clothes piled on the grass nearby, the belt around his narrow waist, his fingers caressing its fur, his human throat chanting the meaningless words, he found that standing naked was a cold business, and that it was easy to void his bladder as the books had said he must.

Then it was all over.

He had done everything just as he should.

At first nothing happened, and the cold white moon looked down at him, and fear rode up and down his spine that he would be seen by one of the two-leggeds who always wore blue clothes, and he would be taken and put back into that other zoo that was not a zoo even though it had bars on the windows.

But then an aching began in his erect back, and he fell to all fours, and the agony began, and the pain blinded him to everything, to all the strange functional changes that were going on, and it was a long, long time before he dared open his eyes.

Even before he opened them, he could sense that it had happened, for crisp and clear through the night wind he could smell as he knew he should be able to smell. The odors came and they told him old stories.

Getting up on all fours, paying no attention to the clothes that now smelled foully of the two-leggeds, he began to run. His strong claws scrabbled at the cement, and he hurried to the grass and it was wonderful and exciting to feel the good feel of the growing things under his pads. Throwing his long head back he closed his eyes and from deep deep inside he sang a song to the wolves' god, the moon.

His baying excited the animals in the cages so near him, and they began to roar, and scream, and those sounds were good too.

Running through the night, aimlessly, but running, feeling the ground beneath his paws was good . . . so good . . .

And then through the sounds, through all the baying and roaring and screaming from the animals, he heard his she's voice, and he forgot about freedom and the night wind and the cool white moon, and he ran back to the cage where she was.

The zoo attendants were just as baffled when they found the wolf curled up outside the cage near the feeding trough as they had been when they had found the man in the wolf's cage.

The two-legged who was his keeper recognized him, and he was allowed to go back into his cage and then the ecstasy, the spring-and-fall-time ecstasy of being with his she . . .

Slowly, as he became used to his wolfhood again, he forgot about the life outside the cage, and soon it was all a matter that only arose in troubled dreams. And even then his she was there to nuzzle him and wake him if the nightmares got too bad.

Only once after the first few days did any waking memory of his two-legged life return, and that was when a two-legged she passed by his cage pushing a small four-wheeler in front of her.

Her scent was familiar.

So too was the scent of the two-legged cub.

Darting to the front of his cage, he sniffed long and hard.

And for just a moment the woman who was pushing the perambulator that contained her bastard looked deep into his yellow eyes and she knew, as he did, who and what he was.

And the very, very last thought he had about the matter was one of infinite pity for his poor cub, who some white moonlit night was going to drop down on all fours and become furred . . . and go prowling through the dark—in search of what, he would never know . . .

LILA THE WEREWOLF
by PETER S. BEAGLE

Originally published as a chapbook in 1974, "Lila the Werewolf" is an ultramodern werewolf story: sophisticated, sexy, satirical. Its evocation of the "young New Yorker" and the free-wheeling contemporary life-style is flawless, the writing is smooth and literate, and the difficult blending of humor and horror is accomplished with consummate skill and flair. In a word, it is a delight.

And no wonder, considering the substantial and diverse talents of Peter S. Beagle: novelist, poet, essayist, writer of short stories and nonfiction, composer and folk singer, civil libertarian. Born in 1938, a graduate of the University of Pittsburgh and of Wallace Stegner's renowned writing course at Stanford University, Beagle achieved literary reputation at a remarkably early age: his superior fantasy novel, A Fine and Private Place, *was published when he was only twenty-one. Other outstanding long works are the novel* The Last Unicorn *(1968) and two nonfiction titles,* I See By My Outfit *(1965) and* The California Feeling *(1969). His short stories and poems have appeared in such quality publications as* The Atlantic Monthly *and* The Texas Quarterly; *one of his* Atlantic *stories, "Come, Lady Death," was included in the prestigious* O. Henry Prize Stories, *1965.*

Now—meet Lila the Werewolf, her lover Farrell, and her very odd and very possessive mother Bernice . . .

Lila Braun had been living with Farrell for three weeks before she found out she was a werewolf. They had met at a party when the moon was a few nights past the full, and by the time it had withered to the shape of a lemon Lila had moved her suitcase, her guitar, and her Ewan MacColl records two blocks north and four blocks west to Farrell's apartment on Ninety-eighth Street. Girls sometimes happened to Farrell like that.

One evening Lila wasn't in when Farrell came home from work at the bookstore. She had left a note on the table, under a can of tuna fish. The note said that she had gone up to the Bronx to have dinner with her mother, and would probably be spending the night there. The cole slaw in the refrigerator should be finished up before it went bad.

Farrell ate the tuna fish and gave the cole slaw to Grunewald. Grunewald was a half-grown Russian wolfhound, the color of sour milk. He looked like a goat, and had no outside interests except shoes. Farrell was taking care of him for a girl who was away in Europe for the summer. She sent Grunewald a tape recording of her voice every week.

Farrell went to a movie with a friend, and to the West End afterward for beer. Then he walked home alone under the full moon, which was red and yellow. He reheated the morning coffee, played a record, read through a week-old "News Of The Week In Review" section of the Sunday *Times,* and finally took Grunewald up to the roof for the night, as he always did. The dog had been accustomed to sleep in the same bed with his mistress, and the point was not negotiable. Grunewald mooed and scrabbled and butted all the way, but Farrell pushed him out among the looming chimneys and ventilators and slammed the door. Then he came back downstairs and went to bed.

He slept very badly. Grunewald's baying woke him twice; and there was something else that brought him half out of bed, thirsty and lonely, with his sinuses full and the night swaying like a curtain as the figures of his dream scurried offstage. Grunewald seemed to have gone off the air—perhaps it was the silence that had awakened him. Whatever the reason, he never really got back to sleep.

He was lying on his back, watching a chair with his clothes on it becoming a chair again, when the wolf came in through the open window. It landed lightly in the middle of the room and stood there for a moment, breathing quickly, with its ears back. There was blood on the wolf's teeth and tongue, and blood on its chest.

Farrell, whose true gift was for acceptance, especially in the morning, accepted the idea that there was a wolf in his bedroom and lay quite still, closing his eyes as the grim, black-lipped head swung toward him. Having once worked at a zoo, he was able to recognize the beast as a Central European subspecies: smaller and lighter-boned than the northern timber wolf variety, lacking the thick, ruffy mane at the shoulders and having a more pointed nose and ears. His own pedantry always delighted him, even at the worst moments.

Blunt claws clicking on the linoleum, then silent on the throw rug by the bed. Something warm and slow splashed down on his shoulder, but he never moved. The wild smell of the wolf was over him, and that did frighten him at last—to be in the same room with that smell and the Miró prints on the walls. Then he felt the sunlight on his eyelids, and at the same moment he heard the wolf moan softly and deeply. The sound was not repeated, but the breath on his face was suddenly sweet and smoky, dizzyingly familiar after the other. He opened his eyes and saw Lila. She was sitting naked on the edge of the bed, smiling, with her hair down.

"Hello, baby," she said. "Move over, baby. I came home."

Farrell's gift was for acceptance. He was perfectly willing to believe that he had dreamed the wolf; to believe Lila's story of boiled chicken and bitter arguments and sleeplessness on Tremont Avenue; and to forget that her first caress had been to bite him on the shoulder, hard enough so that the blood crusting there as he got up and made breakfast might very well be his own. But then he left the coffee perking and went up to the roof to get Grunewald. He found the dog sprawled in a grove of TV antennas, looking more like a goat than ever, with his throat torn out. Farrell had never actually seen an animal with its throat torn out.

The coffeepot was still chuckling when he came back into the apartment, which struck him as very odd. You could have either werewolves or Pyrex nine-cup percolators in the world, but not both, surely. He told Lila, watching her face. She was a small girl, not really pretty, but with good eyes and a lovely mouth, and with a curious sullen gracefulness that had been the first thing to speak to Farrell at the party. When he told her how Grunewald had looked, she shivered all over, once.

"Ugh!" she said, wrinkling her lips back from her neat white teeth. "Oh baby, how awful. Poor Grunewald. Oh, poor Barbara." Barbara was Grunewald's owner.

"Yeah," Farrell said. "Poor Barbara, making her little tapes in Saint-Tropez." He could not look away from Lila's face.

She said, "Wild dogs. Not really wild, I mean, but with owners. You hear about it sometimes, how a pack of them get together and attack children and things, running through the streets. Then they go home and eat their Dog Yummies. The scary thing is that they probably live right around here. Everybody on the block seems to have a dog. God, that's scary. Poor Grunewald."

"They didn't tear him up much," Farrell said. "It must have been just for the fun of it. And the blood. I didn't know dogs killed for the blood. He didn't have any blood left."

The tip of Lila's tongue appeared between her lips, in the unknowing reflex of a fondled cat. As evidence, it wouldn't have stood up even in old Salem; but Farrell knew the truth then, beyond laziness or rationalization, and went on buttering toast for Lila. Farrell had nothing against werewolves, and he had never liked Grunewald.

He told his friend Ben Kassoy about Lila when they met in the Automat for lunch. He had to shout it over the clicking and rattling all around them, but the people sitting six inches away on either hand never looked up. New Yorkers never eavesdrop. They hear only what they simply cannot help hearing.

Ben said, "I told you about Bronx girls. You better come stay at my place for a few days."

Farrell shook his head. "No, that's silly. I mean, it's only Lila. If she were going to hurt me, she could have done it last night. Besides, it won't happen again for a month. There has to be a full moon."

His friend stared at him. "So what? What's that got to do with anything? You going to go on home as though nothing had happened?"

"Not as though nothing had happened," Farrell said lamely. "The thing is, it's still only Lila, not Lon Chaney or somebody. Look, she goes to her psychiatrist three afternoons a week, and she's got her guitar lesson one night a week, and her pottery class one night, and she cooks eggplant maybe twice a week. She calls her mother every Friday night, and one night a month she turns into a wolf. You see what I'm getting at? It's still Lila, whatever she does, and I just can't get terribly shook about it. A little bit, sure, because what the hell. But I don't know. Anyway, there's no mad rush about it. I'll talk to her when the thing comes up in conversation, just naturally. It's okay."

Ben said, "God damn. You see why nobody has any respect for liberals anymore? Farrell, I know you. You're just scared of hurting her feelings."

"Well, it's that too," Farrell agreed, a little embarrassed. "I hate confrontations. If I break up with her now, she'll think I'm doing it because she's a werewolf. It's awkward, it feels nasty and middle-class. I should have broken up with her the first time I met her mother, or the second time she served the eggplant. Her mother, boy, there's the real werewolf, there's somebody I'd wear wolfsbane against, that woman. Damn, I wish I hadn't found out. I don't think I've ever found out anything about people that I was the better for knowing."

Ben walked all the way back to the bookstore with him, arguing. It touched Farrell, because Ben hated to walk. Before they parted, Ben suggested, "At least you could try some of that stuff you were talking about, the wolfsbane. There's garlic, too—you put some in a little bag and wear it around your neck. Don't laugh, man. If there's such a thing as werewolves, the other stuff must be real, too. Cold iron, silver, oak, running water—"

"I'm not laughing at you," Farrell said, but he was still grinning. "Lila's shrink says she has a rejection thing, very deep-seated, take us years to break through all that scar tissue. Now if I start walking around wearing amulets and mumbling in Latin every time she looks at me, who knows how far it'll set her back? Listen, I've done some things I'm not proud of, but I don't want to mess up anyone's analysis. That's the sin against God." He sighed and slapped Ben lightly on the arm. "Don't worry about it. We'll work it out, I'll talk to her."

But between that night and the next full moon, he found no good, casual way of bringing the subject up. Admittedly, he did not try as hard as he might have: it was true that he feared confrontations more than he feared werewolves, and he would have found it almost as difficult to talk to Lila about her guitar playing, or her pots, or the political arguments she got into at parties. "The thing is," he said to Ben, "it's sort of one more little weakness not to take advantage of. In a way."

They made love often that month. The smell of Lila flowered in the bedroom, where the smell of the wolf still lingered almost visibly, and both of them were wild, heavy zoo smells, warm and raw and fearful, the sweeter for being savage. Farrell held Lila in his arms and knew what she was, and he was always frightened; but he would not have let her go if she had turned into a wolf again as he held her. It was a relief to peer at her while she slept and see how stubby and childish her fingernails were, or that the skin around her mouth was rashy because she had been snacking on chocolate. She loved secret sweets, but they always betrayed her.

It's only Lila after all, he would think as he drowsed off. Her mother used to hide the candy, but Lila always found it. Now she's a big girl, neither married nor in a graduate school, but living in sin with an Irish musician, and she can have all the candy she wants. What kind of a werewolf is that. Poor Lila, practicing *Who killed Davey Moore? Why did he die?* . . .

The note said that she would be working late at the magazine, on layout, and might have to be there all night. Farrell put on about four feet of Telemann laced with Django Reinhardt, took down *The*

Golden Bough, and settled into a chair by the window. The moon shone in at him, bright and thin and sharp as the lid of a tin can, and it did not seem to move at all as he dozed and woke.

Lila's mother called several times during the night, which was interesting. Lila still picked up her mail and most messages at her old apartment, and her two roommates covered for her when necessary, but Farrell was absolutely certain that her mother knew she was living with him. Farrell was an expert on mothers. Mrs. Braun called him Joe each time she called and that made him wonder, for he knew she hated him. Does she suspect that we share a secret? Ah, poor Lila.

The last time the telephone woke him, it was still dark in the room, but the traffic lights no longer glittered through rings of mist, and the cars made a different sound on the warming pavement. A man was saying clearly in the street, "Well, *I'*d shoot'm. *I'*d shoot'm." Farrell let the telephone ring ten times before he picked it up.

"Let me talk to Lila," Mrs. Braun said.

"She isn't here." What if the sun catches her, what if she turns back to herself in front of a cop, or a bus driver, or a couple of nuns going to early Mass? "Lila isn't here, Mrs. Braun."

"I have reason to believe that's not true." The fretful, muscular voice had dropped all pretense of warmth. "I want to talk to Lila."

Farrell was suddenly dry-mouthed and shivering with fury. It was her choice of words that did it. "Well, I have reason to believe you're a suffocating old bitch and a bourgeois Stalinist. How do you like them apples, Mrs. B?" As though his anger had summoned her, the wolf was standing two feet away from him. Her coat was dark and lank with sweat, and yellow saliva was mixed with the blood that strung from her jaws. She looked at Farrell and growled far away in her throat.

"Just a minute," he said. He covered the receiver with his palm. "It's for you," he said to the wolf. "It's your mother."

The wolf made a pitiful sound, almost inaudible, and scuffed at the floor. She was plainly exhausted. Mrs. Braun pinged in Farrell's ear like a bug against a lighted window. "What, what? Hello, what is this? Listen, you put Lila on the phone right now. Hello? I want to talk to Lila. I know she's there."

Farrell hung up just as the sun touched a corner of the window. The wolf became Lila. As before, she only made one sound. The phone rang again, and she picked it up without a glance at Farrell. "Bernice?" Lila always called her mother by her first name. "Yes— no, no—yeah, I'm fine. I'm all right, I just forgot to call. No, I'm all right, will you listen? Bernice, there's no law that says you have to get hysterical. Yes, you are." She dropped down on the bed, grop- ing under her pillow for cigarettes. Farrell got up and began to make coffee.

"Well, there was a little trouble," Lila was saying. "See, I went to the zoo, because I couldn't find—Bernice, I know, I *know*, but that was, what, three months ago. The thing is, I didn't think they'd have their horns so soon. Bernice, I had to, that's all. There'd only been a couple of cats and a—well, sure they chased me, but I—well, Momma, Bernice, what did you want me to do? Just what did you want me to do? You're always so dramatic—why do I shout? I shout because I can't get you to listen to me any other way. You remember what Dr. Schechtman said— what? No, I told you, I just forgot to call. No, that is the reason, that's the real and only reason. Well, whose fault is that? What? Oh, Bernice. Jesus Christ, Bernice. All right, *how* is it Dad's fault?"

She didn't want the coffee, or any breakfast, but she sat at the table in his bathrobe and drank milk greedily. It was the first time he had ever seen her drink milk. Her face was sandy-pale, and her eyes were red. Talking to her mother left her looking as though she had actually gone ten rounds with the woman. Farrell asked, "How long has it been happening?"

"Nine years," Lila said. "Since I hit puberty. First day, cramps; the second day, this. My introduction to womanhood." She snickered and spilled her milk. "I want some more," she said. "Got to get rid of that taste."

"Who knows about it?" he asked. "Pat and Janet?" They were the two girls she had been rooming with.

"God, no. I'd never tell them. I've never told a girl. Bernice knows, of course, and Dr. Schechtman—he's my head doctor. And you now. That's all." Farrell waited. She was a bad liar, and only did it to heighten the effect of the truth. "Well, there was Mickey," she said. "The guy I told you about the first night, you remember? It doesn't matter. He's an acidhead in Vancouver, of all the places. He'll never tell anybody."

He thought: I wonder if any girl has ever talked about me in that sort of voice. I doubt it, offhand. Lila said, "It wasn't too hard to keep it secret. I missed a lot of things. Like I never could go to the riding camp, and I still want to. And the senior play, when I was in high school. They picked me to play the girl in *Liliom*, but then they changed the evening, and I had to say I was sick. And the winter's bad, because the sun sets so early. But actually, it's been a lot less trouble than my goddamn allergies." She made a laugh, but Farrell did not respond.

"Dr. Schechtman says it's a sex thing," she offered. "He says it'll take years and years to cure it. Bernice thinks I should go to someone else, but I don't want to be one of those women who runs around changing shrinks like hair colors. Pat went through five of them in a month one time. Joe, I wish you'd say something. Or just go away."

"Is it only dogs?" he asked. Lila's face did not change, but her chair rattled, and the milk went over again. Farrell said, "Answer me. Do you only kill dogs, and cats, and zoo animals?"

The tears began to come, heavy and slow, bright as knives in the morning sunlight. She could not look at him; and when she tried to speak she could only make creaking, cartilaginous sounds in her throat. *"You* don't know," she whispered at last. "You don't have any idea what it's like."

"That's true," he answered. He was always very fair about that particular point.

He took her hand, and then she really began to cry. Her sobs were horrible to hear, much more frightening to Farrell than any wolf noises. When he held her, she rolled in his arms like a stranded ship with the waves slamming into her. I always get the criers, he thought sadly. My girls always cry, sooner or later. But never for me.

"Don't leave me!" she wept. "I don't know why I came to live with you—I knew it wouldn't work—but don't leave me! There's just Bernice and Dr. Schechtman, and it's so lonely. I want somebody else, I get so lonely. Don't leave me, Joe. I love you, Joe. I love you."

She was patting his face as though she were blind. Farrell stroked her hair and kneaded the back of her neck, wishing that her mother would call again. He felt skilled and weary, and without desire. I'm doing it again, he thought.

"I love you," Lila said. And he answered her, thinking, I'm doing it again. That's the great advantage of making the same mistake a lot of times. You come to know it, and you can study it and get inside it, really make it yours. It's the same good old mistake, except this time the girl's hang-up is different. But it's the same thing. I'm doing it again.

The building superintendent was thirty or fifty: dark, thin, quick and shivering. A Lithuanian or a Latvian, he spoke very little English. He smelled of black friction tape and stale water, and he was strong in the twisting way that a small, lean animal is strong. His eyes were almost purple, and they bulged a little, straining out—the terrible eyes of a herald angel stricken dumb. He roamed in the basement all day, banging on pipes and taking the elevator apart.

The superintendent met Lila only a few hours after Farrell did; on that first night, when she came home with him. At the sight of her the little man jumped back, dropping the two-legged chair he was carrying. He promptly fell over it, and did not try to get up, but cowered there, clucking and gulping, trying to cross himself and make the sign of the horns at the same time. Farrell started to help him up, but he screamed. They could hardly hear the sound.

It would have been merely funny and embarrassing, except for the fact that Lila was equally as frightened of the superintendent, from that moment. She would not go down to the basement for any reason, nor would she enter or leave the house until she was satisfied that he was nowhere near. Farrell had thought then that she took the superintendent for a lunatic.

"I don't know how he knows," he said to Ben. "I guess if you believe in werewolves and vampires, you probably recognize them right away. I don't believe in them at all, and I live with one."

He lived with Lila all through the autumn and the winter. They went out together and came home, and her cooking improved slightly, and she gave up the guitar and got a kitten named Theodora. Sometimes she wept, but not often. She turned out not to be a real crier.

She told Dr. Schechtman about Farrell, and he said that it would probably be a very beneficial relationship for her. It wasn't, but it wasn't a particularly bad one either. Their lovemaking was usually good, though it bothered Farrell to suspect that it was the sense and smell of the Other that excited him. For the rest, they came near being friends. Farrell had known that he did not love Lila before he found out that she was a werewolf, and this made him feel a great deal easier about being bored with her.

"It'll break up by itself in the spring," he said, "like ice."

Ben asked, "What if it doesn't?" They were having lunch in the Automat again. "What'll you do if it just goes on?"

"It's not that easy." Farrell looked away from his friend and began to explore the mysterious, swampy innards of his beef pie. He said, "The trouble is that I know her. That was the real mistake. You shouldn't get to know people if you know you're not going to stay with them, one way or another. It's all right if you come and go in ignorance, but you shouldn't know them."

A week or so before the full moon, she would start to become nervous and strident, and this would continue until the day preceding her transformation. On that day, she was invariably loving, in the tender, desperate manner of someone who is going away; but the next day would see her silent, speaking only when she had to. She always had a cold on the last day, and looked gray and patchy and sick, but she usually went to work anyway.

Farrell was sure, though she never talked about it, that the change into wolf shape was actually peaceful for her, though the returning hurt. Just before moonrise she would take off her clothes and take the pins out of her hair, and stand waiting. Farrell never managed not to close his eyes when she dropped heavily down on all fours; but there was a moment before that when her face would grow a look that he never saw at any other time, except when they were making love. Each time he saw it, it struck him as a look of wondrous joy at not being Lila anymore.

"See, I know her," he tried to explain to Ben. "She only likes to go to color movies, because wolves can't see color. She can't stand the Modern Jazz Quartet, but that's all she plays the first couple of days afterward. Stupid things like that. Never gets high at parties, because she's afraid she'll start talking. It's hard to walk away, that's all. Taking what I know with me."

Ben asked, "Is she still scared of the super?"

"Oh, God," Farrell said. "She got his dog last time. It was a Dalmatian—good-looking animal. She didn't know it was his. He doesn't hide when he sees her now, he just gives her a look like a stake through the heart. That man is a really classy hater, a natural. I'm scared of him myself." He stood up and began to pull on his overcoat. "I wish he'd get turned onto her mother. Get some practical use out of him. Did I tell you she wants me to call her Bernice?"

Ben said, "Farrell, if I were you, I'd leave the country. I would."

They went out into the February drizzle that sniffled back and forth between snow and rain. Farrell did not speak until they reached the corner where he turned toward the bookstore. Then he said very softly, "Damn, you have to be so careful. Who wants to know what people turn into?"

May came, and a night when Lila once again stood naked at the window, waiting for the moon. Farrell fussed with dishes and garbage bags, and fed the cat. These moments were always awkward. He had just asked her, "You want to save what's left of the rice?" when the telephone rang.

It was Lila's mother. She called two and three times a week now. "This is Bernice. How's my Irisher this evening?"

"I'm fine, Bernice," Farrell said. Lila suddenly threw back her head and drew a heavy, whining breath. The cat hissed silently and ran into the bathroom.

"I called to inveigle you two uptown this Friday," Mrs. Braun said. "A couple of old friends are coming over, and I know if I don't get some young people in we'll just sit around and talk about what went wrong with the Progressive Party. The Old Left. So if you could sort of sweet-talk our girl into spending an evening in Squaresville—"

"I'll have to check with Lila." She's *doing* it, he thought, that terrible woman. Every time I talk to her, I sound married. I see what she's doing, but she goes right ahead anyway. He said, "I'll talk to her in the morning." Lila struggled in the moonlight, between dancing and drowning.

"Oh," Mrs. Braun said. "Yes, of course. Have her call me back." She sighed. "It's such a comfort to me to know you're there. Ask her if I should fix a fondue."

Lila made a handsome wolf: tall and broad-chested for a female, moving as easily as water sliding over stone. Her coat was dark brown, showing red in the proper light, and there were white places on her breast. She had pale green eyes, the color of the sky when a hurricane is coming.

Usually she was gone as soon as the changing was over, for she never cared for him to see her in her wolf form. But tonight she came slowly toward him, walking in a strange way, with her hindquarters almost dragging. She was making a high, soft sound, and her eyes were not focusing on him.

"What is it?" he asked foolishly. The wolf whined and skulked under the table, rubbing against the leg. Then she lay on her belly and rolled and as she did so the sound grew in her throat until it became an odd, sad, thin cry; not a hunting howl, but a shiver of longing turned into breath.

"Jesus, don't do that!" Farrell gasped. But she sat up and howled again, and a dog answered her from somewhere near the river. She wagged her tail and whimpered.

Farrell said, "The super'll be up here in two minutes flat. What's the matter with you?" He heard footsteps and low frightened voices in the apartment above them. Another dog howled, this one nearby, and the wolf wriggled a little way toward the window on her haunches, like a baby, scooting. She looked at him over her shoulder, shuddering violently. On an impulse, he picked up the phone and called her mother.

Watching the wolf as she rocked and slithered and moaned, he described her actions to Mrs. Braun. "I've never seen her like this," he said. "I don't know what's the matter with her."

"Oh, my God," Mrs. Braun whispered. She told him.

When he was silent, she began to speak very rapidly. "It hasn't happened for such a long time. Schechtman gives her pills, but she must have run out and forgotten—she's always been like that, since she was little. All the thermos bottles she used to leave on the school bus, and every week her piano music—"

"I wish you'd told me before," he said. He was edging very cautiously toward the open window. The pupils of the wolf's eyes were pulsing with her quick breaths.

"It isn't a thing you tell people!" Lila's mother wailed in his ear. "How do you think it was for me when she brought her first little boyfriend—'' Farrell dropped the phone and sprang for the window. He had the inside track, and he might have made it, but she turned her head and snarled so wildly that he fell back. When he reached the window, she was already two fire-escape landings below, and there was eager yelping waiting for her in the street.

Dangling and turning just above the floor, Mrs. Braun heard Farrell's distant yell, followed immediately by a heavy thumping on the door. A strange, tattered voice was shouting unintelligibly beyond the knocking. Footsteps crashed by the receiver and the door opened.

"My dog, my dog!" the strange voice mourned. "My dog, my dog, my dog!"

"I'm sorry about your dog," Farrell said. "Look, please go away. I've got work to do."

"I got work," the voice said. "I know my work." It climbed and spilled into another language, out of which English words jutted like broken bones. "Where is she? Where is she? She kill my dog."

"She's not here." Farrell's own voice changed on the last word. It seemed a long time before he said, "You'd better put that away."

Mrs. Braun heard the howl as clearly as though the wolf were running beneath her own window: lonely and insatiable, with a kind of gasping laughter in it. The other voice began to scream. Mrs. Braun caught the phrase *silver bullet* several times. The door slammed; then opened and slammed again.

Farrell was the only man of his own acquaintance who was able to play back his dreams while he was having them: to stop them in mid-flight, no matter how fearful they might be—or how lovely—and run them over and over studying them in his sleep, until the most terrifying reel became at once utterly harmless and unbearably familiar. This night that he spent running after Lila was like that.

He would find them congregated under the marquee of an apartment house, or romping around the moonscape of a construction site: ten or fifteen males of all races, creeds, colors, and previous conditions of servitude; whining and yapping, pissing against tires, inhaling indiscriminately each other and the lean, grinning bitch they surrounded. She frightened them, for she growled more wickedly than coyness demanded, and where she snapped, even in play, bone showed. Still they tumbled on her and over her, biting her neck and ears in their turn; and she snarled but she did not run away.

Never, at least, until Farrell came charging upon them, shrieking like any cuckold, kicking at the snuffling lovers. Then she would turn and race off into the spring dark, with her thin, dreamy howl floating behind her like the train of a smoky gown. The dogs followed, and so did Farrell, calling and cursing. They always lost him quickly, that jubilant marriage procession, leaving him stumbling down rusty iron ladders into places where he fell over garbage cans. Yet he would come upon them as inevitably in time, loping along Broadway or trotting across Columbus Avenue toward the Park; he would hear them in the tennis courts near the river, breaking down the nets over Lila and her moment's Ares. There were dozens of them now, coming from all directions. They stank of their joy, and he threw stones at them and shouted, and they ran.

And the wolf ran at their head, on sidewalks and on wet grass; her tail waving contentedly, but her eyes still hungry, and her howl growing ever more warning than wistful. Farrell knew that she must have blood before sunrise, and that it was both useless and dangerous to follow her. But the night wound and unwound itself, and he knew the same things over and over, and ran down the same streets, and saw the same couples walk wide of him, thinking he was drunk.

Mrs. Braun kept leaping out of a taxi that pulled up next to him; usually at corners where the dogs had just piled by, knocking over the crates stacked in market doorways and spilling the newspapers at the subway kiosks. Standing in broccoli, in black taffeta, with a front like a ferryboat—yet as lean in the hips as her wolf-daughter —with her plum-colored hair all loose, one arm lifted, and her orange mouth pursed in a bellow, she was no longer Bernice but a wronged fertility goddess getting set to blast the harvest. "We've got to split up!" she would roar at Farrell, and each time it sounded like a sound idea. Yet he looked for her whenever he lost Lila's trail, because she never did.

The superintendent kept turning up too, darting after Farrell out of alleys or cellar entrances, or popping from the freight elevators that load through the sidewalk. Farrell would hear his numberless passkeys clicking on the flat piece of wood tucked into his belt.

"You see her? You see her, the wolf, kill my dog?" Under the fat, ugly moon, the Army .45 glittered and trembled like his own mad eyes.

"Mark with a cross." He would pat the barrel of the gun and shake it under Farrell's nose like a maracas. "Mark with a cross, bless by a priest. Three silver bullets. She kill my dog."

Lila's voice would come sailing to them then, from up in Harlem or away near Lincoln Center, and the little man would whirl and dash down in to the earth, disappearing into the crack between two slabs of sidewalk. Farrell understood quite clearly that the superintendent was hunting Lila underground, using the keys that only superintendents have to take elevators down to the black sub-sub-basements, far below the bicycle rooms and the wet, shaking laundry rooms, and below the furnace rooms, below the passages walled with electricity meters and roofed with burly steam pipes; down to the realms where the great dim water mains roll like whales, and the gas lines hump and preen, down where the roots of the apartment houses fade together; and so along under the city, scrabbling through secret ways with silver bullets, and his keys rapping against the piece of wood. He never saw Lila, but he was never very far behind her.

Cutting across parking lots, pole-vaulting between locked bumpers, edging and dancing his way through fluorescent gaggles of haughty children; leaping uptown like a salmon against the current of the theater crowds; walking quickly past the random killing faces that floated down the night tide like unexploded mines, and especially avoiding the crazy faces that wanted to tell him what it was like to be crazy—so Farrell pursued Lila Braun, of Tremont Avenue and CCNY, in the city all night long. Nobody offered to help him, or tried to head off the dangerous-looking bitch bounding along with the delirious gaggle of admirers streaming after her; but then, the dogs had to fight through the same clenched legs and vengeful bodies that Farrell did. The crowds slowed Lila down, but he felt relieved whenever she turned towards the emptier streets. *She must have blood soon, somewhere.*

Farrell's dreams eventually lost their clear edge after he played them back a certain number of times, and so it was with the night. The full moon skidded down the sky, thinning like a tatter of butter in a skillet, and remembered scenes began to fold sloppily into each other. The sound of Lila and the dogs grew fainter whichever way he followed. Mrs. Braun blinked on and off at longer intervals; and in dark doorways and under subway gratings, the superintendent burned like a corposant, making the barrel of his pistol run rainbow. At last he lost Lila for good, and with that it seemed that he woke.

It was still night, but not dark, and he was walking slowly home on Riverside Drive through a cool, grainy fog. The moon had set, but the river was strangely bright: glittering gray as far up as the Bridge, where headlights left shiny, wet paths like snails. There was no one else on the street.

"Dumb broad," he said aloud. "The hell with it. She wants to mess around, let her mess around." He wondered whether werewolves could have cubs, and what sort of cubs they might be. Lila must have turned on the dogs by now, for the blood. Poor dogs, he thought. They were all so dirty and innocent and happy with her.

"A moral lesson for all of us," he announced sententiously. "Don't fool with strange, eager ladies, they'll kill you." He was a little hysterical. Then, two blocks ahead of him, he saw the gaunt shape in the gray light of the river; alone now, and hurrying. Farrell did not call to her, but as soon as he began to run, the wolf wheeled and faced him. Even at that distance, her eyes were stained and streaked and wild. She showed all the teeth on one side of her mouth, and she growled like fire.

Farrell trotted steadily toward her, crying, "Go home, go home! Lila, you dummy, get on home, it's morning!" She growled terribly, but when Farrell was less than a block away she turned again and dashed across the street, heading for West End Avenue. Farrell said, "Good girl, that's it," and limped after her.

In the hours before sunrise on West End Avenue, many people came out to walk their dogs. Farrell had done it often with poor Grunewald to know many of the dawn walkers by sight, and some to talk to. A fair number of them were whores and homosexuals, both of whom always seem to have dogs in New York. Quietly, almost always alone, they drifted up and down the Nineties, piloted by their small, fussy beasts, but moving in a kind of fugitive truce with the city and the night that was ending. Farrell sometimes fancied that they were all asleep, and that this hour was the only true rest they ever got.

He recognized Robie by his two dogs, Scone and Crumpet. Robie lived in the apartment directly below Farrell's, usually unhappily. The dogs were horrifying little homebrews of Chihuahua and Yorkshire terrier, but Robie loved them.

Crumpet, the male, saw Lila first. He gave a delighted yap of welcome and proposition (according to Robie, Scone bored him, and he liked big girls anyway) and sprang to meet her, yanking his leash through Robie's slack hand. The wolf was almost upon him before he realized his fatal misunderstanding and scuttled desperately in retreat, meowing with utter terror.

Robie wailed, and Farrell ran as fast as he could, but Lila knocked Crumpet off his feet and slashed his throat while he was still in the air. Then she crouched on the body, nuzzling it in a dreadful way.

Robie actually came within a step of leaping upon Lila and trying to drag her away from his dead dog. Instead, he turned on Farrell as he came panting up, and began hitting him with a good deal of strength and accuracy. "Damn you, damn you!" he sobbed. Little Scone ran away around the corner, screaming like a mandrake.

Farrell put up his arms and went with the punches, all the while yelling at Lila until his voice ripped. But the blood frenzy had her, and Farrell had never imagined what she must be like at those times. Somehow she had spared the dogs who had loved her all night, but she was nothing but thirst now. She pushed and kneaded Crumpet's body as though she were nursing.

All along the avenue, the morning dogs were barking like trumpets. Farrell ducked away from Robie's soft fists and saw them coming; tripping over their trailing leashes, running too fast for their stubby legs. They were small, spoiled beasts, most of them, overweight and shortwinded, and many were not young. Their owners cried unmanly pet names after them, but they waddled gallantly toward their deaths, barking promises far bigger than themselves, and none of them looked back.

She looked up with her muzzle red to the eyes. The dogs did falter then, for they knew murder when they smelled it, and even their silly, nearsighted eyes understood vaguely what creature faced them. But they knew the smell of love too, and they were all gentlemen.

She killed the first two to reach her—a spitz and a cocker spaniel

—with two snaps of her jaws. But before she could settle down to her meal, three Pekes were scrambling up to her, though they would have had to stand on each others' shoulders. Lila whirled without a sound, and they fell away, rolling and yelling but unhurt. As soon as she turned, the Pekes were at her again, joined now by a couple of valiant poodles. Lila got one of the poodles when she turned again.

Robie had stopped beating on Farrell, and was leaning against a traffic light, being sick. But other people were running up now: a middle-aged black man, crying; a plump youth in a plastic car coat and bedroom slippers, who kept whimpering, "Oh God, she's eating them, look at her, she's really eating them!"; two lean, ageless girls in slacks, both with foamy beige hair. They all called wildly to their unheeding dogs, and they all grabbed at Farrell and shouted in his face. Cars began to stop.

The sky was thin and cool, rising pale gold, but Lila paid no attention to it. She was ramping under the swarm of little dogs; rearing and spinning in circles, snarling blood. The dogs were terrified and bewildered, but they never swerved from their labor. The smell of love told them that they were welcome, however ungraciously she seemed to receive them. Lila shook herself, and a pair of squealing dachshunds, hobbled in a double harness, tumbled across the sidewalk to end at Farrell's feet. They scrambled up and immediately towed themselves back into the maelstrom. Lila bit one of them almost in half, but the other dachshund went on trying to climb her hindquarters, dragging his ripped comrade with him. Farrell began to laugh.

The black man said, "You think it's funny?" and hit him. Farrell sat down, still laughing. The man stood over him, embarrassed, offering Farrell his handkerchief. "I'm sorry, I shouldn't have done that," he said. "But your dog killed my dog."

"She isn't my dog," Farrell said. He moved to let a man pass between them, and then saw that it was the superintendent, holding his pistol with both hands. Nobody noticed him until he fired; but Farrell pushed one of the foamy-haired girls, and she stumbled against the superintendent as the gun went off. The silver bullet broke a window in a parked car.

The superintendent fired again while the echoes of the first shot were still clapping back and forth between the houses. A Pomeranian screamed that time, and a woman cried out, "Oh, my God, he shot Borgy!" But the crowd was crumbling away, breaking into its individual components like pills on television. The watching cars had sped off at the sight of the gun, and the faces that had been peering down from windows disappeared. Except for Farrell, the few people who remained were scattered halfway down the block. The sky was brightening swiftly now.

"For God's sake, don't let him!" the same woman called from the shelter of a doorway. But two men made shushing gestures at her, saying, "It's all right, he knows how to use that thing. Go ahead, buddy."

The shots had at last frightened the little dogs away from Lila. She crouched among the twitching splotches of fur, with her muzzle wrinkled back and her eyes more black than green. Farrell saw a plaid rag that had been a dog jacket protruding from under her body. The superintendent stooped and squinted over the gun barrel, aiming with grotesque care, while the men cried to him to shoot. He was too far from the werewolf for her to reach him before he fired the last silver bullet, though he would surely die before she died. His lips were moving as he took aim.

Two long steps would have brought Farrell up behind the superintendent. Later he told himself that he had been afraid of the pistol, because that was easier than remembering how he had felt when he looked at Lila. Her tongue never stopped lapping around her dark jaws; and even as she set herself to spring, she lifted a bloody paw to her mouth. Farrell thought of her padding in the bedroom, breathing on his face. The superintendent grunted and Farrell closed his eyes. Yet even then he expected to find himself doing something.

Then he heard Mrs. Braun's unmistakable voice. *"Don't you dare!"* She was standing between Lila and the superintendent: one shoe gone, and the heel off the other one; her knit dress torn at the shoulder, and her face tired and smudgy. But she pointed a finger at the startled superintendent, and he stepped quickly back, as though she had a pistol, too.

"Lady, that's a wolf," he protested nervously. "Lady, you please get, get out of the way. That's a wolf, I go shoot her now."

"I want to see your license for that gun." Mrs. Braun held out her hand. The superintendent blinked at her, muttering in despair. She said, "Do you know that you can be sent to prison for twenty years for carrying a concealed weapon in this state? Do you know what the fine is for having a gun without a license? The fine is Five. Thousand. Dollars." The men down the street were shouting at her, but she swung around to face the creature snarling among the little dead dogs.

"Come on, Lila," she said. "Come on home with Bernice. I'll make tea and we'll talk. It's been a long time since we've really talked, you know? We used to have nice long talks when you were little, but we don't anymore." The wolf had stopped growling, but she was crouching even lower, and her ears were still flat against her head. Mrs. Braun said, "Come on, baby. Listen, I know what—you'll call in sick at the office and stay for a few days. You'll get a good rest, and maybe we'll even look around a little for a new doctor, what do you say? Schechtman hasn't done a thing for you, I never liked him. Come on home, honey. Momma's here, Bernice knows." She took a step toward the silent wolf, holding out her hand.

The superintendent gave a desperate, wordless cry and pumped forward, clumsily shoving Mrs. Braun to one side. He leveled the pistol point-blank, wailing, "My dog, my dog!" Lila was in the air when the gun went off, and her shadow sprang after her, for the sun had risen. She crumpled down across a couple of dead Pekes. Their blood dabbled her breasts and her pale throat.

Mrs. Braun screamed like a lunch whistle. She knocked the superintendent into the street and sprawled over Lila, hiding her completely from Farrell's sight. "Lila, Lila," she keened her daughter, "poor baby, you never had a chance. He killed you because you were different, the way they kill everything different." Farrell approached her and stooped down, but she pushed him against a wall without looking up. "Lila, Lila, poor baby, poor darling, maybe it's better, maybe you're happy now. You never had a chance, poor Lila."

The dog owners were edging slowly back, and the surviving dogs were running to them. The superintendent squatted on the curb with his head in his arms. A weary, muffled voice said, "For God's sake, Bernice, would you get up off me? You don't have to stop yelling, just get off."

When she stood up, the cars began to stop in the street again. It made it very difficult for the police to get through.

Nobody pressed charges, because there was no one to lodge them against. The killer dog—or wolf, as some insisted—was gone; and if she had an owner, he could not be found. As for the people who had actually seen the wolf turn into a young girl when the sunlight touched her; most of them managed not to have seen it, though they never really forgot. There were a few who knew quite well what they had seen, and never forgot it either, but they never said anything. They did, however, chip in to pay the superintendent's fine for possessing an unlicensed handgun. Farrell gave what he could.

Lila vanished out of Farrell's life before sunset. She did not go uptown with her mother, but packed her things and went to stay with friends in the Village. Later he heard that she was living on Christopher Street; and later still, that she had moved to Berkeley and gone back to school. He never saw her again.

"It had to be like that," he told Ben once. "We got to know too much about each other. See, there's another side to knowing. She couldn't look at me."

"You mean because you saw her with all those dogs? Or because she knew you'd have let that little nut shoot her?" Farrell shook his head.

"It was that, I guess, but it was more something else, something I know. When she sprang, just as he shot at her that last time, she wasn't leaping at him. She was going straight for her mother. She'd have got her too, if it hadn't been sunrise."

Ben whistled softly. "I wonder if her old lady knows."

"Bernice knows everything about Lila," Farrell said.

Mrs. Braun called him nearly two years later to tell him that Lila was getting married. It must have cost her a good deal of money and ingenuity to find him (where Farrell was living then, the telephone line was open for four hours a day), but he knew by the spitefulness in the static that she considered it money well spent.

"He's at Stanford," she crackled. "A research psychologist. They're going to Japan for their honeymoon."

"That's fine," Farrell said. "I'm really happy for her, Bernice."

He hesitated before he asked, "Does he know about Lila? I mean, about what happens—?"

"Does he know?" she cried. "He's proud of it—he thinks it's wonderful! It's his field!"

"That's great. That's fine. Goodbye, Bernice. I really am glad."

And he was glad, and a little wistful, thinking about it. The girl he was living with here had a really strange hang-up.

Part Three:

TWO VIEWS OF TOMORROW

A PROPHECY OF MONSTERS
by CLARK ASHTON SMITH

Assume the werewolf does exist in reality, not just in folklore and the imagination of fiction writers. What would the future hold for him? Would he continue to exist in the shadows, alone, or would he be forced out into the light by advances in science and technology, forced to join into packs of his own kind in an effort to survive? And how would man deal with him in any case, in the world of tomorrow?

This story by Clark Ashton Smith, and the one by Brian W. Aldiss which follows, offer two possible answers.

Told with irony and wry wit, "A Prophecy of Monsters" blends the fields of fantasy and science fiction with a deftness not often seen in the short-short. It also presents, in less than a thousand words, an entire future society in perfect microcosm—yet another remarkable achievement.

Clark Ashton Smith began his career as a poet; with the help of San Francisco litterateur George Sterling he published The Star-Treader *(1912) and several other volumes of poetry. But it is as a writer of macabre and science-fantasy stories that he is best known. The quality of his fiction, most of which was published in* Weird Tales *in the '20s and '30s and later collected in such Arkham House books as* Out of Space and Time, Genius Loci, *and* The Abominations of Yondo, *has made him a cult figure among today's aficionados; he is regarded, along with H.P. Lovecraft and August Derleth, as one of the finest craftsmen of the "modern" weird tale.*

The change occurred before he could divest himself of more than his coat and scarf. He had only to step out of the shoes, to shed the socks with two backward kicks, and shuffle off the trousers from his lean hind legs and belly. But he was still deep-chested after the change, and his shirt was harder to loosen. His hackles rose with rage as he slewed his head around and tore it away with hasty fangs in a flurry of falling buttons and rags. Tossing off the last irksome ribbons, he regretted his haste. Always heretofore he had been careful in regard to small details. The shirt was mono-grammed. He must remember to collect all the tatters later. He could stuff them in his pockets, and wear the coat buttoned closely on his way home, when he had changed back.

Hunger snarled within him, mounting from belly to throat, from throat to mouth. It seemed that he had not eaten for a month—for a month of months. Raw butcher's meat was never fresh enough: it had known the coldness of death and refrigeration, and had lost all vital essence. Long ago there had been other meals, warm, and sauced with still-spurting blood. But now the thin memory merely served to exasperate his ravening.

Chaos raced within his brain. Inconsequently, for an instant, he recalled the first warning of his malady, preceding even the distaste for cooked meat: the aversion, the allergy, to silver forks and spoons. It had soon extended to other objects of the same metal. He had cringed even from the touch of coinage, had been forced to use paper and refuse change. Steel, too, was a substance un-friendly to beings like him; and the time came when he could abide it little more than silver.

What made him think of such matters now, setting his teeth on edge with repugnance, choking him with something worse than nausea?

The hunger returned, demanding swift appeasement. With clumsy pads he pushed his discarded raiment under the shrubbery, hiding it from the heavy-jowled moon. It was the moon that drew the tides of madness in his blood, and compelled the metamorphosis. But it must not betray to any chance passer the garments he would need later, when he returned to human semblance after the night's hunting.

The night was warm and windless, and the woodland seemed to hold its breath. There were, he knew, other monsters abroad in that year of the twenty-first century. The vampire still survived, subtler and deadlier, protected by man's incredulity. And he himself was not the only lycanthrope: his brothers and sisters ranged unchallenged, preferring the darker urban jungles, while he, being country-bred, still kept the ancient ways. Moreover, there were monsters unknown as yet to myth and superstition. But these too were mostly haunters of cities. He had no wish to meet any of them. And of such meeting, surely, there was small likelihood.

He followed a crooked lane, reconnoitered previously. It was too narrow for cars, and it soon became a mere path. At the path's forking he ensconced himself in the shadow of a broad, mistletoe-blotted oak. The path was used by certain late pedestrians who lived even farther out from town. One of them might come along at any moment.

Whimpering a little, with the hunger of a starved hound, he waited. He was a monster that nature had made, ready to obey nature's first commandment: *Thou shalt kill and eat.* He was a thing of terror . . . a fable whispered around prehistoric cavern fires . . . a miscegenation allied by later myth to the powers of hell and sorcery. But in no sense was he akin to those monsters beyond nature, the spawn of a newer and blacker magic, who killed without hunger and without malevolence.

He had only minutes to wait, before his tensing ears caught the far-off vibration of footsteps. The steps came rapidly nearer, seeming to tell him much as they came. They were firm and resilient, tireless and rhythmic, telling of youth or of full maturity untouched by age. They told, surely, of a worthwhile prey; of prime lean meat and vital, abundant blood.

There was a slight froth on the lips of the one who waited. He had ceased to whimper. He crouched closer to the ground for the anticipated leap.

The path ahead was heavily shadowed. Dimly, moving fast, the walker appeared in the shadows. He seemed to be all that the watcher had surmised from the sound of his footsteps. He was tall and well-shouldered, swinging with a lithe sureness, a precision of powerful tendon and muscle. His head was a faceless blur in the gloom. He was hatless, clad in dark coat and trousers such as anyone might wear. His steps rang with the assurance of one who has nothing to fear, and has never dreamt of the crouching creatures of darkness.

Now he was almost abreast of the watcher's covert. The watcher could wait no longer but sprang from his ambush of shadow, towering high upon the stranger as his hind paws left the ground. His rush was irresistible, as always. The stranger toppled backward, sprawling and helpless, as others had done, and the assailant bent to the bare throat that gleamed more enticingly than that of a siren.

It was a strategy that had never failed . . . until now . . .

The shock, the consternation, had hurled him away from that prostrate figure and had forced him back upon teetering haunches. It was the shock, perhaps, that caused him to change again, swiftly, resuming human shape before his hour. As the change began, he spat out several broken lupine fangs; and then he was spitting human teeth.

The stranger rose to his feet, seemingly unshaken and undismayed. He came forward in a rift of revealing moonlight, stooping to a half crouch, and flexing his beryllium-steel fingers enameled with flesh pink.

"Who—what—are you?" quavered the werewolf.

The stranger did not bother to answer as he advanced, every synapse of the computing brain transmitting the conditioned message, translated into simplest binary terms, "Dangerous. Not human. *Kill!*"

FULL SUN
by BRIAN W. ALDISS

Brian Aldiss's "view of tomorrow" is similar to the Smith story in that it also postulates a future society in which werewolves are methodically being hunted down by both humans and machines—but in treatment, development, tone, and conclusion it is wholly different. Its last paragraph, in particular, makes it an appropriate final entry for this anthology.

But more than that, "Full Sun" (which was first published in the second volume of Damon Knight's critically acclaimed Orbit *series of original science-fiction anthologies) is notable for its fine writing, careful plotting, and strong extrapolative portrait of what life might be like for humans (and werewolves) in the far future. Balank, Cyfal, Gondalug—and the trundler—are each memorable creations.*

Born in Manchester, England, in 1925, Brian Aldiss began publishing science fiction in the mid-50s. Since then he has established himself as one of the premier writers in the field, with numerous short stories and such novels as Barefoot in the Head *(1969) and the first and best of the "new" Frankenstein books,* Frankenstein Unbound *(1973). He is the recipient of several Hugo and Nebula awards for excellence in science fiction, and the author of a critical history of the genre,* The Billion-Year Spree, *published in 1972.*

The shadows of the endless trees length-ened toward evening and then disappeared, as the sun was con-sumed by a great pile of cloud on the horizon. Balank was ill at ease, taking his laser rifle from the trundler and tucking it under his arm, although it meant more weight to carry uphill and he was tiring.

The trundler never tired. They had been climbing these hills most of the day, as Balank's thigh muscles informed him, and he had been bent almost double under the oak trees, with the machine always matching his pace beside him, keeping up the hunt.

During much of the wearying day, their instruments told them that the werewolf was fairly close. Balank remained alert, suspicious of every tree. In the last half-hour, though, the scent had faded. When they reached the top of this hill, they would rest—or the man would. The clearing at the top was near now. Under Balank's boots, the layer of dead leaves was thinning.

He had spent too long with his head bent toward the brown-gold carpet; even his retinas were tired. Now he stopped, breathing the sharp air deeply, and stared about. The view behind them, across tumbled and almost uninhabited country, was magnificent, but Ba-lank gave it scarcely a glance. The infrared warning on the trundler sounded, and the machine pointed a slender rod at a man-sized heat source ahead of them. Balank saw the man almost at the same moment as the machine.

The stranger was standing half concealed behind the trunk of a tree, gazing uncertainly at the trundler and Balank. When Balank raised a hand in tentative greeting, the stranger responded hesi-tantly. When Balank called out his identification number, the man came cautiously into the open, replying with his own number. The trundler searched in its files, issued an okay, and they moved forward.

As they got level with the man, they saw he had a small mobile hut pitched behind him. He shook hands with Balank, exchanging personal signals, and gave his name as Cyfal.

Balank was a tall, slender man, almost hairless, with the closed expression on his face that might be regarded as characteristic of his epoch. Cyfal, on the other hand, was as slender but much shorter, so that he appeared stockier; his thatch of hair covered all his skull and obtruded slightly onto his face. Something in his manner, or perhaps the expression around his eyes, spoke of the rare type of man whose existence was chiefly spent outside the city.

"I am the timber officer for this region," he said, and indicated his wristcaster as he added, "I was notified you might be in this area, Balank."

"Then you'll know I'm after the werewolf."

"*The* werewolf? There are plenty of them moving through this region, now that the human population is concentrated almost entirely in the cities."

Something in the tone of the remark sounded like social criticism to Balank; he glanced at the trundler without replying.

"Anyhow, you've got a good night to go hunting him," Cyfal said.

"How do you mean?"

"Full moon."

Balank gave no answer. He knew better than Cyfal, he thought, that when the moon was at full, the werewolves reached their time of greatest power.

The trundler was ranging about nearby, its antenna slowly spinning. It made Balank uneasy. He followed it. Man and machine stood together on the edge of a little cliff behind the mobile hut. The cliff was like the curl of foam on the peak of a giant Pacific comber, for here the great wave of earth that was this hill reached its highest point. Beyond, in broken magnificence, it fell down into fresh valleys. The way down was clothed in beeches, just as the way up had been in oaks.

"That's the valley of the Pracha. You can't see the river from here." Cyfal had come up behind them.

"Have you seen anyone who might have been the werewolf ? His real name is Gondalug, identity number YB5921 stroke AS25061, City Zagrad."

Cyfal said, "I saw someone this way this morning. There was more than one of them, I believe." Something in his manner made Balank look at him closely. "I didn't speak to any of them, nor them to me."

"You know them?"

"I've spoken to many men out here in the silent forests, and found out later they were werewolves. They never harmed me."

Balank said, "But you're afraid of them?"

The half-question broke down Cyfal's reserve. "Of course I'm afraid of them. They're not human—not real men. They're enemies of men. They are, aren't they? They have powers greater than ours."

"They can be killed. They haven't machines, as we have. They're not a serious menace."

"You talk like a city man! How long have you been hunting after this one?"

"Eight days. I had a shot at him once with the laser, but he was gone. He's a gray man, very hairy, sharp features."

"You'll stay and have supper with me? Please. I need someone to talk to."

For supper, Cyfal ate part of a dead wild animal he had cooked. Privately revolted, Balank ate his own rations out of the trundler. In this and other ways, Cyfal was an anachronism. Hardly any timber was needed nowadays in the cities, or had been for millions of years. There remained some marginal uses for wood, necessitating a handful of timber officers, whose main job was to fix signals on old trees that had fallen dangerously, so that machines could fly over later and extract them like rotten teeth from the jaws of the forest. The post of timber officer was being filled more and more by machines, as fewer men were to be found each generation who would take on such a dangerous and lonely job far from the cities.

Over the eons of recorded history, mankind had raised machines that made his cities places of delight. Machines had replaced man's early inefficient machines; machines had replanned forms of transport; machines had come to replan man's life for him. The old stone jungles of man's brief adolescence were buried as deep in memory as the coal jungles of the Carboniferous.

Far away in the pile of discarded yesterdays, man and machines had found how to create life. New foods were produced, neither meat nor vegetable, and the ancient wheel of the past was broken forever, for now the link between man and the land was severed: Agriculture, the task of Adam, was as dead as steamships.

Mental attitudes were molded by physical change. As the cities became self-supporting, so mankind needed only cities and the resources of cities. Communications between city and city became so good that physical travel was no longer necessary; city was separated from city by unchecked vegetation as surely as planet is cut off from planet. Few of the hairless denizens of the cities ever thought of outside; those who went physically outside invariably had some element of the abnormal in them.

"The werewolves grow up in cities as we do," Balank said. "It's only in adolescence they break away and seek the wilds. You knew that, I suppose?"

Cyfal's overhead light was unsteady, flickering in an irritating way. "Let's not talk of werewolves after sunset," he said.

"The machines will hunt them all down in time."

"Don't be so sure of that. They're worse at detecting a werewolf than a man is."

"I suppose you realize that's social criticism, Cyfal?"

Cyfal pulled a long sour face and discourteously switched on his wristphone. After a moment, Balank did the same. The operator came up at once, and he asked to be switched to the news satellite.

He wanted to see something fresh on the current time exploration project, but there was nothing new on the files. He was advised to dial back in an hour. Looking over at Cyfal, he saw the timber officer had turned to a dance show of some sort; the cavorting figures in the little projection were badly distorted from this angle. He rose and went to the door of the hut.

The trundler stood outside, ever alert, ignoring him. An untrustworthy light lay over the clearing. Deep twilight reigned, shot through by the rays of the newly risen moon; he was surprised how fast the day had drained away.

Suddenly, he was conscious of himself as an entity, living, with a limited span of life, much of which had already drained away unregarded. The moment of introspection was so uncharacteristic of him that he was frightened. He told himself it was high time he traced down the werewolf and got back to the city: too much solitude was making him morbid.

As he stood there, he heard Cyfal come up behind. The man said, "I'm sorry if I was surly when I was so genuinely glad to see you. It's just that I'm not used to the way city people think. You mustn't take offense—I'm afraid you might even think I'm a werewolf myself."

"That's foolish! We took a blood spec on you as soon as you were within sighting distance." For all that, he realized that Cyfal made him uneasy. Going to where the trundler guarded the door, he took up his laser gun and slipped it under his arm. "Just in case," he said.

"Of course. You think he's around—Gondalug, the werewolf? Maybe following you instead of you following him?"

"As you said, it's full moon. Besides, he hasn't eaten in days. They won't touch synthfoods once the lycanthropic gene asserts itself, you know."

"That's why they eat humans occasionally?" Cyfal stood silent for a moment, then added, "But they are a part of the human race—that is, if you regard them as men who change into wolves rather than wolves who change into men. I mean, they're nearer relations to us than animals or machines are."

"Not than machines!" Balank said in a shocked voice. "How could we survive without the machines?"

Ignoring that, Cyfal said, "To my mind, humans are turning into machines. Myself, I'd rather turn into a werewolf."

Somewhere in the trees, a cry of pain sounded and was repeated.

"Night owl," Cyfal said. The sound brought him back to the present, and he begged Balank to come in and shut the door. He brought out some wine, which they warmed, salted, and drank together.

"The sun's my clock," he said, when they had been chatting for a while. "I shall turn in soon. You'll sleep too?"

"I don't sleep—I've a fresher."

"I never had the operation. Are you moving on? Look, are you planning to leave me here all alone, the night of the full moon?" He grabbed Balank's sleeve and then withdrew his hand.

"If Gondalug's about, I want to kill him tonight. I must get back to the city." But he saw that Cyfal was frightened and took pity on the little man. "But in fact I could manage an hour's freshing—I've had none for three days."

"You'll take it here?"

"Sure, get your head down—but you're armed, aren't you?"

"It doesn't always do you any good."

While the little man prepared his bunk, Balank switched on his phone again. The news feature was ready and came up almost at once. Again Balank was plunged into a remote and terrible future.

The machines had managed to push their time exploration some eight million million years ahead, and there a deviation in the quanta of the electromagnetic spectrum had halted their advance. The reason for this was so far obscure and lay in the changing nature of the sun, which strongly influenced the time structure of its own minute corner of the galaxy.

Balank was curious to find if the machines had resolved the problem. It appeared that they had not, for the main news of the day was that Platform One had decided that operations should now be confined to the span of time already opened up. Platform One was the name of the machine civilization, many hundreds of centuries ahead in time, which had first pushed through the time barrier and contacted all machine-ruled civilizations before its own epoch.

What a disappointment that only the electronic senses of machines could shuttle in time! Balank would greatly have liked to visit one of the great cities of the remote future.

The compensation was that the explorers sent back video pictures of that world to their own day. These alien landscapes produced in Balank a tremendous hunger for more; he looked in whenever he could. Even on the trail of the werewolf, which absorbed almost all his faculties, he had dialed for every possible picture of that inaccessible and terrific reality that lay distantly on the same time stratum which contained his own world.

As the first transmissions took on cubic content, Balank heard a noise outside the hut, and was instantly on his feet. Grabbing the gun, he opened the door and peered out, his left hand on the doorjamb, his wristset still working.

The trundler sat outside, its senses ever functioning, fixing him with an indicator as if in unfriendly greeting. A leaf or two drifted down from the trees; it was never absolutely silent here, as it could be in the cities at night; there was always something living or dying in the unmapped woods. As he turned his gaze through the darkness —but of course the trundler—and the werewolf, it was said—saw much more clearly in this situation than he did—his vision was obscured by the representation of the future palely gleaming at his cuff. Two phases of the same world were in juxtaposition, one standing on its side, promising an environment where different senses would be needed to survive.

Satisfied, although still wary, Balank shut the door and went to sit down and study the transmission. When it was over, he dialed a repeat. Catching his absorption, Cyfal from his bunk dialed the same program.

Above the icy deserts of Earth a blue sun shone, too small to show a disk, and from this chip of light came all terrestrial change. Its light was bright as full moon's light, and scarcely warmer. Only a few strange and stunted types of vegetation stretched up from the mountains toward it. All the old primitive kinds of flora had vanished long ago. Trees, for so many epochs one of the sovereign forms of Earth, had gone. Animals had gone. Birds had vanished from the skies. In the mountainous seas, very few life forms protracted their existence.

New forces had inherited this later Earth. This was the time of the majestic auroras, of the near absolute-zero nights, of the years-long blizzards.

But there were cities still, their lights burning brighter than the chilly sun; and there were the machines.

The machines of this distant age were monstrous and complex things, slow and armored, resembling most the dinosaurs that had filled one hour of the Earth's dawn. They foraged over the bleak landscape on their own ineluctable errands. They climbed into space, building their monstrous webbed arms that stretched far from Earth's orbit, to scoop in energy and confront the poor, fish sun with a vast trawler net of magnetic force.

In the natural course of its evolution, the sun had developed into its white dwarf stage. Its phase as a yellow star, when it supported vertebrate life, was a brief one, now passed through. Now it moved toward its prime season, still far ahead, when it would enter the main period of its life and become a red dwarf star. Then it would be mature, then it would itself be invested with an awareness countless times greater than any minor consciousness it nourished now. As the machines clad in their horned exoskeletons climbed near it, the sun had entered a period of quiescence to be measured in billions of years, and cast over its third planet the light of a perpetual full moon.

The documentary presenting this image of postiquity carried a commentary that consisted mainly of a rundown of the technical difficulties confronting Platform One and the other machine civilizations at that time. It was too complex for Balank to understand. He looked up from his phone at last, and saw that Cyfal had dropped asleep in his bunk. By his wrist, against his tousled head, a shrunken sun still burned.

For some moments, Balank stood looking speculatively at the timber officer. The man's criticism of the machines disturbed him. Naturally, people were always criticizing the machines, but, after all, mankind depended on them more and more, and most of the criticism was superficial. Cyfal seemed to doubt the whole role of machines.

It was extremely difficult to decide just how much truth lay in anything. The werewolves, for example. They were and always had been man's enemy, and that was presumably why the machines hunted them with such ruthlessness—for man's sake. But from what he had learned at the patrol school, the creatures were on the increase. And had they really got magic powers? Powers, that was to say, that were beyond man's, that enabled them to survive and flourish as man could not, even supported by all the forces of the cities? The Dark Brother: that was what they called the werewolf, because he was like the night side of man. But he was not man—and how exactly he differed, nobody could tell, except that he could survive when man had not.

Still frowning, Balank moved across to the door and looked out.

The moon was climbing, casting a pallid and dappled light among the trees of the clearing, and across the trundler. Balank was reminded of that distant day when the sun would shine no more warmly.

The trundler was switched to transmission, and Balank wondered with whom it was in touch. With Headquarters, possibly, asking for fresh orders, sending in their report.

"I'm taking an hour with my fresher," he said. "Okay by you?"

"Go ahead. I shall stand guard," the trundler's speech circuit said.

Balank went back inside, sat down at the table and clipped the fresher across his forehead. He fell instantly into unconsciousness, an unconsciousness that force-fed him enough sleep and dream to refresh him for the next seventy-two hours. At the end of the timed hour he awoke, annoyingly aware that there had been confusion in his skull.

Before he had lifted his head from the table, the thought came: we never saw any human beings in that chilly future.

He sat up straight. Of course, it had just been an accidental omission from a brief program. Humans were not so important as the machines, and that would apply even more in the distant time. But none of the news flashes had shown humans, not even in the immense cities. That was absurd; there would be lots of human beings. The machines had covenanted, at the time of the historic Emancipation, that they would always protect the human race.

Well, Balank told himself, he was talking nonsense. The subversive comments Cyfal had uttered had put a load of mischief into his head. Instinctively, he glanced over at the timber officer.

Cyfal was dead in his bunk. He lay contorted with his head lolling over the side of the mattress, his throat torn out. Blood still welled up from the wound, dripping very slowly from one shoulder onto the floor.

Forcing himself to do it, Balank went over to him. In one of Cyfal's hands, a piece of gray fur was gripped.

The werewolf had called! Balank gripped his throat in terror. He had evidently roused in time to save his own life, and the creature had fled.

He stood for a long time staring down in pity and horror at the dead man, before prizing the piece of fur from his grasp. He examined it with distaste. It was softer than he had imagined wolf fur to be. He turned the hairs over in his palm. A piece of skin had torn away with the hair. He looked at it more closely.

A letter was printed on the skin.

It was faint, but he definitely picked out an "S" to one edge of the skin. No, it must be a bruise, a stain, anything but a printed letter. That would mean that this was synthetic, and had been left as a fragment of evidence to mislead Balank . . .

He ran over to the door, grabbed up the laser gun as he went, and dashed outside. The moon was high now. He saw the trundler moving across the clearing toward him.

"Where have you been?" he called.

"Patrolling. I heard something among the trees and got a glimpse of a large gray wolf, but was not able to destroy it. Why are you frightened? I am registering surplus adrenaline in your veins."

"Come in and look. Something killed the timber man."

He stood aside as the machine entered the hut and extended a couple of rods above the body on the bunk. As he watched, Balank pushed the piece of fur down into his pocket.

"Cyfal is dead. His throat has been ripped out. It is the work of a large animal. Balank, if you are rested, we must now pursue the werewolf Gondalug, identity number YB5921 stroke AS25061. He committed this crime."

They went outside. Balank found himself trembling. He said, "Shouldn't we bury the poor fellow?"

"If necessary, we can return by daylight."

Argument was impossible with trundlers. This one was already off, and Balank was forced to follow.

They moved downhill toward the River Pracha. The difficulty of the descent soon drove everything else from Balank's mind. They had followed Gondalug this far, and it seemed unlikely he would go much farther. Beyond here lay gaunt, bleak uplands, lacking cover. In this broken, tumbling valley, Gondalug would go to earth, hoping to hide from them. But their instruments would track him down, and then he could be destroyed. With good luck, he would lead them to caves where they would find and exterminate other men and women and maybe children who bore the deadly lycanthropic gene and refused to live in cities.

It took them two hours to get down to the lower part of the valley. Great slabs of the hill had fallen away and now stood apart from their parent body, forming cubic hills in their own right, with great sandy cliffs towering up vertically, crowned with unruly foliage. The Pracha itself frequently disappeared down narrow crevices, and the whole area was broken with caves and fissures in the rock. It was ideal country in which to hide.

"I must rest for a moment," Balank gasped. The trundler came immediately to a halt. It moved over any terrain, putting out short legs to help itself when tracks and wheels failed.

They stood together, ill-assorted in the pale night, surrounded by the noise of the little river as it battled over its rocky bed.

"You're sending again, aren't you? Whom to?"

The machine asked, "Why did you conceal the piece of wolf fur you found in the timber officer's hand?"

Balank was running at once, diving for cover behind the nearest slab of rock. Sprawling in the dirt, he saw a beam of heat sizzle above him and slewed himself around the corner. The Pracha ran along here in a steep-sided crevasse. With fear lending him strength Balank took a run and cleared the crevasse in a mighty jump and fell among the shadows on the far side of the gulf. He crawled behind a great chunk of rock, the flat top of which was several feet above his head, crowned with a sagging pine tree.

The trundler called to him from the other side of the river.

"Balank, Balank, you have gone wrong in your head!"

Staying firmly behind the rock, he shouted back, "Go home, trundler! You'll never find me here!"

"Why did you conceal the piece of wolf fur from the timber officer's hand?"

"How did you know about the fur unless you put it there? You killed Cyfal because he knew things about machines I did not, didn't you? You wanted me to believe the werewolf did it, didn't you? The machines are gradually killing off the humans, aren't they? There are no such things as werewolves, are there?"

"You are mistaken, Balank. There are werewolves, all right. Because man would never really believe they existed, they have survived. But we believe they exist, and to us they are a greater menace than mankind can be now. So surrender and come back to me. We will continue looking for Gondalug."

He did not answer. He crouched and listened to the machine prowling on the other side of the river.

Crouching on top of the rock above Balank's head was a sinewy man with a flat skull. He took more than human advantage of every shade of cover as he drank in the scene below, his brain running through the possibilities of the situation as efficiently as his legs could take him through wild grass. He waited without stirring, and his face was gray and grave and alert.

The machine came to a decision. Getting no reply from the man, it came gingerly around the rock and approached the edge of the crevasse through which the river ran. Experimentally, it sent a blast of heat across to the opposite cliff, followed by a brief hail of armored pellets.

"Balank?" it called.

Balank did not reply, but the trundler was convinced it had not killed the man. It had somehow to get across the brink Balank had jumped. It considered radioing for aid, but the nearest city, Zagrad, was a great distance away.

It stretched out its legs, extending them as far as possible. Its clawed feet could just reach the other side, but there the edge crumbled slightly and would not support its full weight. It shuffled slowly along the crevasse, seeking out the ideal place.

From shelter, Balank watched it glinting with a murderous dullness in the moonlight. He clutched a great shard of rock, knowing what he had to do. He had presented to him here the best—probably the only—chance he would get to destroy the machine. When it was hanging across the ravine, he would rush forward. The trundler would be momentarily too preoccupied to burn him down. He would hurl the boulder at it, knock the vile thing down into the river.

The machine was quick and clever. He would have only a split second in which to act. Already his muscles bulged over the rock, already he gritted his teeth in effort, already his eyes glared ahead at the hated enemy. His time would come at any second now. It was him or it . . .

Gondalug alertly stared down at the scene, involved with it and yet detached. He saw what was in the man's mind, knew that he looked a scant second ahead to the encounter.

His own kind, man's Dark Brother, worked differently. They looked farther ahead, just as they had always done, in a fashion unimaginable to *Homo sapiens.* To Gondalug, the outcome of this particular little struggle was immaterial. He knew that his kind had already won their battle against mankind. He knew that they still had to enter into their real battle against the machines.

But that time would come. And then they would defeat the machines. In the long days when the sun shone always over the blessed Earth like a full moon—in those days, his kind would finish their age of waiting and enter into their own savage kingdom.

Bibliography

BIBLIOGRAPHY

Nonfiction:

Baring-Gould, Sabine. *The Book of Werewolves.* Causeway Books, 1973. (Originally published in England, 1865.)
Eisler, Robert. *Man Into Wolf.* Spring Books (London), *ca.* 1960. True crime cases involving lycanthropy.
O'Donnell, Elliott. *Werewolf.* Peter Nevill (London), 1952.
Summers, Montague. *The Werewolf.* University Books, 1966. (Originally published in England, 1933.)

Fiction:

Bill, Alfred H. *The Wolf in the Garden.* Centaur Books, 1972. (Originally published in the U.S., 1931.)
Brandner, Gary. *The Howling.* Fawcett Gold Medal, 1977.
Carr, John Dickson. *It Walks By Night.* Harper, 1930.
Cline, Leonard. *Dark Chamber.* Viking Press, 1927.
Crockett, Samuel Rutherford. *The Black Douglas.* McClure, 1899.
Dumas, Alexandre. *The Wolf-Leader.* Cadot (Paris), 1857.
Endore, Guy. *The Werewolf of Paris.* Farrar and Rinehart, 1933.
Kerruish, Jessie Douglas. *The Undying Monster.* Award Books, 1968; Tandem Books (London), 1975. (Originally published in England by Phillip Allan.)
Koontz, Dean R. *A Werewolf Among Us.* Ballantine, 1973.
Long, Frank Belknap. *The Night of the Wolf.* Popular Library, 1972.
Lupoff, Richard. *Lisa Kane.* Bobbs-Merrill, 1976.

Mann, Jack. *Grey Shapes.* Wright & Brown (London), 1938.
Munn, H. Warner. *The Werewolf of Ponkert.* Centaur Books, 1976. One novelette and one novella.
Phillpotts, Eden. *Loup-Garou!* Sands & Company (London), 1899. Collection of short stories.
————. *Lycanthrope: The Mystery of William Wolf.* Macmillan, 1938.
Reynolds, G.W.M. *Wagner, the Wehr-Wolf.* Dover Books, 1975. (Originally published in England, 1846–47, as a serial in *Reynolds' Miscellany.*)
Service, Robert W. *House of Fear.* Dodd Mead, 1927.
Smith, Robert Arthur. *The Prey.* Fawcett Gold Medal, 1977.
Strieber, Whitley. *The Wolfen.* William Morrow, 1978.
Swem, Charles Lee. *Werewolf.* Doubleday, 1928.
Whitten, Leslie H. *Moon of the Wolf.* Doubleday, 1967.
Williamson, Jack. *Darker Than You Think.* Fantasy Press, 1948. Also published by Sphere Books (London), 1976.

Play:

Manhoff, Bill. *Sidney and the Werewolf's Widow.* Announced for production on Broadway (but actually produced?) fall 1972, starring Geraldine Page and Telly Savalas.

Films:

Boy Who Cried Werewolf, The (1973). Kerwin Matthews, Elaine Devry.
Cry of the Werewolf (1944). Nina Foch, Barton MacLane.
Curse of the Werewolf (British, 1963). Clifford Evans, Oliver Reed. Loosely based on *The Werewolf of Paris* by Guy Endore.
Death Moon (Made-for-TV, 1978). Robert Foxworth, Debra Lee Scott.
Frankenstein Meets the Wolf Man (1943). Lon Chaney, Jr., Bela Lugosi, Patric Knowles, Maria Ouspenskaya.
House of Dracula (1945). Lon Chaney, Jr., John Carradine, Lionel Atwill.

House of Frankenstein (1944). Lon Chaney, Jr., Boris Karloff, John Carradine, George Zucco.

I Was A Teenage Werewolf (1957). Michael Landon, Yvonne Lime.

Moon of the Wolf (Made-for-TV, 1972). David Janssen, Barbara Rush. Based on the novel by Leslie H. Whitten.

Return of the Vampire, The (1943). Bela Lugosi, Nina Foch.

Scream of the Wolf (Made-for-TV, 1974). Clint Walker, Peter Graves.

She-Wolf of London (1946). June Lockhart, Don Porter.

Undying Monster, The (1942). John Howard, James Ellison. Based on the novel by Jessie Douglas Kerruish.

Werewolf, The (1913). Silent film; first werewolf film.

Werewolf, The (1956). Steven Rich, Harry Lauter.

Werewolf in a Girl's Dormitory (European, 1963). Barbara Lass, Curt Lowens. (Released in England as *I Married A Werewolf.*)

Werewolf of London, The (1935). Henry Hull, Warner Oland, Valerie Hobson.

Wolf Man, The (1941). Lon Chaney, Jr., Claude Rains, Warren William, Ralph Bellamy, Bela Lugosi, Maria Ouspenskaya.